HORSES, MUSICIANS, & GODS

HORSES, MUSICIANS, & GODS
The Hausa Cult Of Possession-Trance

Fremont E. Besmer

AHMADU BELLO UNIVERSITY PRESS
ZARIA, NIGERIA

Published in Nigeria by Ahmadu Bello University Press,
P.M.B. 1094,
Zaria, Nigeria

© 1983 Ahmadu Bello University Press

ISBN 978 125 010 0

*To Malam Waziri Jibirin
and to the Memory of Malam Shu'aibu Mai Garaya*

Contents

Appendices

Foreword

Horses, Musicians, and Gods is a scholarly study of the Hausa *bori* cult of spirit-possession or possession-trance as practiced in Nigeria. Basing his book on data collected in 1972 and 1973, Dr. Besmer shares with the reader his methodology in penetrating the thinking and feeling of the adepts of the cult and the musicians who play an important role in its ceremony and ritual. Though the study is concentrated on the organization and operation of the cult, anthropological, sociological, and ethnomusicological interpretations of the material reveal much information regarding the stratification of the Hausa social system. In this system status is ascribed by occupation, the lowest class including musicians, butchers, house servants and menials, clients, and porters.

The possession-trance cult of the Hausa is viewed as a cult of affliction in which the afflicted individual is treated by a formerly afflicted cult member who acts as a medium. This is done with the expectation that the candidate will accept a role as a cult adept through the mechanism of a curing ritual, which is, in reality, an initiation ritual. The individual's affliction may be the mark of some transgression, but it is also taken as evidence that the person has been selected by *iskoki* (supernatural spirits) to become a horse for the gods. In considering a diagnosis, the ailment is matched with those associated with specific spirits. In preparation for the initiation ritual the neophyte is taught the rudiments of possession-trance as well as a body of knowledge about the spirits thought to have caused the affliction. He is also taught the special behavior he is expected to exhibit as a possessed person during the trance ritual.

A study of cult membership indicates that many adepts are deviants from Hausa social standards and that they are drawn together by their common affliction by supernatural spirits. Women provide the bulk of membership for the cult and are stereotyped as prostitutes. As with other possession-trance cults where membership is mainly a female concern, male homosexuals involved with *bori* are usually also transvestites. Psychologically disturbed individuals may find some protection for their behavior within the possession-trance cult, but membership in *bori* stands as a barrier between cult adepts and the general population.

Besmer notes that ritual performances may be divided in one way by describing them in terms of the musical instruments used to invoke the spirits. A list of instruments with their descriptions indicates their significance in the possession-trance rituals. The professional *bori* musician group consists of a leader, who is responsible for insuring that a complete ensemble is engaged for any performance, chorus, praise shouter, and, optionally, vocalist. How curious it is that musicians who are not thought to be afflicted by spirits should occupy such a central position during trance performances, calling and controlling spirits and setting the pace of the event!

The training and apprenticeship of professional *bori* musicians is considered from a sociological point of view, including the way in which they learn their role and the evaluation that society makes of their behavior. In addition to musical training and the shaping of attitudes toward spirits, a young cult musician learns how to behave with respect to other members of the Hausa community. This sometimes manipulative behavior is reminiscent of the calculating, brazen attitude of Senegalese *griots*, with whom a comparison is inevitable.

For most *bori* spirits, two kinds of music are distinguished, one vocal and instrumental and the other purely instrumental. Vocal music honors or calls a spirit and informs the audience. Instrumental music induces trance or otherwise controls the flow of ritual time. Besmer's musical examples support his description regarding the ways music is used in the *bori* cult of possession-trance. One notes the acceleration of the tempo and the density of musical material as it builds up to the induction pace. There is a rhythmic shifting between triple and duple meters as the trancers begin to show the signs of an approaching altered state of consciousness. As with the Hamadsha Muslims of Morocco, both auditory and visual overloading are used in the induction of *bori* possession-trance.

The analysis of the induction and trance-manipulating process is illustrated with examples from actual *bori* events. At the annual harvest ceremony, to cite one such example, *Sarkin Rafi* (Chief of Well-Watered Land, a supernatural spirit) is summoned with a particular trance-inducing song. After he has possessed his medium, he dances with bold leaps in which he extends his legs horizontally and falls to the ground, landing on his buttocks. Another song, completely different in character and tempo, is used to allow *Sarkin Rafi* to 'ride' his mount, that is, to demonstrate possession. Examples of these and many more spirits' songs are included in an appendix [Appendix C].

As described to Besmer, Jangare is the city of the spirits and is governed by a king, *Sarkin Aljan* (Chief of the Spirits). Although no one has ever been there—or, if he has, has never returned—devotees believe that they know how the city is socially organized. Spirits have families and a society stratified according to the principles the Hausa understand. There are twelve houses inhabited by spirits and their families. Besmer has identified the occupants of the houses with reference to such items as personalia, afflictions, sacrifices and medicines, mediums' behavior and dress, and music. In his search for the meaning of *bori* ritual symbols, Besmer focuses on the basic idea that *bori* symbols—in this case, as embodied in the shared ritual knowledge of the spirits' identities—are 'storage units' for concepts the Hausa have about themselves and the people around them.

The possession-trance cult in its true perspective is just one aspect of a comprehensive pre-Islamic Maguzawa religious system centered around the worship of supernatural spirits. These spirits are believed to be infinite in number, although only some are known by name and have definite personalities and powers. In Muslim Hausa communities most of these 'pagan' practices have been replaced by Islamic ones, but the cult of possession-trance still finds considerable expression. Although the cult is officially condemned by devout Muslims, their attitude is not universally shared by the populace. The belief in the efficacy of the curative powers of the cult is an important reason for its popular support.

In a Muslim country where the status of women is low and occasions for change are limited, the *bori* cult provides an opportunity for women to redefine their position in society. To become a mount for a spirit establishes one's identity in the *bori* cult through possession-trance, and, for some, satisfies basic social, physical, and psychological needs. The individual becomes identified with spirit, and the relationship may become a continuing symbiotic one.

Looking back on the cult's past, Besmer reviews reports by other investigators of *bori*. The reader cannot help being impressed with the consistency that is revealed in the comparison of reports over the spans of time and space that separate them. The future of the cult cannot be predicted, but so long as it is sought to explain illness, misfortune, and otherwise unusual circumstances, it is certain to remain a part of the living tradition of the Hausa people.

Willard Rhodes

Preface

The *bori* cult of possession-trance or spirit possession has been an intriguing topic for many observers of Hausa culture. Its ceremonies have been seen by some as colourful, dramatic, and entertaining; by some they have been described as dangerous, frightening, or merely disgusting. During my first trip to Nigeria in 1963 as a Peace Corps Volunteer teacher at Kano's School for Arabic Studies I stayed away from *bori* ceremonies. The Muslim community in which I was working considered the cult polluting at best and probably socially, personally, and morally destructive. My curiosity, however, had been aroused.

After a second trip to Kano, to study the Emir's royal musicians, I became convinced that *bori* was neither a simple entertainment nor particularly dangerous. It seemed that court and *bori* musicians alike were important participants in traditional yet dynamic Hausa culture.

A third trip to Nigeria provided the opportunity to take a close look at the cult as seen through the eyes of its musicians, men who share the stigma of being associated with *bori* but who are not themselves "horses of the gods." I was most curious about the content and organization of *bori* musicians' collective memory; no cult ceremonies or rituals were conducted without these musicians, who controlled the pace and nature (trance vs non-trance) of such events. Also of interest to me were the reasons for the cult's tenacity in the face of periodic attempts to abolish it and a fairly constant criticism of its members and their behaviour. Why would anyone want to be a cult-adept or musician?

This book is presented from two separate but interrelated perspectives. One is the latent urge to stop cultural change as though the ethnographic present were forever. Neither *bori* people nor I believe this to be possible, much less desirable, but we agree that it is "correct" to preserve this slice of Hausa ethnography. This is the reason for the inclusion of numerous musical transcriptions, praise-epithets, and genealogies. Such oral material is held in trust by a few musicians on behalf of the actual members of the *bori* possession-trance cult. It illustrates the actual practice of *bori* and the competence of cult musicians. As a member of a Western culture, which stresses written (or electronic) records of everything, I could not fail to be impressed by the sheer quantity of *bori* esoterica in the memories of *bori* musicians.

The other perspective from which *bori* is viewed here is that of the social and cultural anthropologist. I have sought to understand the complex relationships between the *bori* and non-*bori* aspects of Hausa life; how, for example, the cult adapts, survives, and even thrives in a modernizing northern Nigeria. This book also examines the themes, symbols, and structures in *bori* music, oral tradition, and ritual. Generosity, for example, is an important theme in Hausa life and is underscored in the gift-giving obligations guests seem to have at *bori* events. The guests give to musicians, but it is other *guests* who are obligated to reciprocate with gifts of their own. Musicians are the recipients of these gifts as well: I understand these exchange patterns as containing a kind of social insulation. Guests are "protected" from the dangers of direct exchanges when musicians are used as professional receivers, witnesses to guests' generosity. It is not surprising that these events have been interpreted merely as materialistic entertainment, and as a way for musicians further to extort money from people; but I think that something else is involved here.

I have been asked at what level I understand *bori* explanations of various events. As a social scientist I am usually reluctant to direct a causal arrow at supernatural spirits. However, I have found myself wondering about the extraordinary numbers of "accidents" connected with this project. Cracks in the walls of our Kano house and an uncommon number of cooking accidents involving milk were all explained as having been spirit-caused. But these temporary, on-site inconveniences were not as serious as the misfortunes that have befallen this manuscript. It has been lost, rewritten, misplaced, and otherwise delayed. Doubtless my *bori* friends would be able to explain these misfortunes. And to the skeptics they might say, *"Wanda ya ratsa gari bai san abin da yake ciki ba"* ("He who skirts a town does not know what is inside"). This book will have achieved its purpose if it provides some description of that "town," the cult of possession-trance.

Fremont E. Besmer
City College of New York

Acknowledgements

The following acknowledgements are made with my sincere thanks to the individuals and institutions mentioned for their generous assistance in the conduct and completion of this research project.

The Centre for Nigerian Cultural Studies of Ahmadu Bello University, under the direction of Professor Michael Crowder, provided the necessary financial support in the form of my appointment as a Senior Research Fellow. Without the patience and encouragement of the director and staff of the Centre who indulged my interest in Hausa possession-trance, this study might never have been allowed to develop.

Professor Paul Newman, the Director of the Centre for the Study of Nigerian Languages, Abdullahi Bayero College (ABU), provided a model for scholarly achievement and was invaluable in helping me sort out the structural order of cult events.

The portion of this study which concentrated on Ningi, North East State, could not have been included except for the help and accommodations provided by Mr. Adell Paton from the University of Wisconsin, who was studying the history of the area. Through him I met two others who gave generously of their time and knowledge, Ningi's Senior Councillor, Alhaji Jibril Nayaya, and the chief of the *Bori* cult, Isa Dam Malam.

On a trip to Maiduguri, the capital of the North East State, to gain a different perspective on cult practices, I was confronted with the common problem of how to gain the acceptance of the people involved with *bori*. I could not believe my ears when I heard the voice of one of my cult friends from Kano, Magaji Dan Kukwairi, in the crowd outside a *bori* leader's compound. The touring Magaji provided me with the introduction I needed that day and was later to tell me of his experiences as a trancer. The man for whom the introduction was needed, Sale Mai Nakada, proved to have a wealth of information and insight, and I wish to acknowledge his co-operation and that of the cult-adepts associated with him.

In Kano, where the majority of the material for the study was gathered, I could not have undertaken to be a student of cult practices without the guidance and inspiration of my adopted senior kinsman, Malam Shu'aibu Mai Garaya. An expert musician, Malam Shu'aibu and his ensemble allowed me to record everything I thought I needed and patiently explained the intricacies of cult ritual. He failed to teach me how to play the lute but the fault was mine, not his.

One of the gourd-playing members of his ensemble, Iliyasu Mai Buta, was invaluable as a teacher because of both his skill as a musician and his previous experience as one afflicted by the divine horsemen of Jangare. Iliyasu's knowledge of the social organization of the spirit world was truly impressive, and I count him as one of my primary informants.

To Waziri Kidan Kotso Jibirin I owe a special debt of gratitude. I met Waziri during a previous trip to Kano, but our friendship did not develop fully until this one. As a royal musician, Waziri was risking a great deal to become involved in this study, and I thank him for his help. Whatever needed to be done to ensure the comfort of me and my family or the success of my research activities, Waziri was always available. No task was too large or too small for the best of his efforts.

Countless other Nigerians each contributed to the success of my research, and if I have not mentioned them here it is not that I have forgotten them. To those men and women who were the cult-adepts and musicians of this study I express my sincere appreciation for their frankness and co-operation.

And to my wife and children, who patiently accompanied me on this journey, I cannot begin to express my gratitude. When my spirits were low, they raised them; when I lost the smallest screw from my tape-recorder, they found it; when I needed their understanding, they gave it. Without their enthusiasm for living in Nigeria, this study would never have been undertaken.

F. E. B.
Kent, Connecticut

Chapter 1 · Introduction

Horses, musicians, and gods: these are three of the essential elements of the Hausa cult of possession-trance. The horses are cult-adepts, so described because of the image they have of themselves as mounts for the spirits which possess them; the musicians are non-initiates, professionals, whose function it is to preserve much of the oral tradition of the cult and to invoke the spirits with special songs during possession-trance performances; the gods are the divine horsemen, the residents of the invisible city of Jangare, supernatural spirits who mark their victims with illness and misfortune and then provide the source for its remedy. The purpose of this study is to reach an understanding of who or what each of these groups is, what they do, and how they are brought together in *bori* practice and ritual.

The subject of the bori cult is not new in Hausa studies. As early as 1914 Tremearne published his observations on the cult and its personages in *The Ban of the Bori.* Based primarily on material collected among Hausa immigrants in Tunis and Tripoli but supplemented with notes taken in northern Nigeria, Tremearne's book provides a remarkable record of cult beliefs and practices and of the identities of a long list of supernatural spirits. Some of his explanations and conclusions may be subject to re-interpretation in the light of what is now known about Hausa bori, but the meticulous attention to detail so apparent in his descriptions makes his work a valuable comparative source.

Twenty-five years later Greenberg was doing research in Kano, northern Nigeria, and its surrounding rural hamlets on the effects of Islam on the religious beliefs of the Hausa. The results of his study, published in 1946, constitute a landmark in the understanding of Maguzawa (non-Muslim Hausa) religion. In his monograph the cult of possession-trance is seen as just one aspect of a comprehensive religious system based on the worship of supernatural spirits, an accurate description of bori as practised by the Maguzawa.

King's two-part article on what he termed 'a bori liturgy' (1966; 1967) appeared more than twenty-five years after Greenberg's field trip and marks the beginning of a modern interest in the possession-trance cult. In his Katsina liturgy King provides a full transcription and translation of the text of a specially recorded women's performance.

Roughly coincident with King's publication, Reuke and Monfouga-Nicolas (*née* Nicolas) were studying the Maguzawa in southern Katsina Province and the cult of possession in Maradi, Niger, respectively. Reuke's (1969) main emphasis was on missionary activity, and his sections on the *iskoki* cult add very little to Greenberg's exegesis. Monfouga-Nicolas sees the cult of possession-trance as a product of social change, surfacing only after contact with Islam and a consequent disintegration of Hausa clan structure (Nicolas 1967). In her second book on bori she concentrates on the social aspects of the cult particularly as regards its function as a mechanism to deal with status ambiguity in women (1972).

All of these studies mention or imply the part played by musicians and their music in the performance of cult ritual, but significantly enough few attempt to include musical data in the explanation of ritual behaviour. King, of course, transcribes song texts (1967) and provides his readers with some significant observations on rhythmic organization (1966: 108-9), but, unfortunately, it was not possible to correlate these findings with informant testimony. Monfouga-Nicolas discusses the musicians involved in initiation ceremonies (1972: 157-62) and the physical descriptions of cult instruments in some detail (1972: 168-73), but music and musicians were not an important part of her study.

A significant portion of the following pages is devoted to an examination of the music used in possession-trance performances and of the musicians who play it. Musicians are not usually members of the bori cult, but it would be erroneous to assume, therefore, that they are 'outsiders' or 'strangers'. They are intimately involved in nearly all phases of cult activity and play an indispensible role in cult performances, both public and private. Maguzawa religion, the subject material for Greenberg's study, does not demand the participation of musicians except as they are required for demonstrations of possession-trance. In Muslim Hausa communities, such as those included here, most Maguzawa religious practices have been replaced by Islamic ones. The only one which still finds considerable expression is the cult of possession-trance, hence the importance placed on music and musicians.

No study of the possession-trance cult would be complete without some description of the bori pantheon. Tremearne (1914) is the only author who attempted to be comprehensive in his description, most of the others providing 'representative' lists and explanations. Greenberg's commentary on some of the important supernatural spirits active among the Maguzawa (1946: 39-43) is excellent as far as it goes, but only four of the divine horsemen of Jangare could be included. In addition to the characteristics, illnesses, relationships, and medicines ascribed to a spirit it is important to understand how and when it is called. Supernatural spirits are not mere personalities, each with its own idiosyncracies. They are religious symbols arranged in patterns, and their attributes outline their order in the minds of cult-adepts and participants.

It has been asked whether there is some consistency in the social categories which are drawn to possession-cults (cf. Lewis 1966: 309), and various answers have been proposed by different authors writing about bori and other cults. The way in which bori may be described and analysed as a cult of affliction, deprivation, or deviation are all explored here as are the kinds of people, both men and women, who tend to become its adepts.

The types of rituals used in the Hausa possession-trance cult are implied in the works of Greenberg (1946), King (1966), and Monfouga-Nicolas (Nicolas 1967; Monfouga-Nicolas 1972), but few have attempted to describe their structure or their meaning to the actors except in so far as their curative or therapeutic content combined with initiation is concerned. Periodic possession-trance rituals are largely ignored or treated as 'entertainment'. In fact such performances are commonly used to promote cult solidarity, reaffirm cult obligations, and both separate and bond together distinctive groups of cult-affiliated people, whether or not they include possession-trance demonstrations. All cult rituals reveal a strong diachronic order and structure which transcends any individual event yet which is present in it.

Lastly, with the increase in interest in the subject of altered states of consciousness (ASCs) it was decided that bori had to be examined in the light of current findings. None of the writings on Hausa possession-trance is much concerned with the induction or mechanics of ASCs, and the general arcana of Hausa bori resulted in its exclusion from a significant project which studied dissociational states cross-culturally (cf. Bourguignon 1973). Particularly as regards the induction of possession-trance, this study examines the techniques used by cult-adepts to enter an ASC and illustrates how they are taught during initiation rituals.

DEFINITIONS

In the ethnographic literature on bori frequent mention is made of 'trance' or 'spirit-possession' with little regard as to their distinction or meaning. For the most part these terms have been avoided here and adepts' altered states of consciousness identified with the term 'possession-trance'. Following Bourguignon (1973: 4-15), possession-trance is defined as an altered state of consciousness[1] which is institutionalized and culturally patterned. It is a learned skill, and adepts who enter possession-trance are expected to behave in certain ways, following cult 'rules'. Dissociation is described by initiates as due to possession by supernatural spirits, involving the impersonation of their speech and behaviour, and is followed by amnesia. During possession-trance a medium's personality disappears, and his gestures and speech are interpreted as belonging to the possessing world.

In the absence of an altered state cult mediums, adepts, or devotees are described with the concept of 'possession'. This includes the belief that the supernatural spirits present on a medium at his initiation (or curing) are for ever with him, it being impossible to exorcize them from their victim. Trance in the absence of possession does not occur among the Hausa, and when 'trance' is used it is a shortened form of 'possession-trance'.

Mention should be made of the Hausa terms used to refer to supernatural spirits. Bori has both a general and a specific sense; it is used in this study to refer to the cult of possession-trance—its general meaning. The term is also used by informants to indicate 'supernatural spirit' or 'mediumship'. Thus, when it is said of someone, 'He is able to do bori' or 'He has bori', this means that he is a competent medium. *Iska* (pl. *iskoki*) is the common term used to refer to a supernatural spirit, but its primary meaning is 'wind'. In urban Hausa settlements *aljan* or *aljani* (fem. *aljana;* pl. *aljanu*) which is derived from the Arabic *jinn* is a frequent substitute for iska or bori (supernatural spirit).

DESCRIPTION OF THE DATA

The data for this study were collected between September 1972 and December 1973 while I held an appointment as Senior Research Fellow in the newly established Centre for Nigerian Cultural Studies at Ahmadu Bello University. Tape-recordings of numerous cult events and interviews, photographs of people and of divine horsemen (or at least of the adepts impersonating them), and notebooks full of observations, questions, and answers are all a part of this data. The tape-recordings of performances at which cult musicians invoked the divine residents of Jangare created a familiar problem: how to separate the tightly woven strands of musical and verbal behaviour during such events. The problem was solved by having groups of musicians play especially for me at the Centre's offices in Kano or, if on tour, in a relatively quiet, neutral compound. No illusions were entertained about such 'faked' performances representing meaningful cult events. They were used as a device for understanding what musicians might be likely to do during actual cult rituals. As expected, their musical behaviour in artificial situations differed considerably from that motivated by bori events; however, by studying the tapes of such performances it was possible to develop some competence in the special language of the cult and the nature of its musical expression.

Working with musicians and adepts, using both 'artificial' and 'genuine' tapes, also led to other kinds of information than that actually recorded. Information regarding spirits' genealogies, descriptions, relationships, characteristics, illnesses, and medicines were all prompted by the stimulation of 'hearing what went on last night'.

Thus, the main technique used for gaining an understanding of the cult and its activities was first to witness something and then to ask about it. It was difficult to ask conditional questions (e.g. 'What would happen if . . .' or 'What would it mean if . . .') and expect reliable answers. Accordingly, the data fell into two categories: my observations of what was happening and informants' statements or explanations of the same events. Our descriptions were not always the same, and it quickly became apparent that either I was mistaken about what I had 'seen' or the actors were only partially aware of the significance of some of their behaviour. It was concluded that both sources contributed to the total picture; they simply represented different levels of interpretation. Those of my continually revised conclusions which could be validated with subsequent observations and informal predictions appear in the following pages, none of which conflicts seriously with informant testimony. On the other hand, the actors' statements of the meaning of cult symbols were accepted as they were given, since I viewed part of my task as uncovering the structure or meaning of the meaning.

HAUSALAND

The northern part of the Federal Republic of Nigeria and the southern part of the Republic of Niger is known as Hausaland. The country ranges from the savannah of the south to the sahel of the extreme north. Kano State where most of the fieldwork for this study was conducted is located in the northern part of the savannah belt. Kano City, the state's capital, has a seasonal rainfall of from 40 to 43 inches between May and October. From mid November to January the cool, dry, dust-laden Harmattan wind blows off the Sahara and reduces rainy season temperatures of 65-80° (diurnal range) to 50-75°. The months of February to April are called the hot season; there is no rain and temperatures often rise above 110° during the day.

The Hausa social system is highly stratified, and while other criteria are used socially to place people in the system, for example ethnic membership, kinship, descent and lineage, and sex, the single most comprehensive ranking system is based on occupation. The hierarchical ranking of political offices is a part of this primarily ascriptive system, the highest political and social position being held by the emir. No single hierarchy covers all Hausa traditional occupations, but whichever authority is taken musicians and praise-singers and -shouters are placed in the broadly lowest rank. Among these bori musicians are evaluated least favourably. Mediumship in the possession-trance cult is an achieved status, not an ascribed status. Cult-adepts are therefore not listed in the hierarchy *per se*, but their 'primary' occupations are.

Except for the absence of bori performance during *Ramadan* (the Muslim month of the Great Fast preceding the Lesser Feast) cult activity is sustained for the first half of the dry season and gradually diminishes in anticipation of the rains. During the rains, except for initiations which are sometimes held during the planting and growing season, bori activity practically ceases. Periodic possession-trance performances are coincident with the increase in wealth and the number of social events reaffirming old or creating new obligations following upon the harvesting of crops.

The areas in which this research was conducted may all be described as 'urban'. Following Yusuf, any Hausa settlement with 2,000 or more persons living within a relatively compact area can be considered urban (1974: 205), and those which are (or were) walled may be described as cities. Thus, Kano is a Hausa city while Ringin, Gumel, and Ningi are urban settlements.2 Hausa migrants resident in the Kanuri city of Maiduguri (capital of North Eastern State) being nonetheless 'urban' were also included in the study. Other significant landmarks of an urban settlement include the emir's palace and the market. Weekly markets are usually characteristic of towns while cities such as Kano and Maiduguri have daily markets. Trading is an important occupation among the Hausa though the traditional economy is based on agriculture combined with domestic pastoralism—the raising of chickens, goats, and sheep.

As Yusuf writes, 'gambling, card-playing, drinking, courtesanship and transvestism are some of the major features of Hausa urbanization' (1974: 209), and the venue for such activities is often also a centre of cult organization. Although the iniquities of urban people may occur in places entirely unrelated to bori, female cult leaders often double as house 'madams', gathering many 'mares of the gods' around them as working prostitutes. Male cult leaders sometimes serve a similar function except that they prefer to take a sponsorship rather than a leadership role in the activities of their female-adept clients.

THE MAGUZAWA (RURAL NON-MUSLIM HAUSA) AND THEIR RELIGION[3]

Although the possession-trance cult was once part of a comprehensive Maguzawa religion which is still followed in some isolated areas of Hausaland, this study is not directly concerned with them. The urban populations investigated preferred to view themselves as Muslims and, although the Maguzawa have undoubtedly been influenced by Islam, their conversion has been superficial and has not resulted in replacing their own religious practices by those of Islam.

A conspicuous feature of non-Muslim Hausa social organization is the corporate lineage system which depends largely upon the traditional *gandu* farming pattern. Gandu or ancestral land is inherited through males and is worked by extended families, usually brothers or parallel cousins, their wives, and dependent children. Maguzawa compound organization is based on a rule of patrilocal residence, its core of membership consisting of a number of males related through males. The undisputed head of the compound, its *mai gida*, is the most senior male of this patrilineal group.

Under direct questioning, Greenberg says, the Maguzawa will admit the existence of Allah (1946: 27). But He is believed to be a distant Being, unconcerned with the lives of men. Rituals connected with a belief in Allah are absent, and all supernatural response to worship, whether good or bad, is attributed to spirits called *iskoki* (singular, *iska*) (Ibid.). The Maguzawa cult of the iskoki has four separate aspects: rituals performed for families, public rituals, individual aspects, and the possession-trance cult. Of the four, public rituals performed for the welfare of an entire community have been all but abandoned by the non-Muslim Hausa and, of course, are rarely found among their urban neighbours.[4]

Family rituals are performed by a compound head or mai gida on behalf of his co-resident patrilineal relatives. Consisting of a number of sacrifices addressed to the supernatural spirits inherited by the group, these rituals commonly occur in conjunction with the agricultural season (during the hot season before the first rains and at the harvest) or at the occasion of the marriage of a patrilineal kinsman. The blood of the sacrificial animal is drunk by iskoki and the meat is both eaten by the sacrificing group and given away as alms.[5] Family rituals have totally disappeared from among the urban Muslim Hausa coincident with the absence of corporate extended family structure.

The individual aspects of Maguzawa religious practice are found in the sacrifices made for personal ends. Openly made offerings by members of certain occupational groups to ensure the co-operation of craft-associated iskoki and offerings prescribed by 'medicine men' (s. *boka*) to remedy minor attacks of spirit-caused ailments are examples of legitimate sacrifices with acceptable ends. On the other hand, some individuals privately seek to gain special favour with anti-social spirits, hoping to enlist their aid in one disreputable project or another. According to Greenberg, 'such practices [are] known to the Maguzawa as "keeping a *dodo* (i.e. evil spirit) in the house" ' (1946: 47).

Possession-trance mediums in urban areas follow identical practices, the most common of these consisting of consultations with native doctors for minor ailments. Such other explanatory systems as horoscope casting and the private advice by malams (Quranic teacher-scholars), however, provide fierce competition for a boka, and, as a result, his activities are curtailed by a lack of clientage in all but small urban settlements.

The possession-trance cult, bori, does not seem to play as central a role in Maguzawa practice as it does with the urban Hausa. Greenberg contrasts the 'simple individual performances among the Maguzawa, carried on for specific purposes, [with] the performances of Bori societies [in the cities] whose aim is principally to give amusement, and which require the use of elaborate costumes and other paraphernalia, and are carried on in the presence of a large number of performers and spectators' (1946: 49). While the veracity of city performances will be defended elsewhere in this study, it is certainly accurate to note that Maguzawa possession-trance performances are commonly tied to quite specific crises and events in which supernatural spirits are consulted through their mediums, but urban Hausa performances frequently are not.

ETHNOMEDICINE

As has been suggested earlier spirits are believed to be responsible for a variety of human ailments and misfortunes. But if aljanu are the cause of a malady they are also the source for its cure. Relief from a spirit-caused illness can be obtained through the administration of medicines associated with the afflicting spirit, appropriate sacrifices, and mediumship. Illness thus serves the function of marking an individual for cult membership either as a 'son of the bori' or 'horse' if male or as 'daughter of the bori' or 'mare' if female (the Hausa terms for these will be found in Chapter II).

It should be emphasized that in urban settlements bori explanations for illness represent only one of the possibilities available. Those who deny the value of cult cures may seek treatment in hospitals and clinics where there are Western-trained physicians, the advice of malams who tend to interpret illness in terms of religious poverty, or what Greenberg calls 'the ordinary *mai magani*, "possessor of medicine,"... whose remedies are exclusively vegetal and herbal' (1946: 54). Typically, urban people try non-bori explanations for illnesses before dealing with the 'children of the bori' with cases otherwise incurable.

An important aspect of bori and boka (medicine man) prescriptions is that they restate the conviction that particular supernatural spirits are the cause of specific illnesses. Sacrificial animals are selected on the basis of their breed, colour, sex, and perhaps other physical characteristics, attributes which when taken in combination are symbolic of the afflicting aljan. Medicinal preparations carry the same kind of symbolism. Parts of plants, or small amounts of dirt or debris which are identified as the spirit's resting place are two other examples of their symbolism.

In social terms the possession-trance cult of the cities may be seen as a cult of affliction in which groups of the formerly afflicted treat the currently afflicted (cf. Turner 1968). Since a bori cure includes with it an expectation that the candidate will accept a role as a cult-adept, curing rituals are also initiation rituals and mark the transition from one achieved status to another. Periodic possession-trance events are occasions for the renewal of an adept's commitment to the spirits 'on his head' as well as contexts for an elaborate exchange structure which both unites and separates groups or individuals.

THEORETICAL PERSPECTIVE

Considered by Geertz, the anthropological study of religion is in a state of general stagnation. It seems that more often than not anthropologists have depended upon the 'classical theoretical themes' developed by their intellectual ancestors of fifty or more years ago, 'such well-established propositions as that ancestor worship supports the jural authority of elders, that initiation rites are means for the establishment of sexual identity and adult status, [or] that ritual groupings reflect political oppositions . . .' (Geertz 1966: 1-2). Such themes run through the ethnographic literature on bori and probably have the effect of finally persuading a large number of its readers 'that anthropologists are, like theologians, firmly dedicated to proving the indubitable' (Ibid.: 2).

It is not that this tradition in religious analysis should be abandoned, merely that it should be broadened. To achieve this objective some explanation must be given of what we mean by 'culture' (a term which is likely to attract considerable scorn in some social anthropological circles). As Geertz has succinctly described it, culture 'denotes an historically transmitted pattern of meanings embodied in symbols, a system of inherited conceptions expressed in symbolic forms by means of which men communicate, perpetuate, and develop their knowledge about and attitudes toward life' (1966: 3). Briefly stated, our task here is not simply to relate bori to Hausa social-structural or psychological processes. The sacred symbols of bori must themselves be analysed as to the meaning they hold for cult participants, for without this information the behaviour of actors towards such symbols in both ritual and non-ritual contexts is incomprehensible.

In ritual contexts bori sacred symbols include objects, activities, relationships, gestures, spatial units, music, and texts, all of which may be observed empirically and are subject to interpretation and explanation by cult-adepts and laymen alike. The cult rituals which incorporate these symbols all have a processual form, generally diachronic in character but subject to modification through the use of structural transformations arising out of the specific circumstances in which the rituals are conducted. In other words certain rituals have the same form, broadly considered, but each occasion of the ritual includes separate options—e.g. eliminations, alterations, or additions—which may be taken based on the actors' perception of what has already happened or is expected to happen before the event is concluded.

In non-ritual contexts symbols are found in the rich oral tradition about the lives and activities of supernatural spirits; the identification of places, plants, and phenomena associated with these spirits; and the evaluation of what is appropriate or inappropriate in any given circumstance. Primarily concerned with afflictions and their cures, cult symbols synthesize adepts' ethos: the tone, character, and quality of their lives—and their world-view—the picture they have of the way things in sheer actuality are (Geertz 1970: 325).

This is not to imply that a study of bori can provide all the answers to questions about Hausa sacred symbols. For the urban Hausa especially their dedication to the cult of possession-trance is augmented or tempered by their description of themselves as Muslims, a description with which the general society does not often agree but which provides cult-adepts with few serious problems. For cult initiates the Muslim doctrine of the existence of *jinn* can be directly translated into their ideas about the efficacy of supernatural spirits, an interpretation which is passively accepted by Hausa Muslim clerics and scholars. For this reason urban cult-adepts usually prefer to identify supernatural spirits with the term aljan rather than iska which has a non-Muslim Hausa connotation. In sum, bori sacred symbols are discussed at length in this study both for the significance they hold in cult rituals as the smallest units of ritual structure (cf. Turner 1967) and for the meaning cult participants give to them.

Sociological interest in the possession-trance cult leads to an investigation of the categories of people who become its adepts and an examination of the concepts of affliction, deprivation, and deviation which have all appeared in other contexts (cf. Turner 1968; Lewis 1966; 1971b). When relating cult ritual and symbolism to Hausa social-structural processes a point which frequently appears is that the cult and its symbols are not a reflection of urban Hausa social order (even if at times they are) but that they are shaped or given form by it (cf. Geertz 1966: 35-6). Cult-adepts' feelings about the way the world *ought* to be organized for them become the way it *is* organized. The feedback provided by cult metaphysics creates the conditions for social interaction and survival, and those things which are described as 'necessary' become the same things to be evaluated as 'good' or 'proper'.

PLAN OF THE STUDY

The body of this study has been divided into four chapters covering the membership of the bori cult, the musicians who play for it, the supernatural spirits to which these two groups address their attention, and cult rituals and possession-trance.

In Chapter II the social organization of the 'horses of the gods' is examined together with a description of the kinds of people drawn into cult membership. Bori may be characterized as a community of former sufferers of spirit-inspired afflictions, but only certain kinds of people seem particularly susceptible to infection. These people are otherwise considered by Hausa society as 'deviants' and frequently represent the lowest—some might say 'deprived'—ascriptive social categories. They escape social stigma or at least insulate themselves from it through dissociation states and spirit mediumship which involves them in the bori world of obligations and reciprocities.

Much of the responsibility for the preservation of the cult's oral tradition (songs, praise-epithets, and lore) is vested in the cult musicians, who though themselves not bori initiates stand as mediators between the horses of the gods and the supernatural spirits who 'ride' them. The 'divine horsemen' cannot be called without their music and thus musicians exercise considerable control over cult ritual process. These paid, professional musicians, play special instruments, sing spirits' songs, and shout their praises; their craft is entertaining, their purpose intensely serious. In Chapter III those cult musicians who have developed a competence in other areas than musicianship, e.g. horoscope casting and boka activities, are also discussed.

Divine horsemen live in an invisible city called Jangare. Cult-adepts and musicians have a clear idea of what this city is like, particularly as regards its inhabitants, and their descriptions are given in Chapter IV. It is true that supernatural spirits may be identified according to the special maladies and misfortune they like to cause, but it is also known that they order their lives like the people they are said to resemble—Hausa, Fulani, Maguzawa, Gwari, or 'North Africans'—describing each other with kinship terms and avoiding or joking with appropriate relatives. The old never die and the young never grow old; time is obliterated in the spirit world.

Horses, musicians, and gods all meet in the rituals of the bori cult of possession-trance. In Chapter V cult rituals are examined for what they mean to the actors as well as external observers. Possession-trance, an altered state of consciousness, is considered in detail; also how it is taught during cult initiation and the techniques used to induce it.

NOTES

[1] Bourguignon considers that ASCs 'may be viewed as representing a continuum, in which dreams during REM (Rapid Eye Movement) sleep would represent one extreme, possession-trance linked to impersonation behaviour [the Hausa case] the other, with visionary trance roughly at midpoint between them' (1973: 14).

[2] Ningi (the new town) does not have a wall. Ringin and Gumel might have had walls in the past, but they are not evident now. In any case the important distinction is between urban and rural (sparsely inhabited countryside) and not really between the different levels of urbanization.

[3] Readers wishing a more detailed account of Maguzawa religion than is sketched here may refer to Krusius (1915), Greenberg (1946), or Reuke (1969). Much of the material in this section is from Greenberg (1946).

[4] Combining the orientation of public rituals—the entire community—with the agricultural focus of family rituals, the urban Hausa harvest ritual, *fasa kabewa* (the breaking of a pumpkin), may be considered as a shadowy survival of a Maguzawa practice.

[5] Sacrifices among the urban Hausa follow a similar pattern except that the person or group which offers the sacrifice is not expected to consume any of it, all the meat being given as alms.

Chapter 2 · Horses: Cult-Adepts

SOCIAL ORGANIZATION

Within the Hausa system of ascribed statuses social placement occurs along lines of ethnic membership, kinship (descent and lineage), sex, age, and most importantly, occupational class. In fact the occupation of a person or his kinsmen is a greater determinant of his position in the traditional Hausa social fabric than any other factor. Occupations are most frequently hereditary and are contrasted with those which are freely chosen. The former have a higher status than the latter, and to a considerable extent enjoy greater prestige.

The Hausa do not arrange occupations within a single hierarchy; their number is far too large to accommodate such a system. Smith distinguishes three or four social 'classes' the details for which are vague. In general, the highest level includes *masu sarauta* (s. *mai sarauta*; title-holder) and, occasionally, *malamai* (s. *malam*; Qur'anic scholar or teacher) and wealthy merchants. The vast majority of the traditional sector of the society falls within the next two classes, and the lowest includes 'the musicians, butchers, house-servants and menial clients, porters, and the poorer farmers who mostly live in rural hamlets' (Smith 1959: 249).

This model for Hausa social stratification, however, does not include the social placement of women. As Smith notes, 'there are, in fact, two quite distinct status orders, one regulating the social placement of men, the other applying to women' (1959: 245). Among women the criteria considered for social placement are those of 'generation, age, marriage-order to a common husband, ethnicity and descent, fertility, marital career, the position and prospects of offspring and, to a lesser extent, differences of wealth' (Ibid).

In general the distinction between child and adult is more important than any other status consideration, and a person does not become an adult until the occasion of the first marriage. The condition after divorce and before another marriage is described as *karuwanci* (lit. prostitution), and single persons of either sex are referred to as *karuwai* (s. *karuwa*). Since marriage is the only normal con-

11

dition for adults in Hausa society karuwai are viewed as deviants and are marked with some degree of social distance. For example, during Ramadan such deviants are the subject of ridicule and the taunting of children's groups. Significantly, many of those involved in the bori cult of possession-trance are stereotyped as karuwai, and as Greenberg (1946: 49), King (1966: 105), and Nicolas (1967: 2) observed, the membership of women is predominant. Status within the possession-trance cult, as already observed (Chapter I), is not ascribed but achieved. However, there seems to be some relationship between bori achieved status and the Hausa system of ascribed status, and this is a point to which we will return below.

Cult-adepts are described collectively as *yam bori* (lit. children of the bori) and divide on the basis of sex into *dam bori* (lit. son of the bori) and *yar bori* (lit. daughter of the bori). The relationship between a spirit and the cult-adept possessed by it is stated in the metaphor of a rider and his horse. A male medium is called a *doki* (lit. stallion; horse) and a female medium a *godiya* (mare). This equestrian theme is extended to include the attendants who assist and control the trancers during performances but who do not themselves fall into possession-trance. Such attendants are described as *masu kiwo* (s. *mai kiwo*; lit. herder or groom), and it is their responsibility to ensure both that a 'horse' is properly dressed in the costume symbolic of the riding spirit and that its actions do not cause physical danger for the spectators.

There are two principal leadership positions in the cult which are identified by titles. The first of these is *Sarkim Bori* (Chief of the Bori, principal cult leadership position) and is usually held by a man. In his essay on Katsina bori King reports that this office is held by a woman (1966: 106), but informants in Kano, Ningi, Ringin, and Maiduguri maintain it is inappropriate for anyone except a man to hold this position. All accounts agree that it is the Sarkim Bori in a district who has authority over the mediums who live there and who acts as host for those who tour through it. When the services of the cult are required the Sarkim Bori of the district is normally the first person to be contacted. Through his office the performance is organized and gifts and invitations are sent to the actors. The Sarkim Bori received a considerable portion of the fees for such services and may act as the redistribution point for the participants.

Although the position of the Sarkim Bori is a ritual one and is subject to selection mechanisms within the context of the cult itself, cult members respond to problems of validity in succession and administration in a secular way. In the traditional political system of ranked titles, candidates for office are selected and their rule sanctioned under the authority of the emir; the titles are awarded in a turbaning ceremony itself symbolic of this royal selection and support. The title of Sarkim Bori is usually confirmed in a turbaning ceremony performed by a prominent member of the political hierarchy. This does not, however, represent any royal screening process, but is rather an occasion for public witnessing of a decision arrived at within the cult itself. The office is filled on the basis of expertise as a medium and popular support among cult-adepts in the district. In Ningi, for example, although the Emir himself appointed the present Sarkim Bori it was only after his selection (following upon the position becoming vacant) by popular consensus of the cult members. In terms of cult administration the use of titles borrowed from emirate organization is sometimes found. King notes that the 'practice of transferring *sarautu* titles from a major to a minor social organization [is a result], at least partially from the need for a recognizable system of status definition within the latter'. (1966: 107 n.). The use of a system which is familiar to laymen is certainly important, but such titles are also symbols of socially acceptable grades of authority, tying cult offices to a pre-existing prestige system.

The description drawn above of the Sarkim Bori as the highest authority over the members and activities of the cult shows considerable variation from place to place. In such small urban settlements as Ningi and Ringin the office is strong, and all bori activity centres around it. In urban Maiduguri, the same pattern is evident except that professional musicians play an active part in the schedule of cult performances. In Kano the office is weak, so most requests for cult services first come to musicians who contact individual cult-adepts. The Kano situation is unique in that the most popular musician is also an initiate (although not an active medium) in the cult and is therefore consulted on medicines, initiations, and cult matters.

The other principal leadership position in the cult is that of the *Magajiyar Bori* (Heiress of Bori). This position is always held by a woman, and while individual office-holders may have greater prestige than a given Sarkim Bori the title is generally viewed as subordinate in rank to the Sarki. This is due to the attitude in Hausa society that no titles are superior or equal to that of Sarki. Some title-holders—typically those women who specialize in bori activities alone—exercise authority over districts equally as large as male cult-leaders', but the usual practice is for a Magajiyar Bori to have a smaller area to administer than the Sarkim Bori above her. Through the Magajiya's position the relationship of the cult with female prostitution is underscored, since she is also commonly the head of a *gidan karuwai* (house of prostitutes), and, in fact, her administrative district may correspond to the city ward or small town which the house services.

Women's cult activities only partially intersect with those of men, many of them occurring within the privacy of purdah compounds. Rarely do many women attend the periodic, public performances which have mixed audiences. Secluded performances are presided over by a Magajiya, and the music is provided by women who sing and play *koruka* (s. *kwarya*; large, hemispherical calabash) which are struck with pairs of sticks.[1] Besides their importance as possession-trance events such women's performances reveal patterns of exchange between female cult-adepts, a subject to which we will return later in this chapter.

Whereas the majority of Hausa living units are defined by nuclear or extended families the compounds in which many cult-adepts live frequently emphasize cult, rather than kinship, organization. While some mediums live with their spouses and children in neolocal units thus conforming to a common urban Hausa pattern, the majority of the cult-adepts studied were unmarried and lived in rented rooms. Male mediums are more likely to live with wives than female mediums with husbands, but all compounds are organized under the leadership of a senior person, male or female, who may also be a cult-adept. Commonly, residences headed by women are also gidan karuwai (brothels). The female head is expected to have cult status and operates her compound from commissions received from the prostitutes who live there. Residences headed by men vary in their structure, depending on the cult status of the compound leader. If he does not have a high status in the cult his compound generally has few people in it, but if his status is high or he is a Sarkim Bori as many as twenty unmarried women may share his facilities to ply their trade as courtesans.

In urban Maiduguri, for example, a medium with high status but no specific title is responsible for fifteen women in his own compound and another five in a house still under construction. The economic support he receives from these women—who also take turns with domestic and sexual responsibilities to the master of the house—is large enough for him to continue the construction of his new house. His position in the cult also entitles him to the clientship of a number of male mediums who contribute their talents as mediums at events he schedules in exchange for his financial support of them.

The compound of the Sarkim Bori of Ningi is similarly organized. Although the property itself belongs to his wife's mother, he acts as the compound head and supports a small number of female mediums who are also active prostitutes. Besides the commissions which he collects from the women on an irregular basis, he is able to earn large sums for initiation services held in the compound and regular cult performances held outside it. He receives the balance of his income from farmland on which he raises food crops.

More than anything else these compounds are centers for bori activity and places where mediums gather to socialize with each other. The impediments and medicines (roots, bark, and leaves, primarily) used by the cult are kept in the compound head's quarters, and in small urban settlements the compound often contains a tree or special corner sacred to one or two spirits. For example, this *jigo* (lit. pole) in Sarkim Bori's Ningi compound, is a baobob tree (*Adansonia digitata*), but may only be simple plants identified with one or more spirits of a specific type. It is a place where animals are sacrificed and is usually decorated with spirit-associated tools and clothing.

In both urban and semi-urban compounds cult members feel free to sit in mixed groups and exchange stories, gossip, and personal experiences. Everyone under the nominal authority of the *mai gida* makes at least one visit each day to greet him and get his instructions for the events of the day. Some adepts who live by themselves or with their families may be found at home during the day, but commonly visit 'cult compounds' for conversation after the evening meal.

BORI AND TRADITIONAL HAUSA CLAN ORGANIZATION

It has been suggested in this study that the bori possession-trance cult is one aspect of a comprehensive, pre-Islamic, Maguzawa religious system which still survives among Hausa Muslims many of whom live in urban or semi-urban areas. The urban form of the possession-trance cult is nearly identical to that found among the non-Muslim rural Hausa except that the pervasiveness of other *iskoki* religious activities has been reduced in the cities by Muslim practices. It is believed the use of dissociational states in the worship of spirits pre-dates Islam and that the bori cult did not appear as a result of culture contact. While not denying that Islam has had an impact on the possession-trance cult, it does deny that bori was somehow 'latent' before the spread of Muslim influence in Hausaland.

A different position has been taken by Nicolas (1967) who hypothesizes that the possession-trance cult is primarily a women's organization and is not found among Maguzawa with the 'traditional' pre-Islamic religion and old clan structure deities. In other words Nicolas holds that bori practice depends upon the presence of Islam and the disintegration of Hausa clan structure. Her argument is that old clan spirits are a part of the public domain, and the present bori pantheon consists of mixing these dieties with an inventory of Muslim spirits. She therefore reasons, bori is a product of social change. It is an institution in which women dominate, replacing the participation they enjoyed in the iskoki, clan-related cult with prominent positions in a 'new' cult. This redirection is necessary, it is explained, because women are not allowed to maintain active positions in Islam, such roles being confined to men.

On the surface Nicolas' hypothesis is persuasive. It attempts to define the qualitative differences between Maguzawa bori and the possession-trance cult of the Muslim Hausa, a difference which has been suggested by Greenberg in his studies (1946; 1947). It draws on two obvious features of the urban or post-contact pantheon, namely, that there is a general classification of supernatural spirits into white (Muslim) and black ('pagan') and that the presence of a few of the spirits in the pantheon can only be explained in terms of Muslim contact. It also includes well-documented evidence that traditional Hausa clan organization does not survive the conversion to Islam. However, the question remains as to whether or not Nicolas is justified in drawing a causal arrow from these factors to the urban possession-trance cult. Using data gathered outside the Maradi area where Nicolas did her work, some correlates of her hypothesis may be examined.

In the first place it should be possible to demonstrate an absence of possession-trance elements capable of development into the urban cult among those Maguzawa untouched by Islam. It is not sufficient to demonstrate that *urban* cult organization and practice are not found among the rural non-Muslim Hausa, since the urban form could be the result of any number of factors only one of which may be the disintegration of traditional clan structure. Secondly, where it is possible to show that the effects of Islam have led to the disintegration of traditional rural clan structure and that possession-trance is a part of religious practice, the cult should be of the 'new' type described by Nicolas, i.e. dominated by women and with an 'Islamized' pantheon.

'Pristine' non-Muslim Hausa groups are difficult to find in the ethnographic literature.[2] The term Maguzawa is applied to everything from groups which recognize Islam or place Allah as a figurehead over the pantheon of spirits but do not describe themselves as Muslims, to groups recently converted from 'paganism'. Despite variations in the degrees of acceptance of Islam it seems clear from the reports available that possession-trance (bori) is an integral part of Maguzawa religious culture. Membership in the cult is prescribed by clan affiliation which ties together victims of the same spirits and allows different clansmen to be possessed by different spirits. In other words each clan has an least one supernatural spirit recognized as 'on the heads' of all clan members, but within a clan possession by other spirits is an acceptable occurrence. There would seem to be no reason why this situation could not be directly translated into an urban form where clan organization is absent and clan-related religious functions have been destroyed by Islam. As Greenberg writes, 'the sacrifices to the spirits performed by the compound head in behalf of the entire compound are abolished with conversion' (1947: 210), and this results in a weakening of the extended family structure of the Maguzawa through a discontinuance of family religious functions. Bori practice is apparently untouched by Muslim influence even if Allah is placed above an extended pantheon which includes a few new personalities.

The second case is an outgrowth of the first. After conversion to Islam Maguzawa clans disappear as they are replaced with an economic organization dependent upon small residential units. This does not mean that all new converts move to the cities; they remain on substantially reduced gandu-type farms as rural Muslim Hausa. According to Nicolas's hypothesis as already noted, the disintegration of clan structure should result in a new type of possession-trance cult organization, in which women dominate and which shows the influence of Muslim contact. Taking the second characteristic first, it is true that a spirit known as *Malam Alhaji* (Malam the Pilgrim), for example, can be found in the extended pantheon. But, as Greenberg explains,

> the existence of such a character among the iskoki as Malam 'Alhaji is impossible without an intimate acquaintance with Moslem ways and practices; hence the appearance of Malam 'Alhaji and the other Moslem spirits are phenomena which can only take place under conditions of contact. However, Malam 'Alhaji is not, as one might assume at first blush, a spirit whose cult has been borrowed from Mohammedan sources. It is safe to say that in all the shadowy world of the jinn there is no figure with the characteristics of Malam 'Alhaji. In other words, we have here, under the stimulus of Moslem contact, the creation of new spirits, an invention, indeed, in the field of religion. (1946: 63)

Thus, the 'new' pantheon does not represent a substantive change from Maguzawa practice. A basic idea that spirits resemble the people among whom they live is preserved with the addition of Malam Alhaji and others. The transformation occurs as a Maguzawa commentary on their social existence, an existence which includes Muslims, and not in the form of any serious assimilation of Muslim beliefs.

The other characteristic, a cult dominated by women, is not supported in the ethnographic literature. Rural converts who continue some of their non-Muslim religious practices do not seem to switch to the female domination described by Nicolas for Maradi. There should be no doubt that bori in Maradi is dominated by women, but this must be explained as resulting from a special urban case and not because clan structure has disappeared. The pattern is not unique to the Maradi valley. An identical form of cult organization was cited by King who wrote of Katsina, a large urban settlement not very far from Maradi (1966: 105-6). It must be concluded that the disintegration of Hausa clan structure does not necessarily result in a cult dominated by women unless the settlement in which bori is preserved is also urban.

However, not all urban settlements reveal the same pattern in cult organization. When King and Nicolas describe the possession-trance cult as women-dominated they imply that not only cult membership but cult leadership is in the hands of women. In Kano, Ringin, Ningi, and Maiduguri cult membership is dominated by women since there are more female than male mediums, but cult leadership is not. These urban settlements reveal a leadership pattern which is divided between women and men. Female cult leaders are the undisputed heads of performances which take place in secluded compounds and of the actors who participate in them. Male cult leaders operate in the public sector of the possession-trance cult in which it would normally be considered inappropriate for a female cult leader to sponsor a performance.

As described in the previous section male leadership is not imaginary. The men who hold such positions are identified with an appropriate title (Sarkim Bori; Chief of the Bori) which affords them certain rights and obligations. Men like to think of themselves as superordinate to female cult leaders, and in matters involving periodic public performances women allow them to do this. But since women have a specific authority reference the individual leadership functions must be viewed as parallel rather than vertical in organization. It is, however, inaccurate to characterize these cults as 'dominated' by women.

Finally, some attention should be given to the 'displacement'[3] aspect of Nicolas's hypothesis. Women turned to bori, according to Nicolas, in order to compensate for their exclusion from leadership or other significant roles in Islam as it spread and gradually became adopted by the Maguzawa. Accepting displacement for a moment, it is worth noting that if it occurred it also affected Maguzawa men. Little by little their authority in the iskoki cult was eroded by the intrusion of Islam which led to the abandonment of nearly all but the possession-trance aspects of Maguzawa religious culture. In view of the changes caused by Islam they could take one of two routes: they could become Muslims and give up their Maguzawa past, or they could try to focus their attention on bori, an area of ritual activity in which we are led to believe they had previously played only supportive roles. In Maradi and perhaps Katsina it is said that the predominant pattern is the former, since women control both membership and leadership in bori. Men are excluded from leadership positions or, as Nicolas emphasizes, they are simply not interested in them (1967: 2). In the areas included in this study men have chosen the second alternative; they have tried, usually with considerable success, to secure prominent positions in bori and have kept their participation in Islam to a minimum.

However, 'displacement' is not an easy concept to pin down. In any case it is difficult to understand how it can be applied to an urban situation with much success, since cult-adepts there have Muslim Hausa, not Maguzawa social origins. Perhaps another way of looking at displacement would be to describe it as 'deprivation', emphasizing its synchronic dimension, a view to be discussed in the following section.

What we have attempted to show in this treatment of Nicolas's hypothesis is, first, that the disappearance of the clan structure of the Hausa cannot in itself be used to explain the presence of bori in urban settlements. The cult has different forms depending on whether it is found in rural or urban areas where clan structure is absent from either. Therefore, the rural-urban dimension seems to hold more clues to cult structure than the absence of Hausa clan structure. There is also differentiation between urban patterns. Some, indeed, are woman-dominated, but as many if not more reveal another form in which men hold positions of power and responsibility. Secondly, insofar as Islam defines the urban milieu, placing the possession-trance cult somewhat outside the range of acceptable Muslim behaviour, it can be said to be partly responsible for the social constitution of the cult. However, except for the influence of Muslim symbolism on bori which must be considered as affecting only the surface characteristics of the cult, Islam does not 'create' bori. All the definitions, the vast majority of the supernatural spirits in the bori pantheon, and the use of dissociational states are present in bori before the introduction of Islam or the abandonment of Hausa clan structure. Bori is a product of social change but no more so than any other feature of the dynamic urban scene.

Changing the focus from the origins of bori in the cities to an investigation of the reasons for its continued prosperity despite the efforts of Muslim religious leaders in the nineteenth century and the administrative policy of colonial and post-colonial government in the twentieth, it becomes important to try to understand what kinds of people, both men and women, are drawn to cult membership. It seems almost as if cult mediums have the same specific gravity in some social liquid. They are deviants from Hausa social standards drawn together by what they interpret as their common affliction by supernatural spirits. It is to these factors, deviance and affliction, that we now turn.

BORI DEVIANCE AND DEPRIVATION

In Hausa society people with cult status are stereotyped as capable of unusual behaviour, wild-eyed, personally unclean, religiously ambivalent (according to the tenets of Islam), and generally a bit odd. In short, they are viewed as deviants. Cult-adepts try both to deny this image by dressing in conservative clothing and acting as 'normal' as possible, and to capitalize on it when it seems to be to their advantage.

From a sociological point of view bori participants are drawn from the fringes of Hausa society. For example, they do not fit well in the system which ascribes status positions on the basis of occupations. Mediumship is not considered a craft (*sana'a*) even if many trancers derive most of their economic support from cult activities. As already stated, women provide the bulk of membership for the cult and are stereotyped as prostitutes. As karuwai they choose to ignore the Muslim Hausa practice of remarrying after divorce or widowhood. Their deviance is in prolonging a common temporary social condition into an apparently permanent one.

As Beattie and Middleton have observed, there is an 'association in some cultures between male homosexuality, with transvestism, and spirit possession [i.e. possession-trance], especially where mediumship is mainly a female concern' (1969: xxv). The Hausa are a case in point. 'Yan Daudu (s. *dan Daudu*; lit. son of *Daudu* male homosexual/transvestite) also known as 'yan hamsin (lit. 'sons of fifty') can be found at any gidan karuwai, but their activities there appear to be purely social or economic. Yusuf reports that 'transvestites specialize principally in the processing and vending of luxury snacks' and 'they also operate as intermediaries' between courtesans and their clients (1974: 209). They appear at public bori performances where they dance in an effeminate manner. 'Yan Daudu do not fall into trance at these events and confine their participation to the giving of small gifts of money to cult-adepts who do enter possession-trance, especially when the spirit, *Dan Galadima*,[4] is present.

, Transvestites dress in clothing styles which are nearer masculine than feminine; overshirts and trousers are worn rather than blouses and wrappers. However, the cloth from which these garments are made is distinctly feminine and other male informants say that the collars, and cuffs on the shirt sleeves and trouser legs are too large. Their voices are too high and soft to be male, and their motor behaviour suggests too many female cues. In other words they are socially visible as homosexuals/transvestites and rarely make any attempt to conceal it.

This visibility has its price. 'Yan Daudu are subject to (generally good-natured) caricature, within the context of the cult and in public. During the preliminaries to one possession-trance performance I observed, a royal musician—a 'retired' cult-adept[5]—imitated the dancing style of the 'Yan Daudu, exaggerating it to include a complete female imitation. He tied a wrapper around his waist and put two oranges in his jersey, much to the amusement and delight of the gathering. On another occasion the celebrations for the Muslim festival *Mawlid al-nabi* (Arabic: the Prophet's Birthday) in the small urban settlement of Gumel featured a farcical soccer match between local prostitutes and transvestites. The prostitutes won as the transvestites seemed incapable of doing anything right. Besides, the referee was more liberal in his treatment of the women than he was of the men.

Since all cult-adepts—including prostitutes, homosexuals, and those who exhibit other forms of marginally acceptable, if not unacceptable, behaviour— are considered by Hausa society in general to be deviants, bori takes on the appearance of a cult of deviance. Although musicians in general and bori musicians in particular are not deviants, their social ranking in Hausa society is low, and the popular stereotype of them as lazy, dirty, spendthrift, and obsequious provides a social model having close affinity with bori enthusiasts.

Closely related to deviance is deprivation, if indeed the latter is useful at all as an analytical concept. Which is not to suggest that all deprived or underprivileged people are deviants, but as Lewis comments, 'the incidence of possession afflictions is not purely arbitrary but tends to run in defined social grooves, those particularly subject to such possession belonging to marginal social categories' (1971*b*: 214-15). In other words, such cults may function as socially integrating associations for those who are treated as 'second-class' citizens. In many Islamic societies—and the urban Hausa are an example—the jural position of women is weak, and they are at least partially excluded from full participation in the men's world of Islam. According to Lewis's approach, it could be predicted that women in general and prostitutes in particular would be candidates for cult membership. Jurally deprived categories of men, including both deviants (homosexuals) and despised or lowly ranked occupational categories (butchers, night-soil workers, menial clients, poor farmers, and musicians) constitute the central group of possessed or participating males. Bori membership, however, is not confined to the socially dispossessed, and as Lewis observed for spirit-possession (possession-trance) cults in north-east Africa, it includes 'an element of psychologically disturbed individuals [both male and female] which cuts across social distinctions' (1971*b*: 215).

Thus, bori can be treated as a cult of deviance in the sense that the behaviour of its members is stereotyped as unusual or generally unacceptable, or as a cult of deprivation in the sense that its membership is commonly drawn from marginal social categories. In either case such explanations focus on the significance of bori in terms of social function and not on its historical origins.

Deprivation cults, according to Lewis's framework, do not exist as independent phenomena. Writing about north-eastern Africa, he makes a distinction between 'main morality' and 'peripheral' cults (Lewis 1971*b*: 213). The former are involved in the maintainance of general morality in a society, the latter are not. Cults of the main morality type are those which venerate ancestors, or other mystical powers which reward the morally just with prosperity and success and cause disease and affliction in the unjust or sinful. Cults of the peripheral type, for example the women's cult of *zar* spirits in Omdurman (Sudan), are directed at 'disaffiliated' spirits whose affliction is capricious and without regard for the victim's moral condition (Ibid.: 213-14). Placing Islam in the position of a main morality cult (while being aware it is more than that), bori is a peripheral cult in Hausa urban society. As will be seen in a later chapter bori spirits are not entirely 'disaffiliated', but the broad features of Lewis's dichotomy are applicable. His conclusions about the place of possession-trance in a peripheral cult fit the Hausa situation, and bori is comparable to the case he describes for north-eastern Africa where 'possession [i.e. possession-trance] does not figure at all prominently (if at all), in the main morality cult, [and] only women (or submerged classes of men) and psychologically disturbed individuals (of either sex) are subject to it' (1971*b*: 215).

Corresponding with this 'epidemiological'[6] approach to cult membership is a description of the social function of bori. At the level of observable behaviour, cults of deprivation provide the opportunity for women especially to put pressure on men to pay for expensive initiations and special sacrifices and to 'extort', in Lewis's terms, gifts and favours from them. He describes such cults as having a potential for a sort of reservoir of marginal power to act on the domain of male-dominated public morality (1971*b*: 222). This is not generally true in the case of bori where such power is never brought to bear on the major morality system. For the most part the persons responsible for a cult-adept's deprivation are never compelled to change their attitude towards him or her. Rather the emphasis seems to be on a symbolic form of redress. Thus, devotees appear to be less concerned to use their 'reservoir of marginal power' to obtain material comforts or any genuine social readjustment than they are to state symbolically their separateness as deviants from the major social organization. Achievement within the cult has its own reward in increased ritual status; external social status is unaffected. Membership in the bori cult drives a symbolic wedge between cult-adepts and the general population, a theme which is emphasized in the initiation process.

Lewis's hypothesis that possession-trance may be traced to the innate conflict between men and women in certain types of societies where men monopolize the social structure—a condition which implies the subordination and deprivation of women who in some sense may be described as peripheral—has serious weaknesses. Wilson (1967), for example, takes exception to the idea that deprivation and peripherality generate hostility between men and women and that this situation comes to be expressed in possession-trance where there are no formally sanctioned means of its expression. Rather than viewing possession-trance as a part of the 'war between the sexes', Wilson maintains that it is 'more closely correlated with social situations which regularly, though not necessarily, give rise to conflict, competition, tension, rivalry or jealousy between members of the *same* sex rather than between members of opposite sexes' (1967: 366). Avoiding what he calls the vague and general notions of 'deprivation' and 'social peripherality', he substitutes the hypothesis that possession-trance 'is a means to status or identity definition, and arises in contexts where individual status is jeopardised or rendered ambiguous' (1967: 376-7).

Wilson's statement that possession-trance 'occurs primarily among women, and especially married women' (1967: 374) is applicable to the Hausa situation as long as it is remembered that the participation of men is by no means insignificant and that the category, 'married women', includes divorced women. In his view possession-trance is a form of *rite de passage* through which social identity may be altered and social status defined. His focus is on social status ambiguity arising from such innate personal characteristics as sexual abnormality or specific social conditions (1967: 375), but particularly in the Hausa context this ambiguity is coupled with a negative evaluation, i.e. deviance from 'acceptable' social behaviour. In other words status ambiguity is not completely eliminated through involvement in the bori cult. While an initiated individual achieves a specific, formal social status within the cult since possession is institutionalized it is not possible for him to escape the general social assessment of his behaviour as deviant. Prostitutes, male transvestites, and psychologically disturbed individuals may find some protection for their behaviour within the possession-trance cult, but in Lewis's terms they remain 'deprived' (whether or not this deprivation is seen as an aspect of the denial of an acceptable role *vis-à-vis* non-cult members of the same or opposite sex) and are assigned to the Hausa social periphery.

BORI AS A CULT OF AFFLICTION

In the previous section it was stated that people in certain social positions—women, certain men of low occupational status, and people of either sex who might be described as psychologically disturbed—constitute the 'social groove' from which membership in the bori cult tends to be recruited. In a following chapter the structure and process of their initiation will be examined in detail. This section describes the circumstances surrounding the selection of devotees from the list of likely candidates.

The primary way a person is initiated into the cult is through a curing rite. An element of inheritance is generally involved, initiation being more common for persons whose families have a past history of bori involvement than those who do not. In such cases a person may be said to inherit one or more spirits 'on the head' of a previous generation kinsman. Commonly, the inheritance pattern is patrilineal but women are especially subject to the inhertance of spirits from female kin. During curing rites people with cult status—that is, those who have suffered illnesses believed to have been caused by supernatural spirits and have been healed by initiation into the cult—administer to those seeking relief from a malady diagnosed as having been caused by spirits. These rites for the afflicted are mainly the way membership is recruited for bori and therefore the principles of a cult of affliction are outlined.[7]

With the addition of the concept of affliction to the social characteristics of those likely to become candidates for possession-trance cult membership the cross-sectional view of bori social organization is completed. As an analytical model Lewis's interpretation of deprivation, particularly its jural form, has serious shortcomings, but it would be unwise to reject it altogether. Tempered with the sociological interpretation of deviance and status ambiguity, some of Lewis's deprivation hypothesis can be preserved. These concepts are, however, external to the attitudes cult-adepts themselves hold about the nature of bori membership. For them candidacy is identified by some form of ritual illness which may also be physiological or psychological, and the effective cure is through an acceptance of bori mediumship. Cult social organization then, is that of a society for the formerly afflicted but forever possessed, of people whose obligation is expressed by the acceptance of the role of spirit medium ever after.

The illnesses which can be cured through initiation are extremely varied, ranging from household clumsiness, impotence, and infertility to rashes, boils, stomach trouble, headaches, insanity,[8] incipient leprosy, and paralysis. The results of a bori healing ritual include the attainment of harmony or reconciliation between the sufferer and the spirits believed to have caused his specific trouble, rather than an exorcism of the spirits, and, of course, the recruitment of a new cult member.

Affliction by bori spirits has a dual function. On the one hand it is the mark of some transgression committted by the victim which has angered the spirits. On the other, it is taken as evidence that the sufferer has been selected by iskoki to become a horse for the gods. Bori spirits generally do not strike with the capriciousness of the *zar* spirits of the Sudan. It may be that the transgression is not that of the victim, particularly in the case of children, and no initiation will be required. Greenberg cites a case in which a young girl was inflicted with stomach trouble; her moral condition was not investigated; instead the illness was interpreted as a sign that the spirit, *Danko Dam Musa (Danko,* Small *Musa),* who is believed to cause stomach ailments, had been angered by the actions of the girl's mother in leaving the father of the girl (who was Danko's medium) and the spirit was said to be displeased by the insult to his horse. Danko's spirit mother, *Inna,* added paralysis to the girl's trouble, and became the focus of her affliction. Inna was placated in a special possession-trance ceremony in which the father's mother acted as the only medium and transmitted the spirit's instructions for a special sacrifice for appeasement (Greenberg 1946: 51-2).

Even in cases where the sufferer's own misdemeanour is responsible for the illness it usually takes a cult specialist to analyse the details and call attention to the probable circumstances in which the insult occurred. The diagnostic technique used is first to consider the nature of the illness and match it with those associated with specific spirits. Once the probable identity of the afflicting spirit is known the diagnosis proceeds to an examination of the circumstances in which the spirit could have been angered. With the diagnosis complete a boka (native doctor) who usually also has a cult status will first prescribe the sacrifice of an animal identified with the spirit. If this does not result in an elimination of the symptoms a curing rite (initiation) at the hands of the bori cult may be prescribed. During initiation the patient is treated with medicines symbolically identified with the spirit or spirits believed to have caused the illness. For example, if the illness has been caused by Danko (a snake spirit) the treatment will include the drinking of an infusion made from *kanya* (African ebony; *Diospyros mespiliformis*) wood and *kanwa* (potash), the former being sacred to Danko.[9]

As mentioned above, once a person has been marked by the spirits as a desired 'mount' he is initiated into the cult under the direction of the formerly afflicted. His initiation or 'cure' marks a transition from one achieved status to another; he becomes a minor 'doctor' and is qualified to treat others with similar afflictions. It is through affliction therefore that a person may earn cult status and gradually achieve religious acclaim even if his status among the non-afflicted remains unchanged and low.

POSSESSION-TRANCE

In this study frequent reference is made to an altered state of consciousness (ASC) termed possession-trance. In ethnographic literature it is variously described as a state of 'dissociation', 'trance', or 'spirit-possession'. Following Bourguignon's definition of possession-trance (1973), a number of its aspects may be noted. In general terms possession-trance refers to a state interpreted by the society in which it occurs as due to possession by spirits. As such, it is opposed to states in which spirits play no part. Possession-trance in the bori context conforms to the model of such states as involving the impersonation of spirits, specifically, the acting out of their speech and behaviour. Another aspect of possession-trance is that it is commonly followed by amnesia. Bourguignon comments that a distortion of perception occurs in possession-trance—but it refers to the self, not to other sense objects—and is manifested as a 'radical discontinuity of personal identity' (1973: 12-13). It is probable that this discontinuity is responsible for the amnesia following possession-trance.

Central to the identification of possession-trance is the cultural evaluation of the dissociated person's state. As Bourguignon emphasizes,

> We must not merely observe the subject or note how the state was induced; we must ask his fellows—and afterward, the individual himself—how they explain the individual's transformation. We must note the cultural context in which the observed event occurs. Only in this way can we discover whether we are, in fact, dealing with an individual, private, perhaps deviant event or a patterned and institutionalized one; whether we are dealing with a profane or secular phenomenon, one that is positively evaluated and desired or one that is negatively evaluated and feared (Bourguignon 1973: 13).

If the content of the possession-trance state is culturally patterned then it is necessary to answer the questions Bourguignon has raised with the responses of the actors. This process properly begins with whether or not bori participants even recognize that possession-trance is culturally patterned or that a person in such a state is expected to behave according to some set of rules.

During the initiation ritual a neophyte is taught, directly and indirectly, the rudiments of possession-trance as well as a specialized body of knowledge about the spirits which have caused his affliction. Despite the fact that the actors consider the event to be based on the theme of cure rather than on initiation as such, it is recognized that the initiate must be taught the behaviour he is expected to exhibit while in a dissociated state. He learns the speech patterns and behaviour of the spirit believed responsible for his possession-trance, its praises, songs, rhythms, dances, and distinctive bodily movements. These, in fact, generate the 'rules' for his altered state behaviour.

It will by now be clear that bori adepts employ a supernaturalistic explanation to account for illness and misfortune. Medicines, themselves organic substances, are symbolically tied to iskoki and not directly to the afflictions they are supposed to treat. Under these circumstances possession has a negative connotation. A possessed person is incapable of behaving in a normal way in Hausa society, either because he is totally incapacitated or his behaviour appears inappropriate for a given situation. Possession is transformed into a positive attribute through membership in the bori cult and the activity of possession-trance.

Thus far we have focused on possession-trance as though it was invariably interpreted as genuine. However, if the technique of ethnographic inquiry is to be applied consistently the question of fraud must be considered. When 'simulated' or fraudulent possession-trance has been detected by outside observers their conclusions about the nature of bori have been that its main function is dramatic entertainment (Greenberg 1946: 49; King 1966: 105), an implied kind of cultural hypocrisy. Cult-adepts themselves recognize and identify standards for possession-trance but a bori performance is rarely invalidated by a fraudulent trance.

At the broadest level, horses of the gods recognize possession-trance which is either *na gaskiya* (lit. of truth; authentic) or *na karya* (lit. of lie; fraudulent). They do not doubt the sincerity of bori na karya which may occur within their ranks; it is usually classed as total ineptitude, a problem for the divine horseman but not the cult. This attitude is further expressed in what might be called the 'cancellation rules' for a possession-trance event. It is not possible for an event to be 'broken' with fraudulent trance even if it is a subject for discussion by the participants and generally detracts from the excitement of the performance. Within the class of bori na gaskiya performances by individuals, there are those which are less spectacular in the demonstration of possession-trance than others; these are commonly by the newly initiated. Since possession-trance behaviour is recognized as learned and constitutes a skill, the inexperienced are not expected to be as proficient as devotees with a long history of cult involvement. The single, most important characteristic which native critics use to distinguish 'true' possession-trance from false is body temperature. They state that a person in true dissociation state perspires heavily, and his body should be hot to the touch. Lee also notes that sweat is the most important symbol of dissociation in Bushman possession-trance (1968: 44). For them perspiration is the visible expression of powerful medicines on the surface of the body, for the Hausa it is the visible expression of a spirit's presence 'on the neck' of a devotee.

Later in this study we will return to the subject of possession-trance, examining it in terms of its induction and psychological characteristics and its place in bori ritual.

EXCHANGE: GIVING, RECEIVING, AND REPAYING

As is frequently repeated in the songs of Hausa musicians, generosity is a primary value in the conduct of social relations. In terms of actual behaviour the Hausa translate generosity into gift-giving and evaluate a person's prestige in terms of the appropriateness of his presentations. Individuals may give privately, others receiving and repaying as individuals, but when they give publicly their actions as members of hierarchically arranged or socially equal groups enhance the process. Rosman and Rubel have observed that 'the sequence of these acts of giving, receiving, and repaying serves to create bonds between individuals and groups' and both bondedness and separateness between individuals and groups is inherent in the process of exchange (1971: 2). In the following description of a possession-trance event gifts (which sometimes look like simple transfers of property) are seen as elements in acts of exchange. Each gift implies the separateness of the giver from the receiver and its content is defined by the donor's position in the bori cult and Hausa society. These gifts also outline the ties between separate and, in this case, unequal social levels, since repayment cannot be made in kind. Typically, material wealth moves in one direction and services in the opposite.

The week after *Id al-fitr* (Arabic: the Lesser Feast) I received an invitation to attend a special possession-trance ceremony. It was an event at which seventeen of the twenty people present were women. An elderly male praise-singer who was the husband of one of the female musicians, my male assistant, and myself were the only men present. The woman who had organized the ceremony was ranked as one of Kano City's most senior bori devotees, and with her age of between 70 and 80 she was probably also one of its oldest. Apart from any 'accidental' possession-trance induction by any of those in attendance, she was to be the only active medium. To honour the spirits residing in her ancient, adobe-constructed compound (the main room of which had a twenty-foot-high vaulted ceiling) the Magajiyar Bori had invited her guests as witnesses and intended to allow herself to be 'ridden' by each of the ninety-nine spirits possessing her. As it turned out there was time for only fifty-six. The ceremony began slowly, but it did not take long for the old woman to fall into possession-trance. Paraphernalia of all kinds, clothing, tools, and special cloth, were used in the symbolic impersonation of each of the spirits invoked. Every spirit was greeted at its arrival, and before the Magajiya sneezed—the sign of its departure—we wished it a safe journey back to the spirits' city of Jangare.

Many times after the old woman was possessed by a new spirit her attendant would bring out a tray of kola nuts, sweets, vegetables, perfume, and money which the spirit would give to various members of the audience. Some of the women would anticipate these gifts with small amounts of money of their own which they would give to the Magajiya, pressing each of their coins on her forehead. As the money was given (some of it falling to the ground) the attendant would gather it up and wrap it in a small piece of cloth. The ceremony was long —it took some 6½ hours to complete—and many left before the final spirit was called. As each guest departed they would approach the medium, bow down on one knee, then rise to distribute money to women standing or sitting along the wall, many of whom were engaged in playing the *kwarya* calabashes and singing.

From my perspective as an observer, giving and receiving seemed as central to the occasion as the possession-trance demonstration. Anxious to be accepted by my hosts, I gave a five-shilling note to my assistant who, according to instruction, gave it unceremoniously to the Magajiya or rather to the spirit, Dan Galadima (the Prince), who at that moment was riding his mare. The attendant placed the note in a scarf, and it disappeared—but not for long for when the tray of gifts which were to be distributed by the Prince was brought out the five-shilling note reappeared. There was no doubt that it was the same one since it was the only piece of paper money being used. From the tray it went into the hands of a well-dressed woman sitting near the Magajiya and opposite the musicians. Shortly afterwards as this woman rose to leave the note again came into view and was given to the woman singer who seemed to be directing the activity of the other musicians.

After asking a few of the women sitting near me what they thought of the route the money had taken, the following interpretation was provided. The original gift to the Prince was a sign that its giver was among the followers of the spirit, including its patrons and its horses but the Prince gave it away, since he is incapable of keeping anything.[10] The woman who received the money was being repaid for her service as a mare for the spirit. She later gave it to a musician in exchange for the latter's services in invoking the spirits.

All exchanges during this event implied social inequality between givers and receivers.[11] The first kind of presentation is thought of as a kind of tribute, passing from mere mortals to supernatural spirits, i.e. upwards in the status continuum. All the other presentations represent the donor's largesse or generosity, moving downwards through the system. Besides this directional aspect of each gift it is clear that the focus of its presentation is on exchange, not simple transfer. Each gift demands a return, but repayment comes in the form of service. The recipients both accept their subordinate positions in the ranking system of the cult, a passive service, and provide witness to the aims of the event itself, an active service.

In his classic essay on exchange Mauss describes three rules of obligation: the obligation to give, the obligation to receive, and the obligation to repay (1967: 37-41). For Mauss as well as a long line of social anthropologists after him exchange is an important part of social relations. As the account above suggests gift-giving is a conspicuous phenomenon in cult activity, gifts being given to men and to gods according to recognized conventions and with certain expectations. Rosman and Rubel, taking their inspiration from Mauss's *The Gift* (1967), maintain that different exchange systems are paralleled by different social structures (1971: 1). The Hausa in general and bori in particular provide an excellent example of this. Muslim societies are commonly ranked societies. Thus it is, as Firth notes, 'the custom to send presents to a person of high rank that he may protect the donor; to a person of inferior rank that the donor may obtain his services; and to a person of equal rank that the donor may obtain an equivalent' (1973: 388). In ritual contexts a most frequent exchange is between representatives of unequal rank (persons and gods), and repayment is expected in a form different to the original gift. Money is repaid with service, sacrifice with divine favour. This inequality of objects exchanged is symbolic of Hausa society itself in which differing horizontal levels are interconnected with vertical exchange patterns.

When in a state of possession-trance a bori devotee ceases to be himself; he becomes the physical representation of the possessing spirit. Therefore, during possession-trance events non-possessed mortals have an opportunity, an obligation even, to give gifts to spirits. This obligation is most strongly felt by those who have been marked by the spirit through initiation, for failure to give could provoke the god's disfavour which in turn could lead to the reappearance of the symptoms of an old affliction. Those not possessed by the spirit may offer gifts to obtain answers to any one of a variety of questions—whom to marry, whom to avoid, whether to travel and so on. Just before or during possession-trance ceremonies gifts to the gods consist almost exclusively of cash donations which eventually become the property of their horses.

Another kind of gift and one associated with the Muslim practice of alms-giving, may be given to the gods. To enter into a contract with a bori spirit an animal specifically identified with it may be sacrificed. The circumstances surrounding a sacrifice are usually that a remedy for some non-chronic ailment or personal misfortune is sought, and the spirit responsible is identified by the nature of the affliction. The spirit is appeased by what is considered the life-substance of iskoki, the blood of the sacrificed animal. The meat is given away as *sadaka* (alms or charity) to those in social positions to receive it (Qur'anic scholars and students, the homeless and destitute, and devotees and musicians). A person receiving a gift of meat when told that it is sadaka customarily says, 'May Allah [not a bori spirit] grant your wish'. This witnessing is an important part of the completion of the sacrifice. The concept of Muslim alms-giving oc-casionally predominates over that of sacrifice, and the principle of sacrificial blood is forgotten. Thus, raw meat is transformed into cooked meat, and cooked meat into food dishes with no meat, sadaka for bori spirits now including grain and vegetables as well as chickens, sheep, goats, and cattle. As Mauss notes for alms, 'it is the old gift morality raised to the position of a principle of justice; the gods and spirits consent that the portion reserved for them and destroyed in useless sacrifice should go to the poor and the children' (1967: 15-16).

As gifts to the gods are symbolic of the relationship men have with them, gifts between cult-adepts are symbolic of their social relationships within bori. In non-ritual contexts exchanges between members of the cult outline mutual equality or inequality, depending on the nature of the gift and the specific cir-cumstances in which it is given. In general gifts between people (of the same or opposite sex) with roughly equal cult status are repaid with equivalents, money with money, food with food, and cloth (or clothing) with cloth. Since Hausa so-ciety normally bifurcates male and female relationships, gifts between adepts of the same sex are more common than those between different sexes. A man or a woman's bond friend is treated as a confidant, and commonly the spirits which ride each of them are pictured similarly; men or women whose spirits 'travel to-gether' often become close friends. Inequality in non-ritual contexts follow the Hausa pattern of patron-client relationships. The superior partner who enjoys a prominent status in the cult, is under obligation to give money and goods (mate-rial objects) to the inferior one. The inferior partner reciprocates with his ser-vices (both the demonstration of dissociation and witnessing) at possession-trance events and is always willing to testify to his patron's generosity (non-material acts). The material-non-material content of this relationship may be disrupted, particularly in the case of male-female patron-client relationships in-volving prostitutes and transvestites who are expected to pay 'rent' money at frequent intervals. This is perhaps an example of gifts for 'protection'. Just as cult-adepts who consider themselves social equals often serve gods thought to be in the same generation and 'house' in the spirit world, the social difference be-tween patrons and clients is matched by the social inequality of their respective possessing spirits. It is not uncommon for recently initiated devotees whose cult status is low, to be described as horses for junior gods. Similarly, no cases were recorded of senior cult-adepts being ridden by any except important divine horsemen, either senior generation iskoki, house leaders, or *Sarkin Aljan* (the Chief of the Spirits) himself.

In ritual contexts the same kinds of social relationships are revealed, but, as already mentioned, the emphasis is often on inequality. The only gift-giving observed during women's performances which involved equals was confined to exchanges between spirits. In such cases a devotee in possession-trance gives some item of ritual significance to another dissociating medium, and this is frequently reciprocated on the spot. Their attendants usually try to prevent these exchanges, because all items must be bought back by the spirits' 'followers' immediately after the ceremony. The majority of the gifts given at women's possession-trance performances are considered by the participants to mark social inequality, and no attempt is made to reciprocate. For example, wealthy patrons are expected to make gifts to the senior cult member in attendance, to the leader of the musician's group playing for the performance, and to the host at whose invitation the ceremony was called. Guests and observers are expected to give to mediums in possession-trance (actually, as we have noted, to the spirits riding them), particularly those being ridden by 'their' spirits, and to musicians and praise-singers. A significant aspect of this kind of gift-giving is that a clear distinction is made between givers and receivers. Whereas musicians never seem to act as gift-givers, cult-adepts may be givers when not involved in possession-trance and receivers when they are. As far as devotees are concerned, anyone may receive gifts; the mark of high cult status is demonstrated by a devotee's ability or obligation to give gifts. Thus, the gifts given by a medium with an important cult status validate his position *vis-à-vis* other members of the cult. When the obligation is ignored or the effort judged weak the giver's status is eroded.

The ritual performances included in this study may be divided in one way by describing them in terms of the musical instruments used to invoke the spirits. Participants themselves frequently use this kind of classification which generates the following sub-categorization: *(a) kidan kwarya* ('drumming' on large, inverted, hemispherical calabashes); *(b) kidan garaya* ('drumming', actually strumming, a two-stringed lute); *(c) kidan goge* ('drumming', actually bowing, a singlestringed lute); and *(d) busan sarewa* (blowing a whistle), to name most but not all the ways spirits may be called. Informants generally make a broader classification consisting of two types of possession-trance events based on the sex of the musicians as well as the sex of the participants, and the venue. The first type, *kidan amada*, has songs accompanied by calabash drums (s. kwarya) usually played by non-professional women. Such performances in the 'amada style' are held inside compounds and are attended almost exclusively by women. *Kidan bori* is a general term used to refer to any bori event at which spirits are called, but specifically it is a second type and indicates garaya, goge, or sarewa performances by professional male musicians, held in 'public' places, and attended by mixed audiences.

A significant difference between female amada performances and mixed bori (male musicians) performances lies in the rules for the giving of gifts. Whereas small gifts of money given to trancers at either type of event are presented without formality, larger gifts of money and clothing are presented with the formality of a public announcement by a *maroki* (male praise-shouter) at public events. The praise-shouter's announcement of the exact amount of the gift and the specific identity of the giver is a prominent aspect of a public performance and results in a pause in the tempo of the event. After shouting for the musicians and dancers to stop—even mediums in possession-trance assume an 'at-ease' posture—the praise-shouter begins with the name of the giver, elaborating it with as much of his genealogy (including requests for Allah to grant his deceased relatives peace), and as many of his praise-epithets as can be learned from whispering friends who provide him with his 'material'. He continues with a description of the gift itself, presenting it in such a way as to exaggerate its size or significance. Two shillings is not simply two shillings; it is twenty pennies or forty half-pennies, and five shillings becomes half a naira or fifty pennies. In other words witnessing is far more obvious in public than in private events. For his service the maroki receives a commission which is not included in the original gift. Thus, a gift of five shillings normally costs the giver an additional five to ten pennies.

A gift given to someone not directly involved in the performance may be kept or redistributed out of social view. However, if a gift is given to a spirit or trancer or a performing musician the rule is that it must be brought forward and displayed at the feet of the seated musicians. Usually a number of shoes or hats is used to collect money gifts for each 'authorized' recipient. A glance at the piles of gifts on the lead musician's mat provides an observer with a physical chart of the divisions which will be made at the end of the ceremony.

The rules by which gifts may be given to participants are very strict, but as my assistant tried to explain to me, there are also rules for breaking rules. For example, while watching a public bori ceremony from among the performing musicians I became interested in the obvious talent and excellence of a special singer who had been added to the ensemble for this particular series of events. It was the *salla* octave, the evening preceding the Muslim festival of Id al-fitr (Hausa: *Karamar Salla;* lit. Small *Salla*) and the seven evenings after it, and the participants considered it an important occasion to placate the spirits which had lived in the Emir of Kano's palace since it was built in the fifteenth century. I expressed my delight with the vocalist's artistry, to my assistant, and asked if there was any way I could give him something to reward his efforts. My assistant reminded me that because Malam Hasan, the singer, was under the authority of the lead musician, his services would be paid for with a share from the shoe holding the musicians' money. Since a good singer is customarily acknowledged by the audience with gifts to the musicians as a group, its leader doubtless hoped that Malam Hasan's gift-eliciting potential might require the use of a bigger container than the shoe, perhaps a hat. But I wanted to give him something entirely for himself. I was told that I must catch the singer's eye and then say, '*Zo. Za mu yi wata magana*' ('Come. Let's have a talk'). When he was near I could then give him the *hasatan akebe* (concealed gift). I tried the formula, but as I was handing the money to the singer (which I had been advised would 'warm his voice',) a praise-shouter saw it, making the gift a public matter. The vocalist did not get his concealed gift but, I think, appreciated the effort. I had had a glimpse of the mechanism by which individuals within a group can be given gifts even when the customary mode of giving is to groups.

When a public possession-trance event is concluded the participants gather around the musicians' mat for the first division of the gifts. The money, perfume, and clothing which constitute the musicians' share is left uncounted at the site of the performance, but a small gift is taken from it for each of the praise-shouter announcers. The musician-leader then counts the money and itemizes the other gifts given to each of the participating mediums who had been ridden by one or more spirits. He announces the contents of each shoe and the name of the spirit for which it was collected; the spirit's mount then steps forward to claim his share and is expected to give approximately one-third of the amount to the musicians for their part in calling the spirit. Another third is given to his attendant and any other cult member who may have assisted him during his possession-trance. If he has had a successful night a cult-adept may go home with fifteen to twenty shillings, but most expect only half that amount.

The musicians fare much better than the trancers, since their share includes gifts given specifically to them during the performance as well as small amounts of money given to dancers not in possession-trance (who are expected to pass on all the gifts they receive to the musicians) and commissions from each of the trancers. Individual members of the musicians' group may not receive any more than the average medium, but such payments are made on the basis of the musician's status in his group.

NOTES

[1] For a discussion of a kwarya-accompanied performance by Katsina women see King (1966; 1967).

[2] See, for example, the early accounts of Palmer (1914), Tremearne (1914; 1915), and Krusius (1915).

[3] 'Displacement' is remarkably similar to the concept of 'deprivation' found in Lewis' writings on possession-trance cults in East Africa (cf. Lewis 1966: 1971b).

[4] *Daudu* is a praise name for any *Galadima* (a ranked title), but it specifically refers to the bori spirit, *Dan Galadima* (lit. 'son of Galadima'; the Prince). The Prince is said to be 'a handsome young man, popular with women, a spendthrift, and a gambler' (Greenberg 1946: 42). Informants were unable to provide a reason why male homosexuals should be identified with his name, and the association remains unexplained.

[5] Properly speaking, a medium can never retire, since the spirits which caused his initiation will never leave him. He may, however, cease to be an active trancer and gradually leave the ranks of those who are.

[6] Not to be confused with phenomena (hysteria, spontaneous possession, etc.) occurring among some peoples of Africa and elsewhere and specifically described as 'epidemiological'.

[7] See Turner (1968) for additional material on cults of affliction.

[8] Greenberg observes that the ascription of insanity to the list of ailments caused by supernatural spirits is probably attributable to Islamic influence. Non-Muslim Black Africans, he states, do not commonly interpret insanity as being spirit-caused (1946: 61).

[9] Other spirits and their medicines are examined in Chapter V.

[10] The Prince is a habitual gambler. Within the context of bori ritual, gambling is transformed into gift-giving. In this way the Prince is seen as the very symbol of generosity, but of the interested, obligation-producing kind. 'Gifts' given by the Prince must be returned with heavy interest payments. The symbolic significance of spirits' characteristics is further discussed in Chapter IV, below. See also Besmer (in press, b) and Greenberg (1946: 42-3).

[11] During periodic possession-trance events another dimension is evident in exchange behaviour. Groups of individuals may compete with each other as social equals, attempting to display like amounts of generosity with respect to a third group (see below, Chapter V).

Chapter 3 · Musicians: Their Society, Instruments, and Music

SOCIAL ORGANIZATION

As mentioned in the previous chapter, occupational classification is the most important factor in the evaluation of social status. The Hausa define musicians' work as a craft (*sana'a*) called *roko* (lit. begging), and those engaged in it—instrumentalists, vocalists, praise-singers and -shouters—are called *maroka* (s. *maroki*) and ranked in the lowest social category. The essential aspect of roko is the type of service performed, that is, acclamation, and its social and economic circumstances. That instruments and music may be used in this service is irrelevant for the Hausa. This attitude is exemplified in the case of instrumentalists who play a certain type of royal drum in the emir's court. *Tambari* (royal hemispherical drum) players are not classified as maroka (although music is as much part of their activity as it is for any professional drummer) but as *bayi* (s. *bawa;* slave), a designation which they are careful to emphasize to avoid being confused with low class maroka. As royal slaves the status placement of tambari drummers is higher than other instrumentalists, probably due to their affinity to the royal courts in which they serve.

Musicians, praise-singers and -shouters—all of them professional maroka—can be divided into the following categories:[1] (a) the musicians of craft groups; (b) musicians in political life; (c) musicians of recreational music; (d) musician-entertainers; and (e) musicians for the bori cult. Those in the first category have patrons within craft groups, and much of their economic support comes from performing for them. As Ames notes, musicians tend to concentrate their activities on one or other of the categories, but overlapping can be found especially in the case of *kalangu* (double-membrane, hourglass-shaped, pressure drum) players. Usually associated with butchers, kalangu drummers also perform recreational music for social dancing at marriage and naming ceremonies.

Blacksmiths, hunters, farmers, and other musicians have been listed as the craft groups for which these musicians play (Ames 1973: 135), but the data gathered for the present study indicate that one important qualification should be included. Musicians do not normally play for members of their own craft group. When they do the musician who serves as the patron for the performances symbolically removes himself from the group and becomes host for some special event, for example, a naming or marriage ceremony. This separation of host or sponsor and entertainer is a significant feature of any performance, since gifts or payments publicly given frequently outline a superior-inferior relationship between giver and receiver, specifically, the groups they represent. Where public witnessing is not a feature of the exchange of service for material wealth individuals act as members of the same social group, but it cannot be said that the giver is the patron of the receiver, at least as far as their respective craft affiliations are concerned. Such relationships are properly considered as aspects of the internal structure of musicians' groups, different in quality to those which musicians have with other craft groups.

Musicians in political life formerly included those who performed for political parties as well as court musicians and famous singers. However, political parties have been banned since the end of the First Republic and civilian rule and the musicians who used to play for them have moved into other sub-categories. When the Military Government retires from Nigeria politics it is anticipated that many of these groups will resume their previous activities and count politicians among their patrons.

The only professionals in this category are court musicians[2] and famous singers, of whom many of the latter are, at least nominally, musicians of particular emirs in northern Nigeria. Court musicians live in the same towns as their patrons—an emir, titled court official, Local Government Authority department head, or a district head—and most of them enjoy some titular status in the royal court. Those who reside in cities are expected to perform at least once a week in the emir's palace as well as for special court events and religious festivals. The instruments on which they perform may be considered as symbols of status, since they may be played only for the aristocracy.

The emir exercises his authority (considerably tempered by modern Nigerian governmental structure) through a system of ranked, titled offices. Court musicians' groups are modelled on this pattern. It is customary for the emir to award a title, bestowed in a turbanning ceremony, to the leader of each group of court musicians, who then turbans selected members of his ensemble with titles borrowed from traditional emirate administration. To a great extent the aura and prestige of these courtly titles is passed on to the musicians who hold them. This is part of the reason why royal musicians are consistently ranked above other kinds of musicians by Hausa laymen.

Ames's third category contains professionals who play music for different craft groups and social classes, music which is not restricted by any ceremony or religious ritual (1973: 138). They play for naming ceremonies and wedding feasts, boxing and wrestling contests, and 'for dancing on the streets Friday nights or any pleasant moonlight night, and for special plays put on by young men and girls during the harvest season' (Ibid.).

The musician-entertainers of Ames's fourth category are Hausa comedians. In Kano the most conspicuous musician-entertainers are *'Yan Kama* (s. *Dan Kama;* lit. 'son of catching', from the belief that the original comedians caught their gifts in their mouths).[3] The leader of the group has a title in the Emir of Kano's court, but his attendance there is so infrequent that other royal musicians doubt its legitimacy. Spending most of his time performing for private parties, in the market place, and in the nightclubs of Kano's *Sabon Gari* (Strangers' Quarter), he uses his title as an entrance ticket to play for court events which are both widely attended and lucrative.

'Yan Kama do not dress as 'strangely' as other types of comedians; in fact, they frequently pose as learned men complete with the appropriate attire, but their performances are quite unlike those of 'serious' musicians. In Gidley's words, 'they have never customarily used *habaici* "hurtful innuendo", *zambo* "provocative speech and song", and *batsa* "indecent remarks" to the extent that some other maroka . . . have done' (1967: 53). Their skilful and genuinely amusing performances are very successful, using such themes as the learned pedant, gastronomy, and the domestic scene in a carefully rehearsed style. They customarily contain the following elements: original comical songs on contemporary topics, satires of popular songs or lighthearted imitations of popular musicians, admonitions, and a closing 'prayer'. The following example of a closing prayer was recorded in the palace of the Emir of Kano during festivities marking the Muslim festival of Id al-fitr (Besmer 1972: 247-8):

Dan Kama:	*'Jama'a za ni addu'a ko mu tashi.'* Citizens, I will pray before we leave.
Assistant:	*'Gafarta Malam.'* Attention sir.
DK:	*'Ya Allahu gwaza Allahu rusga fara* Allah koko yam Allah first break off *wa daka namu Uban gijin gayya.'* and pound ours, the Lord God of all people.
Assistant and audience:	*'Amin!'* Amen.
DK:	*'Yini da yunwa dai Alla sauwaki mana.'* Daylight and hunger, may Allah preserve us from them.
All:	*'Amin!'*
DK:	*'Idan muka je nema wanda ba ya da shi* If we go searching for something which somebody does not have *ya karba a gurin danuwansa ya ba mu* he receives it from his relative and gives it to us *in mun tafi warware, jama'a na Annabi,* if we go away untangled, people of the Prophet, *kowa ya ce amin.'* everyone say amen.
All:	*'Amin!'*
DK:	*'To, ba sadaka jama'a, sai amin, amin, amin?'* What, no alms, friends; just amen, amen, amen?

What was particularly unusual about this performance which ended with the comedian asking his audience for alms was that the audience consisted almost entirely of court musicians. The incredulity with which his request was received seemed to underline the point made earlier in this section, that is that musicians do not normally perform for themselves. The fact that gifts were publicly solicited from them by another musician can only be understood in the context of the comedian's performance which included a satire of acceptable musicians' behaviour.

The fifth category of musicians surveyed by Ames consists of those who play for the bori cult of 'spirit-possession' or possession-trance. In many respects such professionals are regarded as a group to be the lowest placed musicians in the maroka class. As individuals they may achieve fame and recognition through their excellence as artists, but such cases are clearly the exception rather than the rule.

The reasons for this extremely low evaluation of their status seem to fall in two main areas, and Ames has touched on one of them. He notes that officially, at least, music has no part in Islamic ritual, and musical instruments are not played in the mosque (Ames 1973: 140). The only exceptions to this practice are the unaccompanied chanting of religious poems and Muslim hymns, and the playing of the *bandiri* (a set of two or more drums, one type of which is a single-membrane circular frame-drum with or without circular metal jingles, and a second type which is a single-membrane bowl-shaped drum).[4] The view that Muslim scholars, teachers, or mosque heads take is that many kinds of Hausa music are evil. They single out goge (single-stringed, bowed lute) music, describing it as the music of the devil (Ibid.: 141). Since one of the two main instruments used in the invocation of bori spirits is the goge, they are somewhat justified in their conclusion that to their way of thinking, bori spirits are devils. It is understandable, therefore, why goge players (bori musicians) are not received with much enthusiasm by devout Muslims.

The second area of criticism of bori musicians is the fact that Hausa society views them as keeping bad company. This is of course a restatement of the stereotype, layman opinion concerning anyone who participates in bori rituals and its other activities. Its members are treated as deviants, and the musicians who play for them must share its social stigma. In other words, it is bad enough to be a musician, but inexcusable to practice one's craft in support of this heathen cult.

Ordinarily, Hausa occupations are limited to one sex, but maroka cannot be so described. Female praise-singers/musicians (s. *zabiya*) perform side by side with men and in ensembles for recreational music frequently act as the leaders of the integrated group, or organize ensembles consisting entirely of women. One example of this latter type may be found among royal musicians where groups of female praise-singers perform for the emir during public court and religious events or on a private basis for his wives who live secluded in the palace. *Zabiyoyi* (pl.) of the Emir of Kano, for example, exercise their privilege as women to enter private areas of the palace closed to men, but reflect their unusual position in an essentially male-dominated craft by wearing male-associated gowns (s. *riga*) which they modify by tying at the waist (Besmer 1972: 46). Another example of a women's ensemble is the kwarya (hemispherical shell of a dried half-gourd) players who perform in secluded compounds for almost exclusively female audiences. Women's bori ceremonies may be the occasion for such performances which include zabiyoyi as vocalists and instrumentalists, and both professional and non-professional women as accompanists.

Ames categorizes group musicians according to the events in which they perform and the patrons whom they serve. The system which Hausa musicians use to classify themselves largely ignores these factors, considering instead the professional's specific performance skill. There is no lexical item in Hausa which can be translated as 'music', rather, the activities of a certain class of professionals are divided into *roko* (lit. to beg), *waka* (to sing; also song[5]), *busa* (to blow), and *kida* (to drum). The first of these is considered to be the primary term, and from it the whole class is named: *maroki* (lit. one who does roko). Any professional in this social category may be described as a maroki, but unless his work is confined to praise-shouting or -singing and he performs without instrumental accompaniment a more specific term than maroki may be used to identify his activity. Thus, a *mawaki* (from waka) is a vocalist; a *mabushi* (from busa) performs on a wind instrument; and a *makadi* (from kida) is a drummer. Bori and other musicians who play such stringed instruments as the goge and the *garaya* (two-stringed, plucked lute) are described as 'drummers', and the Hausa do not have a special term for bowing or strumming.

Thus far the discussion has been confined to professional musicians. Non-professionals who may, nonetheless, be competent specialists are also involved in the performance of Hausa music. Apart from the large number of people who sing to amuse themselves or play informal or perishable instruments, a few non-professionals are conspicuous in organized music performances. As non-professional musicians they do not consider themselves maroka (or zabiyoyi) and earn their living in the practice of some other craft than music or 'begging.' The first of these groups, mentioned earlier in this chapter, consists of certain royal slaves who play tambari drums. They prefer to be identified as slaves and spend all but a few weeks of the year (when they are in attendance at the emir's palace) working on rural farms.

A second group of non-professionals consists of the women who assist professional female musicians at performances inside secluded compounds. Actually, the line between professional zabiya leaders and their non-professional *'yan kwarya* (lit. daughters of kwarya-gourds; hemispherical-gourd or -calabash players) accompanists is not easily drawn. Sometimes the latter may be considered as non-professionals, but in other instances they are not. These performances are generally called kidan amada (drumming for amada), one subsection of which is songs for bori spirits, and are based on *kwaryar kidan ruwa* (the hemispherical gourds for drumming on water).

With the completion of this brief introduction to the description and classification of both professional and non-professional Hausa musicians, we may now examine the internal organization of bori musicians' groups. Similar to the picture drawn for the society as a whole bori musicians place themselves in clearly defined hierarchies. For some groups these positions are formally recognized with titles borrowed from traditional emirate administration, while for others the positions have no further designation other than the ranking implied by a musician's particular skill.

In a study of bori in Katsina, King describes a group of professional female musicians whose members hold ranked titles (1966: 107). The leader of the group was elected by her fellow musicians as *Sarkin Kidan Kwarya* (Chief of the Beating of Kwarya) a title which was then confirmed by turbanning at the hands of a member of the Katsina royal court. Her two assistants hold the titles *Maji-dadin Kwarya (Majidadi[6] of Kwarya)* and *Wazirin Kwarya (Waziri[7] of Kwarya)*, respectively, and are said to have been turbanned by a member of the Katsina royalty.

The use of such titles by bori musicians is not thought to be very common, considering the data for the present study. Only one example could be found in which a cult musician was identified with a title, and this was in the small urban settlement of Ningi. The Emir of Ningi took a positive attitude towards the bori cult, although he did not act as its patron. However, his younger brother, the District Head of the town and in line for the emirate, acted as a royal sponsor for the cult and regularly called its members to perform at his compound. The two of them generated a degree of support for bori in Ningi far greater than any other place surveyed. For example, as mentioned in Chapter II, it was the Emir of Ningi himself and not a royal representative who confirmed the title of the town's Sarkin Bori. He also turbanned the cult's selection of a principal musician, giving him the title *Sarkin Garaya* (Chief of the Garaya). Unlike the practice reported for Katsina, however, no further titles were given to other cult musicians.

The data on the use of ranked titles by bori musicians are sparse, but out-lines of a pattern emerge. Title-holding cult musicians are not chosen by the tur-banning official in the same way as are court musicians. Cult musicians are con-firmed in their titles only after they have been selected or nominated by their associates. This recognition of achieved status is identical to the selection process used for non-musician cult status positions.[8] Court musicians, on the other hand, may be nominated by other musicians, but the emir can and sometimes does make such appointments for personal reasons.[9] The differences in the way leadership is selected in these two types of musicians' groups seems to emphasize the different criteria for status placement in the social sub-systems in which musicians participate. Achievement plays a minor role as a factor in the assign-ment of traditional court titles. The candidate's ascribed status, primarily his genealogical position takes precedence over his deeds. Court musicians, like their patrons, are chosen on the basis of the positions of their relatives and not on their ability as performers. Within the limits of the bori cult, however, achieve-ment is a major factor in the attainment of leadership. Bori musicians must demonstrate their skill as performers before their peers (musicians and cult-adepts) will consider them qualified for nomination.

It might be asked why so few bori musicians actually hold titles. Only one case was recorded in the present study, leaving the vast majority identified only by a personal name plus such designations as *mai garaya* (lit. owner of the garaya; a double-stringed plucked-lute player) or *mai goge* (lit. owner of the goge; a single-stringed bowed-lute player). No satisfactory explanation of this could be found, but one factor, proximity to a royal court, suggests itself. Musicians who are directly associated with royal courts or who count royalty among their patrons—this would include court musicians as well as those bori musicians who have received some official recognition—are more likely to use the status system found in traditional emirate administration (ranked titles) than those who do not have royal support, that is, the majority of cult musicians.

Why this same factor should not also apply to non-musicians' positions in the cult can perhaps be explained in terms of simple transfer of the ranked title system from a major social organization (traditional emirate administration) to

a minor one (cult administration) irrespective of royal sponsorship. This transference is exactly what King observed for both cult and musician organization in
Katsina (1966: 107). While his study implies that both group structures were
produced by the same factor, this conclusion is not supported by data gathered
elsewhere. Clearly King had no reason to suppose that any special conditions
might have existed for the musicians he studied. His data was based on a single
group of musicians whose group structure was similar to that found in the rest of
the cult. However, on the basis of the present material it would appear that the
musicians' use of ranked titles might more probably have been due to their close
association with Katsina royalty than to his 'transferring' principle which
accounted for general cult organization. In other words title transference seems
to occur with non-musician cult-adepts independent of an association with a
royal court. The rationale is an effective, familiar, or prestigious administration.
Title transferring occurs with cult musicians only when they are associated with
a royal court.

As should be clear, most bori musicians' groups do not outline their
structure with ranked titles. Positions in such groups are frequently indicated on
the basis of the performance on a particular instrument and on seating arrangements. It is a general rule among professional musicians that ensembles be divided
into principal and secondary roles whether or not instruments are used. When
instruments are used this division is extended to include principal and secondary
types. Excluding for the moment women's performances which use one 'family'
of kwarya gourds, a family which has senior and junior members, bori groups
generally use instruments of contrasting types. Thus, the garaya plucked lute
is played with *buta* rattles, and the goge bowed lute with kwarya gourds. In such
cases it is the garaya or goge player who holds the principal or leadership position
in the ensemble. The accompanying rattle or gourd players are further divided
into principal and secondary members. The principal member of the group's
chorus, a buta or kwarya player, sits closest to the group's leader. The other
members of the chorus place themselves in descending order of rank down to the
group's most junior member who sits to the leader's extreme left or right. When
the ensemble uses a vocalist not playing an instrument he sits near the lute
player if he is judged especially proficient or near the lowest ranked chorus
member if he is undistinguished. His proximity to the lute player therefore is a
physical representation of his social position in the group. Praise-singers and
-shouters wander about outside the group of seated musicians, and they hold the
ensemble's lowest positions.

Thus, the following levels may be distinguished in professional bori
musicians' groups even when titles are absent: (a) leader; (b) chorus; (c) praise-
shouter; and, optionally, (d) vocalist. The leader is identified with his personal
name or nickname and the instrument he plays, for example, Malam Shu'aibu
Mai Garaya (Malam[10] Shu'aibu, Player of the Garaya). Malam Shu'aibu's lute
playing, like that of other ensemble leaders, is occasionally reinforced by other
garaya players, but it is never difficult to observe which is the group's leader.
The pace of the performance and the transitions between separate spirits' songs
are always dependent upon Malam Shu'aibu's signals. Significantly, secondary
lute players are never treated as members of the chorus and do not join in singing choral responses to the leader's verses. Leaders' assistants, if they may be
termed as such, are not fully integrated into the ensemble, and their presence is

inversely correlated with the main lute player's reputation as a performer. As a general practice well-known and proficient leaders prefer not to use them, whereas young or inexperienced ones do.

It is the leader's responsibility to ensure that a complete ensemble is engaged for any performance, and the host for the event deals only with him. In places where the principal non-musician leadership position in the cult is weak or absent the lute player may also be responsible for inviting the right kinds and number of trancers for the event. This is particularly important for periodic performances which are not tied to special cult rituals the most common of which are weddings and namings.

The principal musician in a bori group may expect each of the members of his ensemble to call on him with greetings every day in much the same way that courtiers visit an emir's palace. This practice is much less common in small urban areas where farming takes a sizeable portion of commoners', even musicians', time. Where the members of the ensemble accept the principal musician's complete authority over their lives group relationships are amicable, but as is often the case senior members of the chorus are envious of the leader's position and only the formality of a relationship between master and apprentice prevents the ensemble from disintegrating.

A most important expectation that a group has of its leader is that he will be generous in his division of the money obtained for performances. In many respects the leader is caught between patrons or sponsors who underpay and the members of his ensemble who appear to want more than their fair share of the 'take' from a performance. As a professional musician the leader must be careful to avoid engagements which might not be particularly well-paid. He must consider whether his assistants' share of the profits will satisfy their expectations of what they should receive for a night's work. When the usual proportions of fifty percent for the leader and fifty percent to be divided (unequally) among the chorus do not result in the assistants' definitions of a fair wage 'good' (that is, generous) leaders voluntarily reduce their own share. 'Greedy' leaders consider their assistants last and group friction results. One gourd-rattle player who performs in two bori ensembles put it this way: when thirty naira (forty-five U.S. dollars) are received for a performance[11] by the group in which he holds a position as second member of the chorus the leader keeps twelve naira and gives eighteen naira to his assistants. The principal assistant may expect eight naira and the second assistant six. When the same amount is received by the leader of the group in which he occasionally acts as principal assistant, this gourd-rattle player complained that only six naira is divided (equally) between the two members of the chorus. His share of three naira is unfair in view of the identical amount given to the lesser member of the chorus and the twenty-four kept by the leader. He maintained that if it were not for the fact that this man trained him in his craft and that he must address him as *Baba* (father) he would withhold his services from the group. Actually, other musicians described this buta player as guilty of *kwadayi* (greediness), saying that he wanted too much all the time.[12]

Whereas the members of an ensemble's chorus hold sarautu (s. sarauta; ranked title) when the group performs frequently for the aristocracy, no special designations are used in the majority of bori musicians' choruses. There are usually as many status positions as there are members of the chorus, but payments in particular indicate at least two and sometimes three separate levels. The first two levels are held by full members of the chorus and the third by apprentices if the group includes any. The principal member of the chorus like all the others is called by his proper name or a nickname and the instrument he plays. If his is the buta (gourd-rattle) it is known that he performs under a garaya-playing leader;[13] if he plays the kwarya (hemispherical gourd struck with two sticks) it is known that he accompanies the goge. In a bori performance the principal gourd player can be identified without much difficulty. He sits closest to the ensemble's leader and is usually the most technically proficient performer of his instrument's type. Unlike court musicians' groups in which the principal musician's role as lead vocalist is rarely assumed by any secondary member of the ensemble, the principal assistant in a bori group is frequently called upon by the leader to sing songs for which no choral response is required. For his work in a performance the leader's 'right-hand man' may expect a greater share of the money and gifts given to the chorus than any other member.

Other full members of the ensemble's chorus arrange themselves in a pattern of descending seniority next to the principal assistant. They are never asked to sing by themselves, being confined to the choral responses for particular songs. Their instrumental performance is usually as good as the group's principal assistant even if it is not as flamboyant. Despite the fact that differences in group rank determine seating order, no distinction is made between their separate shares of the 'take'. Customarily, the leader pays them with equal amounts, tending to overpay those who are his direct descendants. The equal shares described by the disgruntled gourd player above in which the leader failed to make the proper distinction between the principal assistant and an ordinary full member of the chorus were due to the fact that the lower-ranked buta player is the leader's youngest son. This practice is understandable under the general requirement in Hausa society to assist one's relatives in any way possible, but bori musicians consider it out of place in the pseudo-meritocracy of their performing groups.

Apprentices constitute a minor part of an ensemble's membership. Most groups have none, but young (ten to fifteen years old) members are often used in ensembles whose leader has a reputation as a teaching master. Garaya-buta ensembles are the only ones in which the present data record apprentice membership. However, since this is the way in which new performers are trained it is unlikely that they are not used in other types of groups from time to time. Apprentices receive a smaller portion of the group's earnings than its full members, not an unusual practice since they are not considered as adults, socially or professionally.[14]

At least one praise-shouter, an ordinary maroki, is usually affiliated with each bori musicians' group. He is distinguished by his detailed knowledge of the *kirari* (descriptive praise-epithets) associated with each of the spirits which the principal musician is able to invoke with his music. He rarely sits during a performance, walking around in front of the performing musicians and acting as a human microphone. He shouts the praises of the spirits as they are called and announces 'significant' gifts as measured by their size or the status of the giver. When a member of the audience or a participant in the event wishes to speak to the gathering he moves to the edge of the cleared dancing area and calls the maroki to his side. What follows is a most curious sight. Standing beside his temporary employer, the praise-shouter yells for the attention of the assemblage and the music and dancing stops. Then he shouts the praises and genealogy of the intended speaker and finishes his introduction by saying the person he has just named is the *mai magana* (lit. owner of the speech). The mai magana speaks to the praise-shouter in a quiet voice, and at the end of each phrase the praise-shouter proclaims what has been said in his loudest voice, being careful to change all first-person pronouns to third person. When the announcement is completed the mai magana gives the praise-shouter ten kobo (a tenth of a naira) for his work and returns to his former place in the crowd.

The praise-shouter announces gifts in a similar manner. He shouts for the attention of musicians and audience and then describes the gift in its greatest detail. Part of the praise-shouter's skill lies in his ability to flatter the gift-giver into greater and greater prestations. Indeed, the social recognition and approval which accompany even the simplest gifts have exactly that effect on the audience. Again, when the maroki has finished his work as an announcer he expects to receive a small commission additional to the gift. If one's fortune could be made in five- and ten-kobo amounts, praise-shouters provide proof of it.

When the event is concluded and it is time for the leader of the group to make the 'first division' of the spoils, the ensemble's praise-shouter stands patiently but interestedly to one side, awaiting his share. Although rarely more than a fraction of the small portion given to an apprentice during the second division, the praise-shouter may expect to go home with a total income almost as much as any member of the chorus.

The last, and it should be added, optional member of the ensemble, is a *mawaki* (vocalist). Unlike the principal assistant who only sings alone when no choral response is required, the mawaki may sing all of the leader's parts regardless of the chorus's role. He works, however, at the leader's direction and may be required to keep silent or join in with the chorus during the performance. How much he sings depends on the general assessment of him as an artist and the leader's whim. When an acknowledged expert is used by the group its leader allows him to do all the singing, recognizing that a good vocalist adds appeal to the performance and is capable of encouraging gift-giving. After a performance has been under way for a few hours the principal musician is likely to welcome the assistance of even a mediocre singer so that he may take a rest. Both *mawaka* (pl.) and principal assistants may be called upon for relief work.

Expert vocalists, those described as having a clear voice and knowing a large number of verses for as many songs, are seated close to the principal musician, while those of moderate ability find a place on the other side of the chorus. In garaya-buta ensembles the instrumentalists are seated on mats spread in a line on the ground. Vocalists sit on chairs or benches or stand so that their voices may be heard by a greater proportion of the audience than if they were seated on the ground. Many vocalists hold a small half-gourd or brass pan in front of their mouths as they sing. It was never clear whether this practice, confined to vocalists, was for aesthetic or technical reasons.

RECRUITMENT AND CULT MEMBERSHIP

The primary way in which prospective musicians are recruited is through the Hausa system of status ascription and patrilineal inheritance. That is, the son of a musician is expected to become a musician, and his ascribed status will be low. A secondary way in which a musician may inherit his craft is through male relatives on his mother's side, but this is usually given as an additional justification or refinement of his choice rather than as a sole rationale. The principal reason for this is that since musicians have a low status ascription the Hausa believe that no one would choose to become a maroki, using the craft of his mother's male relatives as an occupational source if his father's occupation was different. Thus, if a musician's maternal side is significant in his occupational choice it is generally because he wishes to point to a firm pedigree of patrilineal *and* matrilineal inheritance or because he wishes to support his claim to some musician's title or instrumental proficiency.

These are the general factors involved in any maroki's choice of his occupation, but many bori musicians add another. To become involved with the cult of possession-trance a musician must play the appropriate instrument or be familiar with a special corpus of songs and praises for the spirits. Bori musicians frequently come from families with a history of cult involvement or are maroka who have been initiated into the cult. The latter condition is exceptional since musicians *per se* are not active trancers. However, people who have been marked by supernatural spirits but who do not continue as active cult-adepts after their initiation may fulfill their obligation by participating as cult musicians.

Malam Shu'aibu Mai Garaya is a case in point. He describes his father and father's father as blacksmiths and garaya players, and according to the general rule, he should have been the same—a blacksmith first and a lute player second. He says that he knows smithing but that an illness in his early childhood made him reverse the occupations, and eventually he gave up iron work altogether. His mother's father was a musician, and while this provided further support for the decision to turn him into a bori musician his maternal relatives had no part in his training. It was a kinsman on his father's side who first taught him how to play the buta and the garaya and later acted as leader of the initiation which cured his illness and made him a horse of the gods. For some reason he never became an active trancer, interpreting the spirits' call by serving them as a musician.

TRAINING AND APPRENTICESHIPS

Reporting on his survey of sixty musicians in Zaria (northern Nigeria), Ames states that seventy-five percent of the total received formal training before becoming professionals (1973: 152). He further states that the percentages were higher for certain kinds of musicians, 'e.g. drummers for farmers, drummers for the youth, and court musicians' (1973: 161 n). Twenty-five bori musicians from Kano, Kurna Asabe (near Kano), Ringin, Ningi, and Maiduguri were interviewed during the present study, and all but one of them received training before being allowed to participate in cult ensembles. The single exception was a metal-rattle player—not usually a bori instrument—who had perfected his own style and technique and 'sat in' on garaya performances in Ningi on an irregular basis. He liked to think of himself as a professional musician, but everyone else described his occupation as farming rather than roko. It was concluded from this data that the vast majority of bori musicians do receive formal instruction, 'involving demonstration by the teacher and observation and correction of the learner' (Ames 1973: 152).

Two types of training can be distinguished, depending upon the kinship relationship between teacher and pupil. One type is where the two are related as kinsmen—either through males or females, although the former is more common than the latter—and this is a simple example of expected inheritance of the craft from relatives. The other is where they are not related as kinsmen and falls under the rubric of apprenticeships. About as many Zaria musicians receive instruction from kinsmen as non-kinsmen (Ibid.: 153); for bori musicians, however, kinsmen outnumber non-kinsmen as teachers, but collateral relatives (e.g. father's brother or cousin) predominate over lineal ones (father or father's father). For those trained by non-kinsmen through apprenticeships the decisions have been made on the basis of factors such as the availability of a prestigious teacher (an affiliation with whom is thought to ensure the successful start of a career), or the non-availability of a kinsman-teacher (the pupil may be an orphan or have been ostracized by his relatives for his involvement in bori music and cult activities).

Whether a pupil is trained by collateral relatives (in which case he is adopted by them, his own parents following the Hausa custom of avoidance) or whether he is apprenticed to a non-kinsman, the same pattern prevails. No written contract is made between the pupil or his parents and his master, although it is understood that the teacher assumes social and professional responsibility for the pupil. The pupil addresses his master as 'father' and treats him with the same degree of respect due to any male relative of his father's generation. The master treats his pupil as his son (or son-in-law), but, irrespective of age he will be assigned 'younger brother' status if his teacher has natural sons who are also apprentices, a practice which results in friction when age and achievement do not correspond with this social placement. It will be recalled that a buta player reported earlier objected to his 'father's' equal treatment of him, a principal assistant, and the man's own son, a member of the group's chorus. This musician had been an apprentice in the group and had achieved full membership before the master's son but despite his age and musical achievement he was still regarded as a junior son.

A pupil training to be a member of a Hausa musicians' ensemble is expected to learn to play the simplest instruments before being allowed to try his hand at those thought to require greater skill. If the teacher is a garaya player this means that up to the age of eight or nine, a boy spends his time playing various improvised noise-makers, then his formal training begins with a small buta (gourd-rattle). He is taught how to keep a basic beat with the rattle, his teacher first demonstrating the proper technique and then playing a full-sized version of the instrument with him. When his pupil seems to understand, these early lessons develop into private performances, and the teacher exchanges his own gourd-rattle for his lute. Playing together, the pupil learns how his rattle beat 'fits' with the master's lute. There are many melodic patterns to learn, each gourd pattern with its own series of embellishments, and progress is slow. During this early phase of learning the pupil is encouraged to attend as many of the group's performances as he can stay awake for. Many of them take place late at night and he is permitted to fall asleep after he has demonstrated a scholarly interest in the event. Quite often this means helping out with the singing if not the buta-playing. To encourage him in his attempts the leader recognizes his membership in the group and gives him a small payment from its earnings.

When the pupil feels comfortable with his playing and singing technique he asks to experiment with the garaya within the privacy of the compound and may even buy a small lute with his earnings. He watches and listens, hoping to learn a song or two which he can play for his teacher. He also begins to complain that as he is now thirteen or fourteen years old, his beginner's gourd-rattle is too small and he would like to play a larger one. When he is allowed to play a full-sized rattle his position (albeit lowly placed) as a member of the ensemble's chorus is tacitly acknowledged. He may count on a real share of the group's profits and not simply a token payment. He plays the garaya as often as he can, and if he is lucky the leader may call on him for relief work during long overnight sessions.

For many pupils the master's responsibility ends here. Any further encouragement of a pupil's lute-playing ability would be a threat to the master's position in the group. Young aspiring lute players frequently solve this problem by moving to a 'bush village' where audiences are not too critical and where one or two rattle players can be found as assistants. With added experience the young garaya player may eventually move back to the town in which he was taught, but it is an unwritten rule that he avoids competition with his former master, seeking his engagements in parts of the town in which his master does not play or waiting until he sends prospective clients to him. It is a serious breach of etiquette for an anthropologist to try to interview a bori musician if his former teacher has not suggested it.

SOCIALIZATION, SOCIAL VISIBILITY, AND SOCIAL ACCEPTANCE

Two aspects of bori musicians' presentations of themselves to Hausa society are considered in this section. The first is the way in which these musicians learn their role and the second is the evaluation society makes of their behaviour. Being a cult musician involves more than simply learning to play certain kinds of musical instruments. Underlying their participation in bori is an attitude about the power of cult music and the efficacy of supernatural spirits. For many this involves a constant tempering of Muslim beliefs with the conviction that iskoki shape and cause events around them. Such behaviour is considered reprehensible by the overwhelmingly Muslim population, and coupled with the popular stereotypes for musicians, frequently renders cult maroka quite sensitive about their social image.

Sons of musicians begin to learn their place in society from the perspective of their immediate families and the people with whom they live. For the sons of cult musicians, particularly those who live in urban rather than rural settings, non-kinsmen can be most important in teaching a boy how to observe signs of the presence of supernatural spirits and to seek their meaning. Urban bori musicians frequently live with or near cult-adepts and sympathizers in the compounds in which they rent rooms. Bori people maintain this is because they are not wealthy enough to afford their own houses or would not want to own a compound and thereby hinder their geographic mobility. The second reason is probably a rationalization for the first, since cult-adepts and musicians with few exceptions rarely have more resources than are needed to keep them from total destitution. Drawn together both by their common association with the cult and their meagre incomes, compound residents cooperate with each other in teaching their children the names and relationships of the iskoki and a proper respect for their power.

One common but informal institution for these lessons is the evening gossip sessions held inside or immediately in front of most Hausa compounds. A boy old enough to have 'sense' (which the Hausa say should come to him by the time he is five or six years old) normally sits on the outside of the group presided over or attended by his father. Talking is a popular pastime and story-telling is an art, elderly bori musicians regularly claiming to be experts at both. The day's events are discussed and the society's problems solved during these sessions, and when spirits are the topic tale after tale is enjoyed by young and old alike. 'Have I ever told you the secret of so-and-so's wealth?' or 'Do you know the reason why such-and-such is a strange place?' an old man might ask. If his audience should reply 'no' he would ask them how many ears they had. Each listener would answer 'two' and he would retort, 'Well increase them to three and listen to this', the signal that a 'true' story was about to be told.

Learning to play a musical instrument, as was noted earlier, has both informal and formal components. Before a boy is old enough to be taught to play small versions of his father's or other instruments he is encouraged to experiment and play any number of toy drums, rattles, lutes, and whistles, according to his own fancy. His father or guardian frequently assists him in the construction of these instruments and usually takes a friendly attitude towards his efforts to play them. Ames reports that formal instruction on a regular instrument may begin as early as seven to ten years of age. He gives the following as a typical example of such instruction.

> The child is told how to hold the instrument and his hands are positioned properly. He is told to observe his father demonstrate how to manipulate it and then he is told to imitate him as closely as possible. If the child makes a mistake, he is beaten or harshly rebuked. This insistence on exact imitation and severe punishment for mistakes may explain, in part at least, the dearth of creative artists. (Ames 1973: 153).

The present data do not include examples of such early instruction, but if severe punishment is used during the first formal lessons it is less obvious in the training of advanced beginners or apprentices. Only one master-teacher was observed in the present study, and punishment did not seem to be an important part of his teaching technique. Perhaps the learning environment depends more on the individual musician's style than on conformity to the general pattern of primary or Quranic school instruction.

Ames's conclusion that exact imitation and severe punishment may be part of the reason why creative artists are not particularly evident among Hausa musicians is supported, albeit in a negative way, by examples provided by a few bori musicians. The master-teacher mentioned above is a case in point. Acknowledged by the community to be an unusual and creative musician, he was selected by the Federal Military Government for a tour of Kenya, and his former students have received more than their usual share of community recognition in the form of prestige, money, and special favours. Possibly teachers who avoid excessive punishment in their training methods may be those most successful in leaving a legacy of creative students.

In addition to musical training and the shaping of his attitude towards spirits a young cult musician learns how to behave with respect to other members of the Hausa community. Hausa musicians recognize most people as potential patrons and try to cultivate a social superior's obligation to be generous with the social classes under him, including maroka. Musicians do not hesitate to use what the Hausa describe as *fadanci* (lit. court language; obsequiousness or flattery) and display a willingness to do *durkusa* (the squatting down of a social inferior when greeting a superior) more often than non-musicians do. It is of interest to observe that while non-musicians condemn this kind of behaviour as fawning and insincere they are quick to criticize those maroka who do not conform to expected patterns. Cult musicians include within their ranks more non-conformists than other musicians' groups. Thus, a young bori musician grows accustomed to being singled out by his critics for 'not knowing his place' and sometimes violates these standards of etiquette to fulfill a social expectation of him as a deviate. He is instructed that it is proper for him to visit the compounds of bori patrons—the practice being that persons of inferior rank visit those of superior rank as a sign of respect—but the example his teachers set for him seems to indicate that unless his financial affairs are in a state of chaos he may elect to stay at home on Fridays when such visits are appropriate, simply to underline his independence. With this attitude is the conviction that he and the cult will be contacted soon enough when a patron is troubled by one of the spirits which made him a patron in the first place, and more often than not this conviction is correct.

It has been noted that musicians in Hausa society are socially visible not only by their behaviour but by two badges of their status, musical instruments and a particular kind of clothing (Ames 1973: 154). Bori musicians like other instrumentalists may be recognized as maroka because of the musical instruments which they carry with them, but unless they are actually performing they tend to conceal their impedimenta by transporting them in plain cloth bags. Further, since cult musicians are not generally the recipients of elaborate and conspicuous gowns—the gifts of clothing which they receive are usually quite ordinary and undecorated—and since their wealth does not normally permit them to buy expensive clothing, bori performers are less noticeable as musicians than, for example, royal maroka who may receive two or more distinctive gowns every year. This unwillingness to display publicly a bori-associated instrument and the practice of wearing commonplace clothing renders cult musicians a fairly inconspicuous group in Hausa society, a situation which they perhaps prefer to avoid any criticism of the cult which undue public attention to it provokes.

Ames also notes an element of pollution with respect to musicians, in that non-musicians customarily refuse to eat from the same bowl with maroka or lodge in the same dwelling with them (1973: 155). Cult musicians are more 'polluted' than other maroka, and many non-cult musicians express their social distance from bori performers by applying the general practice of avoidance to anyone involved in bori. It is thus unusual for even Hausa musicians to associate voluntarily with bori musicians either at meal-times or in residential units. This results in residences in which cult musicians live by themselves as compound owners (rare) or with other 'deviates' as tenants.

The majority Muslim population view the activities of the cult of possession-trance with a great deal of suspicion—even if sometimes spectacular results are reported for their 'cures'—and bori musicians do not escape this evaluation. Cult musicians for the most part consider themselves as Muslims, enthusiastic advocates of the five Pillars of the Faith (alms-giving, regular prayer, the observance of the fast during the Muslim month of Ramadan, the pilgrimage to Mecca, and the assertion that there is only one [supreme] Being whose name is Allah and Muhammed is His Prophet), but this does not prevent their acceptance of a belief that the everyday affairs of the world are profoundly influenced by spirits. Hausa Muslims publicly reject this theory of causation even when, privately, they may seek bori explanations of events which they consider inadequately explained within the Muslim framework.

When times are difficult for this agriculturally-based society—typically, when the annual rains are late—deviates from the Muslim 'way' become the scapegoat. During the annual purges designed to drive out social misfits, religious backsliders, and infidels, bori people assume a low social profile. Musicians are usually more successful, however, in weathering such purification movements than are cult devotees in general or prostitutes (many of whom are cult-adepts) in particular. Nevertheless, cult musicians and devotees generally acknowledge that it is Allah's displeasure which is ultimately responsible for drought, but they also recognize that it is *Sarkin Rafi* (The Chief of Well-Watered Land), a bori spirit, who is an immediate cause and must be pacified with special sacrifices aimed at ensuring his co-operation.

If bori musicians are socially despised in Hausa society they are not rejected to the point where they are forced into the position of an endogamous (in-marrying) group. Life-histories reveal that cult musicians frequently marry the daughters of both other musicians and non-musicians, although no instances were recorded of them as being able to choose their spouses from significantly higher social groups. The social distance between bori musicians and non-musician social groups is wide, but farmers and blacksmiths, more than other craft groups, have shown willingness to allow their daughters to marry cult maroka. Such marriages are one way in which cult musicians as individuals are able to overcome the group stereotype of them as irreligious, irresponsible, lazy, dirty, obsequious, and spendthrift.

RANK

Ranking, that is, the evaluation of individuals and roles, as it applies to bori musicians has entered into the discussion at various points above. Its inclusion here is intended as a summary, adding evidence to the conclusion that cult musicians are regarded as 'unusual' in much the same way that cult-adepts are. This has important implications for a sociological description of bori as a cult of deviance, a factor which acts both as a rationale for recruitment and as a model for behaviour.

As already mentioned status ascription is far more common in the traditional Hausa social hierarchy than status achievement, although the latter is frequently important in the internal organization of cult musicians' groups. The status of Hausa musicians is placed near the bottom of the system, non-musicians regularly rating maroka lower than maroka do themselves. Inferences concerning the status placement of musicians are based on answers to questions about social rank *(daraja)*, and Ames's conclusions (1973: 155-7) are particularly relevant here. He reports that 'butchers are generally known to have low rank among the Hausa', citing Smith (1959: 248), 'but the court musicians and the farm drummers [who represent the society's ideal of the highest placed maroka] were ranked below even them' (Ames 1973: 157). Significantly, Ames's survey cites ninety to one hundred per cent of the non-musicians asked as assigning a low rank to bori musicians. In fact, bori musicians are placed at the bottom of his list, fifteenth out of the fifteen types of musicians rated.

Why cult musicians should have such minimal daraja is obvious when the nature of their association with known deviants, including prostitutes, male homosexuals, and the psychologically disturbed is considered. In short they share the social stigma which a Muslim society places on what it regards as a pagan group in spite of the fact that musicians themselves are not generally active cult-adepts. Cult musicians usually recognize their low social rank, i.e. the paucity of their daraja, and govern their lives accordingly, maximizing or minimizing their social visibility in response to the mood of their critics. When times are difficult they are all but socially invisible. For those who associate with the bori cult the occasions when it is thought unsafe to schedule cult activities are during the uneasy period before the onset of the rainy season and the important fast-month of Ramadan, two occasions for minor revitalization movements in Hausa society. When the harvest is complete bori activity is tolerated; musicians' fees increase and they can afford to be socially visible, even brazen, in their behaviour.

ECONOMIC SPECIALIZATION AND PROFESSIONALISM

It should be clear that cult musicians are regarded by Hausa society as social specialists. Whether they may also be described as economic specialists depends upon the percentage of their income derived from music-making. In general, urban-dwelling cult musicians receive over half their income from their efforts as maroka and therefore may be regarded as economic specialists. Bori musicians as a group in small urban settlements are less able to live on their cult-related earnings, most of them depending upon farm incomes for their economic support. Strictly speaking these musicians are farmers who occasionally act as maroka, but Hausa society tends to ignore this fact, classifying them with musicians who cannot claim any other craft specialization.

If a 'true' professional is someone who is both a social and economic specialist who has been formally trained and can demonstrate technical competence in his craft, then only the leaders of cult musicians' groups may be regarded as professionals. Similarly, only those subsidiary musicians who live in large urban areas may be classified as professionals, since their semi-urban counterparts are merely social, not economic, specialists. Ames has already commented that this is not the case. According to him, 'these musicians [living in small urban settlements] and their public agree that they should be classed *primarily* as musicians in the occupational or craft sense' (1973: 131). He finds support for his conclusion from Merriam who states that the 'ultimate criterion' for a musician to be considered a professional is that he first be accorded the recognition as a social specialist, regardless of his economic support (1964: 125).

The present data are clear on this matter. The assignment of the status of 'professional bori musician' is made on the basis of social, not economic, criteria.

But an important feature of this social classification is frequently lost in analysis. In addition to those social criteria which apply to a musician's craft, e.g. formal training, musical competence, and particular behaviour, musicians seem to be subject to a subtle pressure to assign them to the lowest possible occupational classification. This pressure works both between craft groups and within the maroka class. Thus, if a man is both a farmer and a musician he is classed as the latter since the former represents a higher ranked occupation. Similarly, a hunter- or blacksmith-musician is a musician, not a hunter or a blacksmith. Within the maroka class, a musician or praise-singer who occasionally works during bori performances is classed as a cult musician regardless of his activities with other, higher ranked musians' groups.

The nature of this pressure could be the result of the inheritance of an occupational designation as Ames suggests (1973: 131), but this merely pushes the question back one generation. Clearly other factors contribute to the process of assigning the lower of two or more possible classifications. In her essay, 'Secular Defilement', Douglas describes an anomaly as 'an element which does not fit a given set or series' (1966: 37). Musicians who practise two crafts and musicians who mix cult with non-cult activities are anomalous in the Hausa social system. As such, they are the subjects of defilement and are treated in a particular way. One way of minimizing this anomaly is by assigning one or other craft as primary; in the case of farmer-musicians this rank assignment is down-graded because of the holder's contamination with maroka. The same principle applies to musicians who have been defiled through their association with the bori cult, itself a 'dangerous' contamination of pure Islamic belief.

PARALLEL ROLES

As described in the previous section, cult musicians, particularly semi-urban ones, frequently divide their time between the possession-trance cult and some other occupation. These two types of roles are not properly described as 'parallel', since as we have seen, they result in an occupation anomaly which Hausa society attempts to resolve by allotting the primary role to maroka activities. A cult musician's parallel roles do not conflict with the general description of him as a cult-associated person and include his activities as a diagnostician (boka), diviner, or purveyor of cult paraphernalia. Only urban musicians were found to supplement their incomes with such pursuits and then not unless their circumstances allowed them to do so.

To qualify as a bori diagnostician a musician must have been initiated into the cult. To be initiated means the same as to be cured, and only the formerly afflicted are thought to be qualified to administer to the presently afflicted. The Sarkin Bori is normally the person consulted in matters of diagnosis and cure, thus a musician cannot assume this role unless the cult lacks any generally recognized leadership or such leadership is weak and ineffective. In Kano the Sarkin Bori does not receive much cult support and demand for the cult's healing services is fairly large. Since the town's most important cult musician, Malam Shu'aibu Mai Garaya, had been initiated as a cult-adept, the organization of the cult in Kano produced an ideal climate in which he could act as a diagnostician, prescribing specific sacrifices to particular spirits and organizing initiation (curing) rituals. That Malam Shu'aibu has never been an active trancer, (indeed seems never to have fallen into trance), is disregarded. Everyone is aware that at least six iskoki are 'on his head' and that he knows enough about 150 more to cure ailments caused by them.

As a musician Malam Shu'aibu has to maintain a careful balance between his activities as a maroki and those as a bori healer; it is not proper for a musician to be an active cult-adept. For minor consultations this is simple as music is not involved. In the privacy of his compound, he is able to receive visitors who describe the affliction or ill-fortune of the person they represent. He then proffers specific advice on what to do to appease the spirit responsible. Each remedy, which consists largely of roots, bark, and leaves of plants symbolically associated with the afflicting spirit, is paid for separately. When food must be given as alms or an animal sacrificed to achieve the desired result Malam Shu'aibu can expect to receive a portion of the offering, particularly the skin, head, and feet of any sacrificed animal. This he does as a musician and not as a diagnostician.

Chronic illnesses require a more drastic course of treatment than a single remedy or sacrifice and a diagnostician customarily prescribes an elaborate curing ritual which, as already indicated, is actually an initiation ritual. Whereas such rituals organized by a senior cult-adept emphasize the attainment of a new status, those organized by a musician focus only on curing the sufferer. Consistent with a musician's avoidance of any demonstration of possession-trance, such skills are not encouraged in the neophyte. Musician-diagnosticians operate on the assumption that to invoke the afflicting spirits (at which they are particularly proficient) and beg their assistance in making the sufferer well—offering in exchange recognition of their power and a promise to provide them with regular sacrifices—is sufficient to achieve a 'cure'. In such cases it is thought the spirits will remain dormant on the heads of the neophytes and thus no active trancing will be necessary. Such cures—the only ones musician-diagnosticians are able to provide—are regarded as incomplete or worse by practising cult-adepts, but because the sufferer and his relatives believe they can 'work' they are a popular alternative to total cult involvement.

The important consideration in initiation or curing ritauls organized by musicians is the danger of overstepping his authority as a cult participant. He may not instruct the neophyte on any trancing skill for that would be to declare himself as an active trancer, and this is inconsistent with his role as a musician. Hence, musicians conduct only the limited initiation curing rituals as described in the previous paragraph.

For his part the initiate does assume a new status; he becomes a 'horse of the gods', but is not expected to demonstrate this by participating as a trancer in bori ceremonies. Although he must regularly attend such ceremonies, he is only obliged to give gifts to the spirits left on him (exorcism being impossible) when they appear riding other, active cult-adepts.

Properly speaking, when a musician or anyone else acts as a diviner or astrologer, deciding whether some trip or decision is in harmony with 'the stars', he does not come in conflict with bori explanations which tend to focus on present or past events. Horoscopes in the sand are cast by specialists and paid for by clients who may or may not have any connection with the cult of possession-trance, and in this connection it is perhaps easier to be a Muslim and admit the efficacy of *tauraro na kasa* (stars for divination) than it is to subscribe to bori ontology.

Musicians who attempt 'star divination' are not subject to any conflict with either their roles as maroka or as cult enthusiasts, but as it is not a skill normally cultivated by them a fairly good record of 'correct predictions' must be achieved before an individual's integrity in the practice is recognized. For example Malam Shu'aibu has attained recognition as a diviner-astrologist, but from observation it seems based more on his skill as interviewer and consultant than his expertise with the marks in the sand. The predictions he makes and the advice he gives appear to depend heavily on the kinds of answers received to the casual questions asked as the horoscope is cast. He draws out solutions to the problems with which he is presented, tempering his answers with his respected opinion of what ought to be done in any particular instance. In this way his work may be described as divination, but it more closely resembles expert counselling. He is able to achieve this because horoscopes in the sand are subject to considerable interpretation by those who cast them. The rules for the generation of the sixteen symbols used in tadauro na kasa are quite strict and actually easy to follow; what it all means, however, is another matter and a function of the imagination of the diviner.

Another activity engaged in only by cult-associated people is that of supplying cult ritual paraphernalia. Cult-adepts are expected to own enough materials to be able to demonstrate possession-trance for each of the spirits on their heads, but complete 'costumes' are generally limited to only a few spirits on anyone's list. The materials are expensive, and thus most spirits must be content for their horses to use only a few *damaru* (s. *damara*; medicine belt), a *zane* (body cloth), and one or two other items. While the leader of the cult and other senior cult-adepts freely lend materials for specific performances, individual 'children of the bori' are under considerable pressure to own the items they need. Those who supply ritual materials either have skill in making the items themselves or, more commonly, merely act as agents for their sale.

Musicians participate less as manufacturers and more as agents, but their involvement is secondary to that of cult-adepts acting in the same capacity. Only cult musicians who have some claim to being classed as initiates are thought qualified to handle transactions involving ritual paraphernalia, so that few are observed to count such sales as any part of their economic resources. Musicians who sell ritual materials frequently limit themselves to such basic items as medicine belts and body cloths (worn by male and female devotees during possession-trance events) and commonly wait for cult-adepts to come to them with specific orders. Cult-adepts also use musician middlemen to convert ritual materials into cash, musicians accepting the items and paying the seller when a buyer can be found.

INSTRUMENTS

Both men and women play instruments for bori performances, but instruments played by one sex are never played by the other. The men who play for the cult are always professional musicians, whereas women may be either professionals or non-professionals. Briefly, women play *kwaryar kidan ruwa* (hemispherical gourds for beating on water) in their performances which, as noted earlier, are attended almost exclusively by women and are classed under the heading, kidan amada (drumming for amada music). Male cult musicians play such instruments as the garaya (two-stringed, plucked lute), buta (gourd-rattle), goge (single-stringed, bowed lute), kwarya (large hemispherical gourd played with two sticks), and a few others quite infrequent in their occurrence. The Hausa group all of these instruments into ensembles comprising two or three timbres, and independent combinations or substitutions are avoided. Before considering these ensembles in detail it should be emphasized that their performance is intended to accomplish the same primary goal: to invoke the divine residents of the city of Jangare.

According to the classification by Ames and King, kidan amada (drumming or music in the amada style) includes such song types as *wakar nashadi* (songs of happiness), *wakar siyasa* (songs for clemency), *wakar yabo* (songs of praise), and *wakar kishiya* (songs for jealous co-wives) (1971: 91). None of these types is in any way related to cult performances which Ames and King imply belong to a parallel category. Informants interviewed for the present study, however, take exception to this classification, describing *wakar bori* (songs for bori spirits) as a part of the amada category when they are performed by professional and non-professional female musicians. Thus, the use of calabash drums of a particular type and the performance of female musicians are regarded by these informants as the distinctive characteristics of the event, not the presence or absence of possession-trance music.

Songs for bori spirits performed by women are accompanied by kwaryar kidan ruwa (calabashes for beating on water) which consist of three instruments. The first of these, a *masakin kadawa* (a large calabash for beating), also known as a *ganga* (lit. double-membrane, cylindrical drum), is frequently played by a zabiya (professional female musician) and is described as the lead-instrument, although this is a matter of opinion since superordinate-subordinate alternations in the instrumental group are not always present. It is a large, half-calabash which is inverted on a blanket on the ground and beaten with the fingers of both hands. Some women put metal rings on their fingers when playing this calabash which sharpens its percussiveness.

The second instrument, a *tulluwa* (lit. summit), is a small calabash inverted and floated in a larger calabash partially filled with water. It is beaten with a single stick. Both this instrument and those of the third type in the ensemble are played by women who are not generally recognized as professional musicians. Members of the *amada* chorus are described collectively as *'yan kwarya* (lit. children of the kwarya) and singly as *'yar kwarya* (lit. daughter of the kwarya), whether or not they are professionals. Whereas it is common practice for only one masakin kadawa and one tulluwa to be used during a women's performance, as many *kazagin amada* (the kazagi for amada music), the third instrumental timbre in the ensemble are used as are needed to provide chorus members with an instrument. Most ensembles include at least two calabashes of this type, but large groups may have as many as four. The kazagi for amada performances is a small hemispherical calabash which is inverted on the ground and beaten with a pair of sticks.

Male bori musicians, all of them professional maroka, divide themselves into two principal kinds of ensembles. The first contains one or more garaya plucked lutes and generally, a larger number of buta gourd-rattles. The second contains one or more goge bowed lutes and again, a larger number of kwarya calabash 'drums'. Significantly, the types of instruments used in one ensemble are never mixed with those of the other. The data also include one example of an ensemble consisting of two *sarewa* end-blown flutes accompanied by the kwarya calabash drums used in a goge ensemble. The performers in this ensemble state that they have never used a goge in their group, but as a point of observation it was noted that the flute melodies, distinctive in themselves, closely resembled and perhaps imitated the playing of the bowed lute. Ames and King comment that this flute is not commonly used during possession-trance events (1971: 52), a point with which the present data agrees, so it is included here as a minor addition to the two principal ensembles.

On one occasion a small tin can, fixed on a stick-handle and partially filled with small stones, was observed being used by a non-professional[15] to fill in for a buta player who was late for a performance. The garaya-leader did not consider this *akayau* (as he called it[16]) player as a regular member of the ensemble, seeming to tolerate his quite spectacular performance technique only because the buta gourd-rattle player had not arrived. No 'serious' bori music was played; this unusual ensemble was engaged in filling the time before the beginning of a possession-trance event.

Garaya is the generic name for a two-stringed, plucked lute, and two main sizes are distinguished. The smaller of the two is known simply as a garaya and has an over-all length of about twenty-two inches (fifty-six centimetres). The larger is known as a *babbar garaya* (big garaya), occasionally as a *komo*, and has an over-all length of about thirty-five inches (eighty-nine centimetres).[17] Only the garaya of the larger type was examined closely for the present study.

Of the babbar garaya's length fifteen inches (thirty-eight centimetres) is in its exposed neck and twenty inches (fifty-one centimetres) in its gourd body. The neck piece which is thirty-three inches (eighty-four centimetres) long ends in a two-pronged fork inside the instrument. It is fitted over the top of the ovoid gourd-body resonator and partially covered with a skin wrapped around the gourd. The wooden parts of the instrument are chosen from the *alilliba (Cordia abyssinica)* tree and the gourd is described as either *zumbulutu* or *duma*. The skin used is from a *gada* (crested duiker; *Cephalophus grimmi*), noted for its durability and malleability. The instrument's two strings, the thirty-inch (seventy-six centimetres) 'upper' string (as the garaya is held for playing) and the twenty-eight inch (sixty-nine centimetres) 'lower' string, are made of *leda* (plastic or artificial cat-gut), the best type being said to have been imported from Mecca. The upper string is lowest in pitch and is called the *tambari* (lit. royal hemispherical drum) and the lower string, highest in pitch, the *sha kidi*, but these names are subject to regional variation.[18] The vibrating lengths of the strings are the same, twenty-eight inches (sixty-nine centimetres), since the longest string is stopped by the leather thong which fastens the shortest one. At the base of the garaya both strings pass over a compound bridge and are tied to the forked end of the neck. The bridge is called a *jaki* (lit. donkey) and consists of a two-inch (five centimetres) wooden piece under the skin which is anchored to the top of the two sides of the gourd resonator and a one-inch (two and a half centimetres) piece on top of the skin. When tuning the garaya the performer first finds an appropriate pitch for the 'upper' (base) string and then tunes the 'lower' (treble) string about 550 cents (an expanded interval of a fourth) higher. A perfect fourth (500 cents) is considered dull, and a performer handed an instrument so tuned immediately adjusts the pitch of the treble string upwards.

The hole in the top of the skin-covering at the instrument's lower end is strengthened and ornamented with red goatskin called *cim baki*. Through it the forked end of the neck can be seen and the knots holding the strings checked. All instruments include a carrying strap, a *maratayi*, used for support in the playing position. The usual material of which this strap is made is goatskin, but some performers use other materials, woven cloth, for example, as a mark of their individuality. This attitude that one's own instrument is unique is also achieved by other means. The plastic ornament at the end of the neck is chosen by the performer, and one instance was recorded of a garaya musician painting the top of his instrument with blue enamel and then inscribing his name on it with black writing-slate ink.

As these descriptions suggest, the manufacture of the instrument is a complex affair, and frequently many people are involved in the process. Few garaya musicians collect the materials for the instrument themselves, urban musicians especially buy what they need from various kinds of suppliers. The wood, gourd, leather, and duiker skin are obtained from separate sources, but one person usually takes charge of the basic assembly. A specialist in leather working is contracted to cover the instrument, and if it has been made under commission a trader may handle its final sale.

Both the garaya and the babbar garaya are held at the neck-end by the left hand with the fingers used to stop either of the two strings. Partially supported by the carrying strap, the body of the instrument rests in the player's lap as he plucks it with his right hand. The smaller garaya is played with a plectrum made of stiff cowhide, whereas the longer babbar garaya is plucked with a pair of cowrie shells (*wurin kida*) tied end to end. For bori performances the player is normally seated on a grass mat on the ground, although younger players prefer to sit on a chair or bench over the heads of the accompanying buta gourd-rattle players.

There is some question regarding how long the garaya (either type) has been used in possession-trance events. Originally, as Ames and King comment, the garaya was used to honour hunters with praise-songs, 'in particular for praising hunters in their traditional rivalry with malamai' (pl. Quranic scholars) (1971: 41). Garaya players still recognize this affinity with hunters; many of them claim hunting as a former occupation. Writing about his observations of the Hausa at the turn of the century, Tremearne says that he only saw the 'violin' (goge) used for bori events, implying that the garaya was not an instrument then associated with the cult (1914: 284). How far this is a statement of actual practice is uncertain, however, since bori ensembles are subject to regional variation. In some places goge ensembles are preferred, in others garaya groups predominate.

Garaya players, while admitting that the instrument was used to praise hunters, insist that it is as old as the cult of possession-trance itself. On one hand, this seems to be more a justification for current practices in support of the claim that spirits are most easily invoked by garaya music, then a statement of historical fact. Conversely, there is at least a fragment of historical truth in it. Tremearne observed a 'guitar' called a *gimbiri* being used for bori in both Tunis and Tripoli at the turn of the century (1914: 251, 283), and it might be suggested that the garaya is a variation of the same instrument. The *gunibri*, as Farmer transliterates it, is a non-Arabic instrument, and its description and dimensions (1939: 575, 579) closely approximate to the modern garaya. Thus, it is possible that the garaya and the gimbiri or gunibri are related in some way even if the exact genealogy of the relationship remains a mystery. If the connection can be established it would place the proto-grarya as being 'known in the Western Sudan between the eleventh and sixteenth centuries' (Farmer 1939: 575), although whether or not it was played by Hausa musicians for the possession-trance cult during this period is not settled.

The instrument which is used to accompany the garaya lute is a buta gourd-rattle. According to Ames and King, any one of a number of gourd-rattle types is suitable as a garaya accompaniment (1971: 5, 41), but musicians interviewed for this study were specific in stating that buta gourds alone are appropriate. Ames and King also state that the *kasambara* (a brush-like instrument made from a length of guinea-corn stalk) 'held between the palms of the hands and rotated by the rubbing motion of the latter' (1971: 7) may be used as an accompaniment, but bori musicians described such a practice as 'improper' or 'bush', some even denying its existence.

Buta bottle-shaped gourd-rattles come in a variety of sizes, ranging from those played by apprentices which are only ten inches (twenty-five and a half centimetres) to those played by seasoned experts which may be as much as fifteen inches (thirty-eight centimetres). The average size is around thirteen inches (thirty-three centimetres) in height with a bottle circumference of approximately twenty-four inches (sixty-one centimetres). The hand-held rattle is made from a common gourd which when dried is emptied of its contents and partially filled with small stones or corn (maize or guinea-corn) seeds. One buta player said that there were exactly ninety-nine seeds in the instrument, a number said to represent the names of the spirits which could 'hear' its music.[19]

In preparing to play the buta a right-handed performer ties two to five pairs of cowrie shells (*wurin kidam buta*) to the middle joints of his left hand with strips of leather. The instrument, held in the right hand, is both shaken and beaten; in all three kinds of sounds are produced. Moving the right wrist in a circular motion causes the seeds to roll in the rattle, and moving the right hand in a brisk forward and backward motion causes the seeds to bounce off its walls. The rhythm is punctuated by the player's left hand which is used to strike the cowrie shells on the gourd-rattle. Particular combinations of right- and left-hand movements produce distinctive rhythms each of which is identified with a single garaya melody and a specific spirit. Players are judged both on their knowledge of basic patterns for all the spirits for which their garaya-leader plays and their ability to embellish these basic patterns with displays of individual virtuosity.

Beside garaya-buta ensembles, goge-kwarya groups may be used to summon spirits from their mythical eastern town of Jangare. The goge is a single-stringed, bowed lute whose tone is much more penetrating than that of the plucked lute. As the Hausa say, '*Goge mai kashe wa molo kaifi*' (lit. Goge, owner of killing of the three-stringed guitar's sharpness; Goge who silences the mob) (Ames and King 1971: 43). The over-all length of the goge is twenty-six inches (sixty-six centimetres), the length of the exposed neck fifteen inches (thirty-eight centimetres), and the length of the vibrating string fifteen inches (thirty-eight centimetres). The following have been listed as the parts of the instrument (Ames and King 1971: 41-2):

a. *fata*: membrane covering body-resonator from the skin of the Nile monitor (*guza*)

b. *izga* or *yazga* or *tambara*: iron- or bronze-backed bow with hairs from a horse's tail

c. *jaki*: the bridge between the string and the body-resonator made from a three-pronged twig of the *urkure* tree

d. *kahom butsiya*: a small horn-like wedge inserted between the lower end of the string and the body-resonator to increase string tension

e. *kallabi*: the leather binding thongs securing the string at the upper end to the neck

f. *kankara*: a smooth egg-shaped stone inserted under the membrane covering of the body-resonator to increase the tension of the covering

g. *kanwa*: potash used to remove the natural oils from the body and bow strings

h. *karo*: resin for the body and bow strings taken from the Copaiba balsam tree (*Pardaniellia Oliveri*)

i. *kumbo*: the hemispherical body-resonator which is made from a latitudinally cut half-gourd

j. *tsagiya*: the string on the body-resonator made from hairs from a horse's tail

k. *wuri*: a cowrie shell used as the *kankara* (f.) listed above.

The goge player holds his instrument with his left hand which is also used to stop the string. Seated on a bench or chair, he rests the gourd body on his lap and bows in a nearly vertical direction with his right hand. An interesting characteristic of goge-playing for possession-trance events is that many of the instrument's musical phrases have textual referents. Except for transitional passages and occasional displays of the performer's virtuosity which have purely musical 'meaning', goge music is said by informants—musicians and cult-adepts alike—to be readily translatable into words (praise-epithets, mostly) or song texts. For example, it frequently happens that when a devotee is being ridden by the spirit which the goge has 'called' a kind of verbal-musical exchange may ensue in which the lute player both speaks to and praises the spirit with short musical phrases. For its part the spirit (through the mouth of his medium) answers each phrase with additional self-praise. As long as the 'conversation' is confined to ritual topics or praise-epithets the musician limits his participation in it to what he plays on his instrument. Further, participants in the event seem to have no difficulty in understanding both sides of the dialogue even though one is musical and the other a distorted form of ordinary speech.

The case for the origin of the goge is much clearer than that for the plucked lute, but again the chronology is problematic. It is most certainly the Algerian or Moroccan *ghugha* which provided the source for the Hausa bowed lute (Farmer 1939: 578; Hause 1948: 20), and the date of its borrowing is probably coincident with the spread of Islam to northern Nigeria. The goge is not an instrument generally related to either Islamic ritual practice or court ceremony, however, so it was most likely borrowed when the contacts between north Africa and northern Nigeria had been firmly established rather than with the earliest of the Muslim travellers. We might suggest the sixteenth or seventeenth centuries as a period during which the goge could have been brought to northern Nigeria—Islam having been established as the official state religion in Kano, for example, during the reign of Muhammad Rumfa (A.D. 1463-99) (Palmer 1928, vol. III: 111-12)—but no confirmation of this exists in the Hausa chronicles. Further, no mention is made of any role musical instruments might have had in pre-Islamic religious worship.

However, whatever the origin of the practice may have been it is clear that the bowed lute has an important place in current bori ritual. It is invariably accompanied by a type of large hemispherical gourd inverted on the ground and played with a pair of wooden sticks. The *kwaryar goge* is similar to one of the gourds used in kwaryar kidan ruwa, the masakin kadawa, but the male musician who plays it puts it directly on the ground without using a blanket to muffle the sound. Kwarya players sit on the ground with the gourd between their legs, and experts use the heel of one foot to lift it off the ground, producing both 'open' and 'closed' sounds. Additionally, the impact of the gourd on the ground is used to punctuate kwarya rhythmic patterns.

Most of the instruments mentioned above are owned by the musicians who play them. Certainly this is true when professional musicians, men who play the garaya, buta, goge, and kwarya are involved. Professional female musicians frequently own sets of gourds for use in women's performances, but it is usual for the hostess for the event to provide calabashes from her own collection for amada music. Garaya and goge musicians, the leaders of their respective groups, own extra gourds, cowrie shells, and playing sticks which may be borrowed by group members. These are usually kept at the leader's residence and are not included (unless at the specific request of a group member) in the common carrying bag used to transport the performance paraphernalia to the site of an event.

MUSIC

Reserving any detailed discussion of the structure of bori music for later sections in this study, it is intended here to answer general questions on artistry, composition, content, and the inheritance of cult music.

Artistry in musical production is a topic Ames has dealt with at some length (1973: 144-51), and it is worth summarizing his observations. It is important to understand that Hausa musicians do not view music as created for what might be described as aesthetic purposes, their emphasis being directed to what is situationally appropriate or socially useful, but the behaviour of both musicians and audiences provides some clues as to artistic discrimination. Broadly considered, Ames states that 'we can speak of a Hausa musician as being an artist if he is an especially inventive individual or a clever improviser who is unusually effective in stimulating intellectual interest or emotional response in his Hausa audiences' (1973: 145). He also comments that, generally, creative musicians are singers rather than instrumentalists (Ibid.).

Taking the second point first, the present data confirm that musical creativity is clearest in the case of singers. Bori vocalists are judged on the basis of vocal clarity and their ability to make an audience understand the words of a song, the amount of testual repetition they use, and, to a lesser extent, their skill in working out original textual material within song structure 'rules'. A good singer's voice is described as pleasant to listen to, and enabling the audience to follow the textual meaning of his songs from word to word and phrase to phrase. He does not resort to more repetition than is necessary to allow the audience to understand a phrase, carefully avoiding the common practice of repeating the same verse over and over in order to gain time to think of something else. Expert bori vocalists are never 'at a loss for words'. They demonstrate a refined talent in knowing a large number of suitable texts and descriptive praise-epithets and are able to describe unusual events in which the spirit whose song they are singing has participated, all within the formal limits of the song. Their singing is flexible, inspiring a confidence in the audience that any piece of text they may include will conform to the song's melodic and rhythmic contour.

Exceptional bori vocalists are not usually required to perform on an instrument while delighting audiences with their singing. Singers who are also engaged in instrumental playing (or instrumentalists who also sing) are not usually subject to the careful scrutiny described above, and perhaps are able to conceal an occasional memory lapse or textual flaw with a bit of instrumental flourish. In either case Hausa musicians recognize the importance of song texts and devote less attention to their playing when singing than when someone else is singing. But bori vocalists are not the only cult performers who achieve recognition by their audiences. Remembering that 'usefulness' is an important consideration, there are frequent occasions in a possession-trance event when the focus of the performance is on the instrumentalist and not the vocalist. The dissociative state is seen as primarily instrumentally, not vocally, induced. Instrumentalists carry a significant 'functional load' during any possession-trance performance. Employing the criteria of an ability to induce trance in any devotee with the minimum delay and of individual instrumental agility, Hausa audiences have little difficulty in deciding if an individual is an exceptional musician, that is, an artist.

Thus, we may return to Ames's general definition of an artist as someone who is especially inventive, a clever improviser, and particularly effective in stimulating intellectual or emotional responses. In terms of bori musicians both vocalists and instrumentalists fit this description. It might be asked how audiences show their approval of a musician of such excellence. Ames concludes that 'the immediate response to an artistic performance is not obvious—it is internalized, so to speak' (1973: 146). However, in addition to the size of an audience and the gifts given to a musician, which Ames describes as the best indications of opinion, a great deal of observable audience behaviour reveals their assessment of the performers. After a particularly commendable verse from a vocalist, members of an audience may say 'exactly' or 'good' and there is a release of tension shown by bodily movement and I have heard '*A dawo lafiya, Malam*' (Return well, Sir) during a display of skill by an instrumentalist. When dancing to music performed by an exceptional lute-player the enthusiasm of the dancer and the instrumentalist reinforce one another, and the audience recognize and encourage this with their exclamations. Gift-giving enters into the list of acts of approval, and as Ames notes, a pleased listener can walk up to a musician and place a coin on his forehead, symbolic of his approval (1973: 146). Significantly, the size of the gift is not important, the act of giving is.

The assessment of a bori musician as an artist is not really an either/or proposition. Most vocalists and instrumentalists seem to have their moments of greatness; acknowledged experts simply have more of them than run-of-the-mill performers. Bori musicians' groups which feature 'experts' in all the musical parts are exceedingly rare, and it even more unusual for a performance by any member of the group's chorus (or a gourd-player) to eclipse that of a lute-playing leader. Before such a situation is allowed to develop the group disintegrates and the aspiring junior member assumes the leadership of an entirely new ensemble.

Considering what has been said about the artistry of bori musicians, it is clear that musical composition plays a special part in the assessment. Composition, that is, in its widest sense, and not the act of creating an entirely new piece of music. Similar to royal musicians who count among their repertoire traditional songs of praise associated with the offices held by their aristocratic patrons, cult musicians mostly confine their efforts to performing songs associated with individual spirits. This repertoire is conservative, consisting essentially of the same songs which were performed by cult musicians before them. There is no stigma attached to this and no cult musician feels inferior because of a lack of inventiveness in creating new songs. Deviation is avoided, primarily because it would result in 'meaningless' music. As the participants say, 'What would be the use of a cult song if it were not able to be heard by some spirit?' But if new composition is avoided great value is placed on 're-composition', i.e. embellishment and improvisation. Song texts and melodies, vocal and instrumental, are subject to re-composition, and by this means a performer is able to imprint a standard piece of music with a mark of his own individuality.

Two kinds of music are distinguished for most bori spirits, one vocal and instrumental and the other purely instrumental. Each of these types implies a specific kind of activity or situation involving cult-adepts at a possession-trance event. Vocal music honours or calls a spirit, and informs or entertains the audience. As outlined earlier its content consists of kirari (descriptive praise-epithets or praise-words and -names) for spirits, anecdotes involving the spirit or ceremonies held in its name, and invitations to possess a particular devotee. The first of these categories is rigidly set in the oral tradition of the cult and changes little from generation to generation. For example, an examination of the song texts recorded by Tremearne (1914) in North Africa at the turn of the century reveals an impressive continuity between what he heard and what is performed in Kano today for the same spirits. Anecdotes change from musician to musician but in fact constitute a small part of total song content. The content of the actual call for a spirit's presence which immediately precedes a cult-adept's altered state of consciousness depends heavily on the pace of the induction and the vocalist's style. It is not primarily the linguistic content of the call wherein its effectiveness lies; it is its melodic and rhythmic accompaniment.

Specific song texts are linked to specific melodic, rhythmic, and structural complexes. It is an unusual spirit which has only one 'song' (vocal or instrumental); many of them have three or more. Whereas it is clear why certain texts should be associated with certain melodies and rhythms in so far as consideration of linguistic tone and vowel length is essential in Hausa, there appears to be no linguistic reason why one song should be sung by a soloist while another involves the participation of a leader and chorus. In other words structural types do not vary directly with linguistic types.

In addition to instrumentally accompanied songs for separate spirits one or more purely instrumental pieces are usually included. Described as *cashiya*, these have a faster tempo than vocal pieces and are intended for dancing. During a performance vocal usually precede, and sometimes also follow, instrumental pieces. The only time a cashiya-type rhythm is not initiated by a slow vocal form is when the 'trance sequence' of an event is under way and the instrumental piece is used to induce a reluctant devotee's dissociation state. A cashiya provides the opportunity for the instrumentalists to display their skill, but it is not performed for that reason alone. Consistent with the attitude that music must have a social or ritual use, musicians prefer to use a cashiya piece when a dancer requires it to demonstrate movements and gestures symbolically associated with a particular spirit or to fall into a trance state.

Part of the corporate, yet intangible, property of the cult of possession-trance is the music used to invoke spirits. Music is not owned by any individual and descendants may only lay claim to it if they meet certain other requirements. Where the membership core of a performing group consists of men who are patrilineally related it is tempting to assume that songs are inherited patrilineally. It is group membership, however, irrespective of how it is recruited, which describes specific lines of inheritance. Further, instrumentalists have a claim to the inheritance only of the music performed on the instruments which they themselves play. For example, goge-kwarya music is quite distinct from garaya-buta music, and musicians in one type of group would consider it inappropriate to claim or play the music of another. Inheritance, of course, is closely related to the system of musical instruction and apprenticeships, and bori musicians make no attempt to separate them.

The case for the transmission of vocal music is slightly different. Kirari epithets are a part of every cult-adept's vocabulary, and a vocalist may widen his collection with every opportunity he has for conversation. Since descriptive praises constitute a large part of song texts, vocalists—even when they are also instrumentalists—often count among their teachers a large number of unrelated people. Generally, however, singing instruction on song texts (no attempt has ever been observed of a teacher making any serious attempt to change his pupil's vocal quality) is given by one or two masters, and the limits of the vocalist's knowledge are frequently circumscribed by his teacher's familiarity with bori songs. Similar to instrumentalists, vocalists make no claims of ownership over the songs they sing. They are flattered by pupils who imitate them, and they pass their songs freely to those willing to take the time to learn them, unlike court musicians who, on the other hand, only sing songs which have been inherited within the limits of their individual groups.

NOTES

[1]Ames (1973: 134-42) counts these groups as those professionals who perform music as their primary craft. He emphasizes the production of music as an essential element for each group, but, as has been indicated, the criteria the Hausa use are primarily social and not artistic.

[2]See Besmer (1972) for a detailed study of court musicians and their music in Kano.

[3]See Gidley (1967) for additional information on Hausa comedians.

[4]*Bandiri* drums are used by members of the *Kadiriyya* sect on Thursday evenings during the recitation of *zikiri* (a creed-formula whereby a person acknowledges that he is a Muslim; this formula in Arabic is called *Kalimatush shahadati* and begins *ashhadu an la ilaha ill'Allahu* (Abraham 1962: 461-2) and neighbourhood mosques. According to Ames and King, 'it comparitively recent introduction into the religious worship of this sect in Nigeria is attributed to *Alhaji* Nasiru Kabara [who lives in Kano], present-day head of the *Kadiriyya;* justification for its use in worship is claimed from the behaviour of Sidi Abdulkadiri, grandson of the Prophet, who performed' *zikiri* to the accompaniment of handclapping' (1971: 13).

[5]Since poetry is normally sung in the Hausa (and Arabic) tradition, it is also described as *waka*. While the nomenclature for the two is undifferentiated, it is easy to recognize and distinguish a poet from a musician as the latter almost invariably implies the presence of either some leader-chorus division or an instrumental accompaniment. Poets sing their songs unaccompanied by instruments or a chorus. Further, a poet is called a *mawaki* but never considers himself as a *maroki*.

[6]The Majidadi is the title of a district headship in Katsina and is held by one of the Emir of Katsina's brothers (King 1966: 107).

[7]The title Waziri (Vizier) is usually given to a member of the aristocracy who is not in the royal family.

[8]The head of the cult, its Sarkin Bori, is chosen by other cult members, and this decision is presented to the turbanning official for appropriate action (see above, Chapter II).

[9]The appointment of the *kotso* (single-membrane, hand-struck hourglass drum) players in Kano is a case in point. Earlier in this century an Emir of Kano turbanned his own choice as *Sarkin Kidan Kotso* (Chief of the Drummers of the Kotso) despite musicians' recommendations to the contrary (Besmer 1972: 42-3).

[10]Malam is a title normally reserved for Quranic scholars, but the Hausa apply it to any man who is either elderly or distinguished.

[11]To get as much as this for one performance would be rare, but the assistant was trying to make a point. Actually, the usual income is closer to ten naira.

[12]They would quote the proverb which says, '*Sannu bat ta hana zuwa*' (Going slowly does not prevent arrival), but he could counter with '*Amma ka dade ba ka zo ba*' (But it has been a long time and you still have not arrived).

[13]This only applies if the person in question is first identified as a maroki (professional musician). If he plays the gourd-rattle but is identified as an *almajiri* (Quranic 'pupil') then he has nothing whatever to do with bori and performs for a *'Yan Lela* troupe of dancers (cf. Vilee and Badejo 1973).

[14]Apprenticeships are discussed in detail in the following section.

[15]He considered himself a professional, but no one else agreed with his assessment.

[16]*Akayau* normally refers to the metal rattles dancers wear around their ankles. Since this was an 'unclassifiable' instrument, the performer gave it a name closest to both the sound it produced and the material (metal) out of which he had made it.

[17]Ames and King report that the babbar garaya they saw was seventy inches (178 centimetres) in length, but that this included a thirty-inch (seventy-six centimetres) jingle out of the top of the instrument's length (1971: 40). No particular significance should be attached to the exact length of either instrument. It is sufficient to observe as the Hausa do themselves that the babbar garaya is simply larger than the ordinary garaya. It is of some interest, however, that unwieldly jingles are not now currently used by plucked-lute players, but that some of them seem to feel the need for such as appendage and replace it, occasionally, with a small plastic ball or some other simple ornament.

18Ames and King record *amale* (lit. huge camel) and *giwa* (lit. elephant) as other names for the low-pitched string and *magudiya* (lit. the ululator) for the high-pitched one.

19Since there are many more than ninety-nine spirits in the bori pantheon it is said that particular buta rattles must be used to call particular spirits. The overlap between any two instruments may be great, few garaya players knowing the songs and rhythms for more than 125 iskoki, but each buta, in theory at least, has its own pecularities. It is of further interest to note that the number ninety-nine has special significance for Muslims. There are ninety-nine beads on the Muslim rosary, representing the names of Allah known to man (Allah's 100th name is known only by Him).

Chapter 4 · Divine Horsemen: The Bori Pantheon

In this chapter the reader is introduced to the spirit world of Jangare, the mythical city in which bori spirits are said to live. Far from being an idiosyncratic universe defined separately by different cult members removed from each other by time or space, a student of cult practices cannot avoid being impressed by the broad consistency revealed by a comparison of accounts such as Tremearne's (1914) in 1913 in North Africa (Tunis and Tripoli), Greenberg's (1946) conducted in the Emirate of Kano in 1938-9, and the present data gathered between Kano and Maiduguri in 1972-3. Despite the distances which separate the sources for these works, and the purposes of the investigators themselves, the identities of many spirit personalities continually reappear and provide a striking example of cultural consistency, or perhaps tenacity. Thus, while individual circumstances colour interpretative statements—spiritual genealogies are a good example of this—there is little argument about who the spirits are and the specific kinds of things they may be expected to do.

CLASSIFICATION

In an important sense Maguzawa theology is monotheistic in that one spiritual force is believed to be responsible for the ultimate control of the universe. In the present situation that spiritual entity is Allah, and clearly this is part of the legacy Islam has placed on the Hausa. Before the addition of Allah to the system it is likely that this force was within the bori hierarchy itself, and that that role was held by the spirit, Sarkin Aljan (the Chief of the Spirits), all other spirits being described as subordinate to him. An obvious difficulty with this reconstruction is that aljan is an Arabic loan word and could only have been used after the introduction of Islam. However, whatever his Hausa name might have been his position as head of the city of Jangare is stated by informants time and time again.

The supernatural order may have Allah or a [proto] super Sarkin Aljan at its apex, but its character is that of a group of spirits who mediate between mortals and the Ultimate. Where Allah is identified as the Ultimate it is important to note that He is a distant, unapproachable Being who does not come into direct contact with ordinary people. And to some extent in marginally Muslim areas this distant Being is Sarkin Aljan. To explain daily events and problems, the most recurrent of which are illnesses variously described and defined, bori enthusiasts turn to mediating spirits which constitute all but the highest level of supernatural organization.

Iskoki (s. iska), as all these mediating beings are known, are said to be infinite in number and found everywhere. In practical terms informants know the names, characteristics, favourite resting places, appropriate sacrifices, and the like of anywhere from 125 to 275 spirits, and this knowledge forms the basis of cult practices for each of them. A general classification of spirits into one of two categories, white or black, is followed, but this does not seem to be a major factor in cult worship. The descriptions white and black are usually taken to follow the broad division of iskoki into two groups, Muslim and pagan. This is not a hard and fast distinction, and other factors are sometimes considered. A white or Muslim spirit may be described as black either because its 'work' is considered particularly evil (causing paralysis is 'evil' work) or its identifying costume consists of dark blue or black cloth. Another possible factor is the urban-rural distinction. White spirits are said to be from towns, black spirits to live in the 'bush'.

The black-white system of classification is Muslim in origin, and includes the belief that black is identified with evil and white with good. However, as Greenberg notes, 'a spirit may be white for the man who worships him, while he is black for everyone else' (1946: 29). In sum, the widespread uncertainty of whether to classify a spirit as white or black is 'largely due to the fact that these categories have been superimposed on a native division of the spirits into those of town and bush' (Greenberg 1946: 29-n).

LORE

To illustrate the point that iskoki in the minds of informants are identified with places and not primarily with the Muslim black-white system one has only to hear the stories told late at night by people both in and outside the cult. One tale I recorded in Ningi was recounted by an important councillor in the emir's court. He was not a bori devotee nor I think had he ever been one, and his story was told to explain why a royal servant had gone mad nearly forty years ago.

'Have you ever heard of *Kukar Makau* (a baobob tree known as Makau)?' he asked those gathered around him. 'It is in Old Ningi and is a place where spirits are said to live'.

When the British 'pacified' the Ningi area in the early twentieth century they decided that the mountainous location of the town was inappropriate for their purposes and far too inaccessible for the roads being built there. Old Ningi was evacuated and replaced with a new town down from the Kabara Hills.

'As you know,' he continued, 'Kukar Makau was a place where criminals were taken for execution. Or if you were mad you were taken there to be cured.

No aljan could hold you because of the power of the tree; you had to be cured.'

'Shortly after Old Ningi had been abandoned,' he said, 'there is a story of a certain *Sarkin Dogarai* (a royal servant and head of the king's bodyguard) named *Shagamba* during the reign of Sarkin Ningi Adamu.[1] While he was sleeping he was awakened by the sounds of drumming and riding, a procession headed towards Old Ningi. It was two or three in the morning just before *Babbar Salla* (the Muslim festival Id al-Kabir; the Greater Feast). He got up and said, "Are you riding without me?" As he joined the parade with sleep in his eyes he realized that it was not Sarkin Ningi who was riding but Sarkin Aljan (the Chief of the Spirits). He tried to get close to the Chief, but when he touched him he went mad. In his madness he kept insisting that Sarkin Ningi would be returning to Old Ningi. All the people said, "No, see him still here?" but he could not believe them. Inhabiting this impossible world, he eventually died.'

Hausa tales generally end with the words, 'Believe it or not!' which is the teller's invitation for the listener to identify the narrative simply as a fable. On this occasion, however, the story-teller ended his tale with what he viewed as a confirmation of the 'truth' of the story. He described an interview he had heard over Radio-Kaduna in which an old and venerable man had been asked if there were such things as spirits. The old man was reported to have said that such an idea was against Muslim law, but that there were spirits. When the interviewer asked where these spirits might be found, he was told, 'At Kukar Makau!'

Another of the many stories recorded in the present data concerns a special place between Dala and Gwauran Dutse hills within the Kano City walls. A man was to be taken on a journey to see his parents, and was to be escorted by a Malam. The Malam directed him to ride a horse which had been provided for the occasion but which lacked both bridle and saddle. The man mounted this ill-equipped beast and followed an instruction to keep his eyes closed as they rode. They dismounted near Dala Hill and entered the ground. The man then realized it was an aljan which had taken him there. The horse which he had ridden was his own mother, and that of the aljan, his father. He then became aware of other very old people sitting along the walls of the cavern. He learned they had not been allowed to die because of the spirits' hold over them. He wanted desperately to leave but could not; there was 'no transport' to take him out.

Many themes are emphasized in such stories—the power of spirits to impersonate mortals; the tenacity of their hold over those whom they afflict; the special lessons in a particular narrative and the frequent reference to the *places* where these things happen. An old baobob tree in a deserted town; an underground place near a hill around which the first inhabitants of Kano lived some 1,000 years ago: these are venues for the dangerous activities of supernatural beings.

THE CITY OF JANGARE

Jangare is the city of the spirits, the place from which they move 'like the wind' when they wish to intervene in the lives of mortals. No one has ever been there, or if he has he has not returned. Yet devotees know or believe they know how the city is socially organized because spirits have families and a society stratified according to principles the Hausa understand. Jangare is governed by a king,

Sarkin Aljan (Chief of the Jinn or Spirits), and he is surrounded by a royal court. Informants in Kano see the court as the primary governing body of this 'City of the East' and the Chief of the Spirits as its absolute head. Ningi devotees, however, prefer to think of Jangare as having a ruling lineage headed by Sarkin Aljan but dividing authority among the heads of various other 'houses'. The Kano version of Jangare is of an organization more centralized than that described by other informants whose experience is expressed in milder feudal terms.

All informants agree that there are twelve 'houses' in Jangare, but usually little agreement is found regarding the leadership or membership of these groups. Generally, the principle of primogeniture is followed in determining *zaure* (house) leadership, and the groups are separated according to ethnicity, occupation, and descent. Spirits complicate matters in that (1) they are difficult to pin down on matters of genealogy, classifying distant relatives by the same terms used for close ones; and (2) they practise an elaborate system of child avoidance and adoption in successive generations. Devotees learn the social organization of Jangare in spirits' praise-songs, -epithets, and by their behaviour when riding their mounts during possession-trance events, but the data are subject to individual interpretation and much disagreement results. The reconstructions given in the following pages are subject to variation, but it is significant that the informants who gave them successfully withstood the cross-checking designed to substantiate internally their information. With that qualification the general outline of the twelve houses of Jangare may be given as follows:

1. *zauren Sarkin Aljan Sulemanu* (the house of the Chief of the Spirits, Sulemanu): includes subsections for blind spirits *(zaurem makafi)*, the chief's bodyguard *(zauren dogarai)*, and smiths *(zaurem makera)*

2. *zauren Sarkin Aljan Biddarene* (the house of a chief of the spirits, Biddarene; a younger brother of the Paramount Chief of the Spirits, 1)

3. *zaurem malamai* (the house of the Quranic teacher-scholars) headed by *Malam Alhaji* (Malam, the Pilgrim; a younger brother of 1)

4. *zaurem kutare* (the house of the lepers) headed either by *Kuge* or his son, *Kuturu* (the Leper), the latter of which is 1's senior councillor *(Madaki)*: includes a subsection for snakes *(zaurem macizai)*

5. *zaurem Filani* (the house of the Fulani) headed by *Sarkin Filani Dukko* (the Chief of the Fulani, Dukko)

6. *zauren Sarkin Aljan Zurkalene* (the house of a chief of the spirits, Zurkalene; a younger brother of *Sarkin Filani*, 5): includes a subsection for butchers *(zaurem mahauta)* and musicians *(zaurem maroka)*

7. *zauren Sarkin Aljan Shekaratafe* (the house of a chief of the spirits, Shekaratafe): they are said to live in water

8. *zaurem maharba* (the house of the hunters) headed by the Owner of the Bush *(Mai Dawa)*: includes a subsection for Tuareg serfs *(zaurem buzaye)*

9. *zauren Sarkin Arna* (the house of the Chief of Pagans)

    10. *zauren Sarkin Gwari* (the house of the Chief of Gwari—a 'pagan' group)

    11. *zauren Turawa* (the house of the North Africans)

    12. *zaurem mayu* (the house of sorcerers) headed by *Batoyi*.

The houses of Jangare are linked in various ways, providing a symbolic model of Hausa social relations. Adoption, clientship, office, kinship, and affinity are all expressed in the model. For example, through the mechanism of successive adoptions adjacent generations which include many avoidance relationships are separated but alternate generations (joking relatives) live together (cf. Besmer 1973a). This is clearly outlined in the relationship between Houses 1 and 2:

FIGURE 1. Adoptions

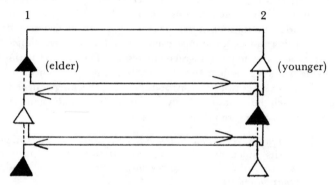

    Looking at the house of the Fulani spirits, the complexity of the social fabric becomes impressive (figure 2). Besides adoptions, the Fulani are linked with other houses through marriage. At first glance the marriage patterns resemble those of the Hausa after the influence of Islam, that is, they are endogamous (cf. Greenberg 1947: 207). But as Fulani spirits they are described as practising a form of preferential marriage which among the Pastoral Fulani is regarded as traditional (Stenning 1959: 42). Marriages between the offspring of two brothers or half-brothers are expressly contenanced by Islamic custom, and the only instances of their occurrence in the Jangare census involve Fulani spirits. It would not be practical to reproduce the census of Jangare here, so the reader is invited to consult the appendices at the end for additional information.

SOME IMPORTANT SUPERNATURAL SPIRITS

It is difficult to separate the important bori spirits from the unimportant ones, every devotee having his own list of special iskoki. However, such factors as frequency of appearance at possession-trance events, household position, and comprehensiveness of data may all be used in a rationale for selection. Following the pattern of division into houses used in previous pages, each section of Jangare is explored to present the reader with a description of its central members, their relationships, characteristics, illnesses, medicines and sacrifices, praise-epithets and -songs, and music.

FIGURE 2. Fulani Spirits' Ties With Others

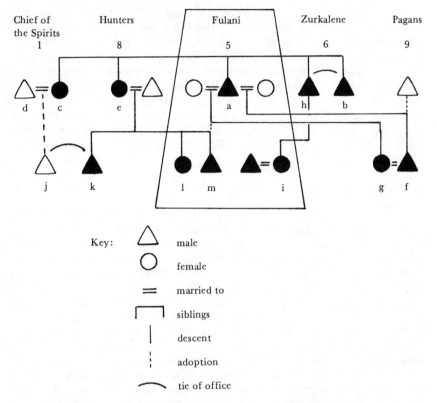

Key:

△ male

○ female

= married to

⎍ siblings

│ descent

⦙ adoption

⌒ tie of office

a. *Sarkin Filani* (the Chief of the Fulani): household head of 5

b. *Sarkin Aljan Zurkalene*: *a*'s younger brother; household head of 6

c. *Bakar Doguwa* (the Black Tall-Woman): wife of the household head of 1

d. *Sarkin Aljan Sulemanu* (the Paramount Chief of the Spirits, Sulemanu)

e. *Barhaza*: *a*'s sister; wife of the household head of 8

f. *Mai Gizo* (Owner of Matted Hair): *a*'s son adopted by the Pagans because of his evil character, becoming one of them

g. *Zainaba*: *a*'s daughter who married her stepbrother, *f*

h. *Ja'e*: younger brother of *a* and *b*, appointed as *b*'s senior councillor

i. *Hajjo*: daughter of *h* who married a Fulani man

j. *Dan Galadima* (the Prince): adopted son of *c* and *d*

k. *Wanzami* (the Barber): son of *e* and holder of the office, Muslim Judge

l. *Tsatsuba*: daughter of *e*, adopted by *a*

m. *Kura*: son of *e*, adopted by *a*.

House 1: Zauren Sarkin Aljan Sulemanu (Chief of the Spirits)

Sulemanu's house, which symbolizes palace organization has four subsections and in common with other houses thus divided, the zaure head is responsible for all the spirits living with him, but each subsection has its own minor leadership. Sulemanu's own subsection contains his wives, and his younger brother's children (whom he has adopted), his own son's children (adopted by one of his stepsons), and additionally, titled officials and their slaves. As the leading house of Jangare Sulemanu's compound provides a place for blind spirits who have their own subsection. His bodyguards are given as a third subsection and the fourth is populated with blacksmiths. It is said the Chief of Jangare has smiths living in his house in order to control the products of their craft, both weapons and articles for his cavalry.

Sarkin Sulemanu

PERSONALIA. Sarkin Sulemanu is thought to be the adopted son of two inactive spirits, *Taiki* (m. Large Hide-Bag) and *Mabuga* (f. Corn-Threshing Place). He is the elder brother of two other compound heads, Sarkin Aljan Biddarene (House 2) and *Malam Alhaji* (Malam, the Pilgrim: House 3). His wives are Fulani sisters (from House 5), and his six sons have all been sent to his brother Biddarene's house for adoption. In exchange Biddarene gave Sulemanu six sons for adoption, this change being explained as necessary in so far as the expected avoidance between parents and their children would be difficult if the children were too near their parents. Suleman's son's children, born in Biddarene's house, came to live with him, having been adopted by one of his stepsons. These adoptions may seem confusing to the casual observer, but the reason for the practice is not. Over three generations kinsmen who are expected to avoid each other are separated and those who may joke with each other united. The Hausa say that grandparents and grandchildren are joking relatives, and through the mechanism of adoption they may become co-residents. As indicated above Sulemanu is the Paramount Chief of Jangare and its inhabitants. How he came to be selected for this position is problematical. Two explanations are offered. The first, given by informants who also consider themselves Muslims, states that it was Allah Himself who selected Sulemanu and that it was the minor prophet Sulemanu who actually tied the turban, symbol of royal office, around his head. The second account, given by those further outside the Islamic fold, is that Sulemanu seized or simply assumed responsibility for the spirit world, appointing household heads in the process. Among his appointments was *Wanzami*, the Barber, who was given the title, *Alkali* (Muslim Judge), and immediately after this he turbaned Sulemanu as the Chief of Jangare. Only mild dissatisfaction regarding the circularity of this story is expressed by those relating it who prefer to emphasize the functions of Jangare offices without over much concern for 'first causes'.

AFFLICTION. Greenberg describes the illness caused by Sulemanu as headache (1946: 30), but no direct statement to that effect was recorded in the present study.

SACRIFICES AND MEDICINES. While it is said that a white ram may be used as a sacrificial animal, genuinely to please Sulemanu the offering of a bull (any colour) is mandatory. It is recorded in one of his praise-epithets,

jumuna ta fi saukar reshe, sarki ya fi yankar rago: the ostrich is too large to land on a branch, the chief exceeds the sacrifice of a ram

Ingredients for medicines used to treat a patient possessed by him are on an equally extravagant scale. The items are rare due either to the circumstances under which they must be collected or the animals from which they are taken. Ingredients such as three plants, all of which must have roots in the same well, the liver and heart of a lion, elephant bone marrow, a piece of hippopotamus hide, are only obtained through very special effort which is translated into cost.

MEDIUM'S BEHAVIOUR AND DRESS. A person possessed by Sulemanu is described as 'bossy', declining to do anything himself and directing others to wait upon him. He acts as a chief and is 'distant from people'. Interestingly enough the only person I observed who was possessed in this way was a woman.[2] One who is possessed by Sulemanu and has also been initiated into the bori cult confines this haughty attitude to occasions when he is 'ridden' by the spirit when it has been called in a possession-trance event; at other times these characteristics are submerged. In addition to displaying a stereotypical chiefly posture the medium dances or perhaps rocks rhythmically while seated, and attendants (usually not in trance themselves) agitate the air around him with ostrich-feather fans.

Considerable financial resources are necessary for those possessed by the Chief of Jangare. The accoutrement essential in order to demonstrate complete obedience—because it is 'royal'—commands an artificially high price. Only the best gown, trousers, shirt, and accompanying insulating garments, shoes, staff, prayer beads, and fans may be used.

MUSIC. In contrast the music used either to honour, invoke, or accompany the trance of one possessed by Sulemanu is limited. Garaya players in Kano use only two pieces, one which has a sung text[3] and one which has an underlying (but not sung) text.

In general garaya music for spirits is not divided on the basis of text (though it can be extremely important), but on what informants call *kida*, that is rhythmic/melodic patterns. When a performance is well under way the first song, sung by a soloist without vocal accompaniment, is heard. In the senior lute/gourd ensemble in Kano the garaya player himself performs the majority of such solos. The song incorporates the special garaya melody identified with Sulemanu, interwoven with the soloist's text. It will be noted that the transcription given below includes frequent interjections by the ensemble's praise-shouter, a conspicuous feature of bori performances (see Example 1).

The second song for the Chief of Jangare, Sulemanu, is without a sung text, but since the lute imitates the playing of the tambari drums an underlying text is implied.[4] Within the context of the courts of Hausa First-class chiefs such royal drums are typically played by royal 'slaves' (not socially classified as musicians, as we have noted), and announce the praises of the chief. While the lute is being thus played in the manner of royal drums, the gourd-rattle players eliminate all but the basic beats of their accompaniment (see Example 2).

Inna (Fulani: Mother)

PERSONALIA. Inna also known as *Bafilatana* (Fulani Woman); *Bakar Doguwa* (Black Tall-Woman); *Doguwa Ta Kwance* (Tall-Woman of Lying-Down) or, her personal name, *Hadiza*,[5](referred to hereafter as Inna), is one of Sulemanu's two wives. Her sister is his other wife and both were born in the house of the Fulani (House 5) as sisters of its head. Additionally, she is involved in an adulterous relationship with Sulemanu's senior councillor, *Kuturu* (the Leper), and in order not to anger Sarkin Aljan, every care is taken during possession-trance events to ensure that these two spirits do not appear together. The sons of Inna and her co-wife, as already noted, were given to their husband's younger brother (Biddarene, House 2) for adoption and in exchange his six sons (the most important of whom is *Dan Galadima* (the Prince)) were given to Inna.

Greenberg devotes a special part of his study to a description of, and commentary on, Inna (1946: 39-40). According to him the Maguzawa combine two spirits—one Fulani and the other Hausa—under one identity, but informants for this study conceive of her as wholly Fulani; an idea which requires elucidation. To say that Inna is Fulani is merely to identify her according to the Hausa taxonomy. The bori cult is not part of any Pastoral Fulani religious tradition, thus to say she is a Fulani woman does not mean her spiritual identity or cult practice is borrowed from them. It does mean that her behaviour and comportment are a product of the stereotype entertained by the Hausa about their pastoral neighbours.

Greenberg also reports that the Maguzawa believe Inna to be mother of all the spirits (1946: 40). Illustrative of local conditions which seem to generate conflicting interpretations of spirits' roles, Kano City informants in particular assign the responsibility for motherhood of spirits to *Magajiyar Jangare* (Heiress of Jangare; 'Jangare's Madam', cf. House 2) supporting their conviction by praise-epithets said to be hers.

AFFLICTION. Inna is feared by the Maguzawa who believe that 'she guards the property of her worshippers, pursuing thieves and causing their bellies to swell with fatal results' (Greenberg 1946: 40). In the present data she is feared for her ability to cause paralysis (a sickness also recorded by Tremearne (1914: 333)), and only brief mention is made of any abdominal swelling. Actually all the female 'Fulani' spirits are said to be responsible for paralysis. To say *'Bafilatana ta taba shi'* (lit. the Fulani Woman has touched him) means 'He is paralysed' (Abraham 1962: 56). Paralysis may be attributed to Inna if it takes a specific form: one hand and foot, usually the left, is twisted back into an immobile position; one hip and side of the lower back become rigid; the muscles around the mouth cause it to open at one side and give a contorted expression; the victim's eyes tend to bulge, he drools and is unable to stand, instead lying in a semi-curled position. As is said in one of her praise-epithets

> *dungu uwar shanu, karkata kugu juya baki baya,*
> stump-of-maimed-arm mother of cattle, twist the hip turn the mouth back
>
> *yanzu ya ga hannun mutum kamar wutsiyar mushen*
> now he will see the person's hand looking exactly as the [dried, curled] tail

muzuru a makwantai.
of a decayed wild-cat in a grave.

And in another:

dungu uwar shanu, kina kisa ana cewa Alla,
Stump-of-maimed-arm mother of cattle, you are killing it is being
said that it is Allah,

kisanki ba jini sai yaba.
when you kill there is no blood just the quivering after death.

SACRIFICES AND MEDICINES. If stricken by Inna's paralysis it is considered essential for the victim to be taken to the 'children of the bori' for
treatment as soon as possible. The illness is known to grow progressively worse
within literally days, so that delay could mean death. When Inna is the suspected
cause of a sickness normally the first step is to sacrifice either a black chicken or
a black goat. A white sheep has been described as appropriate (Greenberg 1946:
51), but present informants insisted the colour must be black. If the sacrifice
fails, serious treatment must be undertaken consisting of an initiation and specially constituted 'cure'. Greenberg lists an infusion of wood taken from trees which
grow in Fulani cattle camps as ingredients for an appropriate and adequate medicine. They are *kadanya* (shea tree; *Butyrospermum parkii*), *kanya* (African ebony
tree; *Diospyros mespiliformis*), and *madaci* (African mahogany tree; *Khaya
ivorensis*) (Ibid.: 55). Ingredients for a potion to be drunk by Inna-stricken sufferers as described in Kano and Ningi are considerably more extensive. Eight ingredients were represented in a medicine belt to be used by her devotees in Kano.
The Ningi list, which did not distinguish between medicines drunk and those
washed with, contained thirty-five ingredients and had recently had a successful
test of its effectiveness.

MEDIUM'S BEHAVIOUR. Greenberg and Tremearne describe devotees
when possessed by Inna as '[twirling] the churning stick used in making butter
while first drinking milk from a calabash and then spitting it out' (Greenberg
1946: 40) or as '[going] through the movements of milking' (Tremearne 1914:
333). Kano devotees, however, do not behave in this manner; their altered state
forces them to the ground, one hand bent close to the body. They may shake
slightly, but that is the extent of their dancing or distinguishing activity. The
preparation and training of the devotee is obviously focused on the affliction
Inna causes and not on her behaviour as a Fulani milkmaid.

MUSIC. When Inna is being 'called' in Kano possession-trance ceremonies
the lute ensembles use three or four songs, the exact number and their length
depending on the specific involvement of either the devotees or members of the
audience present. Invariably the invocation begins with some of her praise-epithets,
partially sung and partly chanted, incorporated into a leader/chorus song form.
The ensemble leader alternates his playing with a declaration of her praises. The
gourd rhythm which is maintained throughout the songs which call the spirit is
changed only when serious final efforts are necessary to induce a devotee's
trance. Example 3 (below) is Inna's first song.

The second song is given in Example 4. The garaya melody changes, but the buta rhythm remains constant, slightly embellished only near the end of the transcription. It may also be noted that the alternation between the lute-playing leader and his gourd-playing chorus is firmly established in this song.

The third song illustrates some of the difficulties involved in creating a visual representation of expert lute-playing. The first four 'measures' are a fairly phonetic transcription of the garaya line, but when the voices enter the realization of any detail becomes impossible. The barest outline of the accented pattern in the earlier measures is given, but it is emphasized that this is a grossly simplified verson of what the garaya player is actually doing. The gourd-rattle pattern continues with its previous shape, although the tapping of the players' fingers (to which a set of cowrie shells are tied, producing a percussive effect) and a slightly elaborated shake of the gourd give the second half of the pattern a complex character (see Example 5).

Dan Galadima (the Prince)

PERSONALIA. Dan Galadima has been said to be the son of Malam Alhaji (the Pilgrim) (Greenberg 1946: 42), and one of his praise-epithets recorded in Kano agrees with this. Informants stress that he is not his real son but his brother's son. As already noted, it seems Dan Galadima is the real son of Sarkin Aljan Biddarene (House 2) but was given for adoption to his father's brother Sarkin Aljan Sulemanu.[6] In the manner customary among the Hausa he may be described as the son of any or all of these three senior male spirits.

Dan Galadima has four wives and one concubine: *'Yar Mairo* (who is the daughter of a musician), *Ciwo Babu Magani* (Illness with no Medicine: the daughter of a sorcerer), *Ci Goro* (Eat Kolanuts), *Azurfa* (Silver), and *Mai Fitila* (Owner of a Lamp; his concubine). His children by these women have all been adopted by his father's brother's son, *Sarkin Rafi* (Chief of Well-Watered Land), in exchange for the children of his male parallel cousins. The result of these adoptions is that his own and his parallel cousin's children live with their real grandfathers with whom they have a joking relationship.

A spendthrift and habitual gambler, providing for his wives is not easy for Dan Galadima.

AFFLICTION. It is said in one of his praise-epithets,

katala turu bawam modi, turu dan na gode
spendthrift, one heavily in debt, slave of gambling; one heavily in debt, son of 'I give thanks'/
bad da naka, bad da na danginka.
lose your own, lose that of your relatives.

For one possessed by Dan Galadima the compulsion to give everything away has another side since it is believed that all will come back with interest. In fact the gifts in return are so large they must be carried one at a time:

sha makara ganji mai fatan ganye, ganyen ganji
enjoy brimfulness, gutta-percha tree *(Ficus platyphylla)* with wide leaves, the leaves of the gutta-percha

akwiya dauki da dai-dai da dai-dai.
are carried by the goat one at a time.

He is not considered a particularly harmful spirit, since total generosity, one of the illnesses ascribed to him, is very much part of the Hausa ethos. Conversely, excessive gambling and the embarrassing nature of such redistribution are not generally admired. A person thus afflicted is frequently a nuisance to his relatives and is taken to the horses of the gods for treatment.

SACRIFICES. One or both of two sacrifices are appropriate for Dan Galadima, the choice depending upon the severity of the affliction. A *zakara mai sirdi* (a red cock with a saddle-shaped design on its back), the lesser sacrifice, or a *rago mai tozali* (a ram with black rings around the eyes), the greater sacrifice, may be offered. His medicines include a variety of plants and parts of his two sacrificial animals, the former tracing a particular theme in that being a handsome man he always uses much perfume and thus his medicines are fragrant, being either from sweet herbs or of commercially obtained toilet waters.

MEDIUM'S BEHAVIOUR AND DRESS. In a seated position Dan Galadima throws cowries on to his mat, simulating gambling. It is very difficult to persuade him to stand or relinquish his gambling posture though sometimes he moves rapidly round and round in a kind of whirling dance. He is one of the spirits who perform *jifa* (jumping into the air or from a height and landing on the buttocks with legs outstretched), and when he begins must be allowed to complete a set of three jumps and may then be restrained by stepping lightly either on his leg below the knee or his body-wrapper between his outstretched feet. In addition to his whirling dance he is likely to have a spasm of gift-giving, his medium removing articles of costume and presenting them either to other possessed mediums, the musicians, or bystanding cult members. His attendants try to prevent this, as everything must be bought back, which constitutes a drain on their resources.

When he is called in a possession-trance ceremony his devotee is covered with a large *saki* (cotton material of black and blue strands woven into a tiny check pattern) cloth by an attendant. This cloth becomes a cape when fully in trance and the medium is then dressed with a turban, given a small fan, kola nuts (the largest, white type are said to be his), a handkerchief with cowries for gambling, and bottles of commercial scent with which his clothing is saturated.

MUSIC. Part of Dan Galadima's most important song is given in Example 6, below. After his medium is fully possessed and has been dressed in the special clothing identified with Dan Galadima he may be called to perform with this song. The only singing is by the ensemble leader or his representative.

Example 7 is actually part of song 1 and is described as a *cashiya* (speeded-up tempo for dancing). Malam Shu'aibu, the primary garaya player in Kano, uses it as a display piece to demonstrate his technique. As he plays he is encouraged by the other musicians with such phrases as '*A gaishe ka Malam Shu'aibu*' (You are greeted Malam Shu'aibu) and '*A dawo lafiya Malam*' (Return well Malam). The short lute interjections toward the middle of the transcription are examples of musical phrases with an underlying text; the garaya 'speaks'. In his enthusiasm the lute player moves slightly out of phase with his gourd accompaniment, but they adjust their rhythmic pattern when he returns to the theme for song 1. This example concludes with the beginning of the next song for Dan Galadima.

The last example illustrates music which may be used to induce the trance of his mediums. Normally, Kano mediums depend upon the music for Maga-jiyar Jangare to provide the final stimulation to reach an altered state of consciousness. But when this fails a devotee may be encouraged into trance state with some quick tempo piece associated with his own particular spirit. In Ningi and Maiduguri, for example, there is no general piece to induce trance, and such music as that in Example 8 below is all that is used, each different spirit requiring a separate piece. It seems necessary, in order to induce the trance state, that a fast tempo be established by the ensemble and then varied rhythmically, particularly in the gourd part. The lute signals the change melodically by creating the illusion through hemiola of a pattern organized in twos instead of the previous threes. Thus, in the second part of the example the triple beat becomes a duple beat:

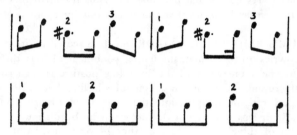

The gourd players respond to this signal by changing their rhythm as follows:

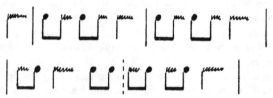

Wanzami (the Barber)

PERSONALIA. As noted above Wanzami was given the title Alkalin Jangare (Muslim Judge of Jangare) by Sulemanu, and his first official act was to turban him as King—Chief of the Spirits. Some informants maintain he is under Dan Galadima's authority; others that he serves the Chief of the Spirits and merely travels with Dan Galadima who is his close personal friend.

His family relationships are extremely involved and various informants emphasize different aspects of his residential history. The most comprehensive explanation was given by one informant as follows. Wanzami was born in the house of the hunters (House 8) as the eldest son of *Mai Dawa* (Owner of the Bush; the house head) and *Barhaza*. His mother is the younger sister of the head of the Fulani House (5) and of the wives of Sulemanu (Chief of the Spirits), which is why he is frequently described as a 'Fulani' son. He was adopted and raised by his mother's brother, *Sarkin Filani* (the Chief of the Fulani), thus emphasizing his Fulani ethnicity. Finally he left the Fulani house for that of Sulemanu (House 1) where he currently resides as a member of that chief's court.

His position as Judge of Jangare is not recorded in literature dealing with the possession-trance cult. Tremearne says that in North Africa Wanzami is 'the tonsorial expert, scarifier, and circumciser of boriland' (1914: 316) and that only in northern Nigeria is he also known as a judge (1914: 488). Neither Mon-fouga-Nicolas (1967: 1972) nor Greenberg make any mention of him, and Reuke (1969) and King (1967) recorded nothing to connect him with judgeship. In the present data, however, Wanzami as a judge is supported by examples from Kano, Ningi (not particularly emphasized), Maiduguri, Gumel, and Katsina (indirectly documented by Katsina residents on tour in Kano). In Kano the fact that he is a barber is overshadowed by the emphasis on his role as Mulsim Judge.

a. *In da gaskiya shara'a, im ma babu gaskiya a dauri.*
   If [a person is true or tells] the truth [there is] justice, if there is no truth [he is] incarcerated.

b. *Ni na tambayi mata Wanzami gyara yai ko ya yi barna*
   Me I asked women, does the Barber repair or does he do damage

   na Inna, kashin shanu bayan ya bushe cikin da daita.
   one of Inna; [it may be replied that] cattle excrement may look dry on the outside but inside it is wet (i.e. his justice can be deceptive).

However, another of his praise-epithets refers to a by-product of his ritual duties.

Masojini ya bi ka da kuttu.
A lover of blood (any spirit) follows you with a gourd-receptacle.

Further, a line in the text for one of his songs alludes to his function as a scarifier.

Kai ne ka kaiwa mutum rauni a ba ka lada.
You are the one who gives a person a wound, and you are given a reward [for it].

AFFLICTION. Wanzami causes baldness in his victims, not a particularly serious affliction, but he is also said by Tremearne to be responsible for shaving rashes and slow healing following a surgical operation (1914: 316).

SACRIFICES AND MEDICINES. His proper sacrifices are either a male red goat or a red cock, the colour being consistent with the red thread of his clothing. An infusion used to treat any of his illnesses contains ten items, the most noteworthy of which are plants, animal parts, and a piece of clothing associated with a spiritual kinsman. For example, *makau* (a type of grass) is included because it is also the name of one of his senior male kin. Blood from a cow's heart because he is a Fulani son. A small quantity of blacksmith's slag is said to be representative of a group of co-resident pseudo-kin. One piece of baobob *(Adansonia digitata)* wood represents both his adopted mother, Inna (who occasionally visits these trees), and Malam Alhaji (his adopted father's younger brother), who holds his Quranic school at their feet. Finally, a piece from a blind man's turban is included because a co-resident blind man has treated Wanzami as his own son.

MEDIUM'S BEHAVIOUR AND DRESS. When in possession-trance his

dancing which includes jifa incorporates stylistic shaving movements and periods of inactivity during which he is said to be acting as a judge. He frequently visits ceremonies in which his close friend, Dan Galadima is present. Wanzami's medium is dressed in a red body cloth, has various of the spirits' medicine belts (which must be exclusively his) around his lower chest and is given a red sword-sling and a special wallet with two compartments in which he keeps his shaving and scarifying materials.

MUSIC. There are said to be three songs for Wanzami; the second and third each have a separate, purely instrumental section used especially for his dances. In Example 9, below, an excerpt from his first and identifying song is given. As the soloist 'calls' him he uses the spirit's praise-epithets in his text. The performance order is not rigidly fixed, although participants have a fairly good idea of which spirits may be expected to follow others. Therefore it is interesting to observe exactly how little musical information needs to be given for listeners to make a positive identification of the spirit about to be invoked. In Example 9 it will be noticed that the ensemble's praise-shouter, as a case in point, knows the name of the spirit for whom the song is intended within one beat following the repeated notes which signal a change.

House 2: Zauren Sarkin Aljan Biddarene (Chief of the Spirits)

Biddarene, one of the Chief of the Spirit's younger brothers and a minor chief of spirits himself, heads a house in which a number of both important and popular spirits are members. His wife is Magajiyar Jangare (Heiress of Jangare), who is listed as the spiritual mother of all cult-adepts. Two of his adopted sons, Sarkin Rafi (Chief of Well-Watered Land) and *Barade* (a warrior) are among the most active spirits in both Kano and Maiduguri. Their wives, *Nana'aishe* and *Badakuwa* especially afflict women, and are responsible for some of the difficulties co-wives have with each other. An abbreviated diagram of Biddarene's house illustrates part of its membership:

FIGURE 3. House 2: Biddarene and Some of His Kin

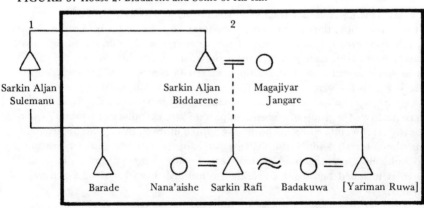

$\approx$ indicates adulterous relationship.

Magajiyar Jangare (Heiress of Jangare)

PERSONALIA. Wife of the household head and a most important spirit in Kano, Magajiyar Jangare is hardly mentioned elsewhere. Part of the reason for this lies in the way in which Kano mediums fall into trance. Unlike Ningi and Maiduguri where spirits are called individually with their own songs—their mediums entering possession-trance one at a time—Kano ceremonies are usually organized so that all the mediums present fall into trance to the accompaniment of the same music. The event is described as unusual if a medium needs a special spirit's song played to induce trance. The single piece which provides the final inducement for trance is one song for Magajiyar Jangare. (An introductory period precedes this sequence during which relatively slow invocational music to prepare the trancers is played.)

In Kano City at least Magajiya is known as the 'mother' of all cult-adepts. Her only praise-epithet alludes to this.

Mai Babban Zane na goya 'ya 'ya.
The Owner of a Large Body Cloth for carrying children.

Kano informants have a clear idea as to her identity and insist that the report in Greenberg (1946) must be mistaken. Greenberg's information led him to list *Mai Iyali* (Owner of a Family) as the wife of Sulemanu and as a spirit who 'has a large cloth to carry children' (1946: 30). The problem here, say Kano native critics, is that Mai Iyali is not the same as the Heiress of Jangare. Mai Iyali, they say, is male not female and is also known as *Kunnau* or *Ali*, Sarkin Rafi's brother. King comments on this point, stating that many of his informants thought Mai Iyali and Ali were identical 'there being strong supporting evidence for this in the song text' (1967: 11 n). King's liturgy does not include Magajiyar Jangare, so it cannot be unconditionally stated that Katsina devotees distinguish one from the other. However, it is likely that they would, since they regard Mai Iyali as male, and Magajiyar Jangare is certainly female.[8]

AFFLICTION. The illnesses ascribed to her are headache, pneumonia, and impotence in men. The data, however, include no examples of anyone ever having been afflicted by her and this is perhaps due to the attitude in Kano that she is not easily angered. As it is sung

Algaje a bar fada Magajiya; Ga Magajiya ba ma
Algaje (Magajiya), fighting has ceased Magajiya; Here is Magajiya
we shall probably not

sha wuya ba.
have any difficulty.

SACRIFICE. The appropriate sacrificial animal for her is either a white hen or a white sheep.

MUSIC. After a Kano City possession-trance event has been in progress for the time during which the trancers and guests arrive and are settled, the host or his representative will say to the lute player, '*Bismilla*' (Pray begin). With this the actual trance-including section of the event may begin, and the lute player modulates into a song for Magajiyar Jangare. The music begins rather slowly ($\flat$ = 160 or less), but the tempo is allowed to build up to induction pace ($\flat$ =200+). Within ten minutes of playing at this speed and barring unusual circumstances, all the adepts who have been selected have fallen into trance. In the excerpt given in Example 10 the two melodic patterns which constitute the basis for Magajiya's song are shown. The beginning includes a simple and repeated text, but this is soon abandoned when the tempo reaches its peak and the trancers begin to show signs of approaching an altered state of consciousness. When the music finally changes again, assuming all of the cult-adepts have entered trance successfully, no one is possessed by Magajiyar Jangare. It is other spirits who ride, Magajiya's music serving as the vehicle to prepare their horses (see Example 10).

Sarkin Rafi (Chief of Well-Watered Land)

PERSONALIA. He is also known as *Ibirahim* (personal name), *Sharu* (praise-name), *Totsi* (One Who Forces his way through Crowds) or *Zugu* (praise-name) (but will be referred to here as Sarkin Rafi) is one of Magajiyar Jangare's adopted sons and for this reason lives in House 2 although he is the real son of Sarkin Aljan Sulemanu (House 1). His wife is Nana'aishe who causes stomach ailments and incessant itching and the joking relationship he has with Badakuwa, his younger brother's wife, has been inflated into an adulterous one. His children live in House 1 where they have been adopted by his parallel cousin Dan Gala-dima whose children are being raised by Sarkin Rafi and their paternal grand-father.

King notes that Sarkin Rafi is regarded as Alkali in Katsina (1967: 13), but in Kano as we have seen, this position is held by Wanzami. Interestingly enough, this statement is not supported in any of the song text given for Sarkin Rafi later in King's work (cf. King 1967: 90-7). One point on which all sources agree, however, is that he is a violent madman. Kano informants say that his title and character were given to him by his real father Sulemanu, Chief of the Spirits. An examination of a few of his praise-epithets reveals the theme of his special characteristics (cf. Besmer 1973b: 25-8).

a.   *Totsi maci kasuwa ran fashi, mahaukaci da ya yi kwari*
     Totsi (praise-name), one who shops on the day when there is no market, the mad one with a quiver of arrows

     Ya yi baka, ya ce da kasuwa, 'kulleru.'
     and a bow, he said to the market, 'lock up' [as he shot an ar-
     row straight up not caring where it might come down].

b.   *Mai raban fada da tabarya.*
     One who settles quarrels with a large pestle (which he swings at the disputants).

c.   *Mai girbi a gonar surukai, tun bai fid da kai ba.*
     One who harvests corn at his in-laws' farm, even before it has headed out.

d. *Shi ya tad da yara guda uku suna fada; ya kama daya*
He happened to find three children who were fighting; he caught one

ya karya, ya kama daya ya jefa rijiya, ya kama daya
and broke him, he caught one and threw him down a well, he caught one

ya kwakule ido; ya ce 'ba don na zo ba da fadan ya baci'.
and scraped his eye out; 'if I hadn't come the fight would have been spoiled'.[9]

e. *Na Nana ya yi gabas, hankalinsa ya yi yamma*
One belonging to Nana, he went east, his good sense went west.

AFFLICTION. It will be clear from the above that the affliction visited upon his victims by Sarkin Rafi is madness in its various manifestations. Some forms of unsocial behaviour may be attributed to other spirits though it may be said that they assist Sarkin Rafi.

SACRIFICES AND MEDICINES. A speckled cock, a black-and-white ram, or a duck of any colour serve as sacrifices, but commonly it is necessary for a patient to undergo a lengthy treatment during which a large variety of medicines are administered. All of Sarkin Rafi's mediums interviewed for this study spent many months residing in the compounds of their curers, one having returned to his senses only after two years of treatment. A specific example of a formula to heal a patient suffering from insanity is recorded at the end of this (House 2) section (p.81).

MEDIUM'S BEHAVIOUR. His behaviour when possessing a medium during a trance ceremony unmistakably identifies him. He mounts his stallion or mare as it violently coughs, retches, and vomits or froths at mouth and nose. The medium is fully under his control when he scoops up handfuls of dirt to pour over his head and rub into his staring eyes. With a scream he stretches one slightly raised arm forward and the other back and slightly lowered, his fists clenched. Reversing the position of his arms he is said to be swimming and he looks for any water or mud to jump into. If a muddy place must be prepared by flooding with tins of water, he passes his time by performing spectacular jifa on the dry ground as a greeting to the assemblage. He prefers, however, to slap around in mud and may march off in disgust if his attendants are slow. The audience give him wide berth when he stamps near them as it is dangerous to block his path; one of his praise names, Totsi, alludes to this (see above). Those who may speak to Sarkin Rafi utilize the fear of his unpredictability as an excuse to enlarge the dancing area which often becomes over-crowded by curious onlookers. Directed to one place or another, the Mad Man scatters the audience, threatening to jump on them if they refuse to move.

During the annual ceremony held to commemorate the harvest, a large pumpkin is brought into the arena where it is broken for distribution among the 'children of the bori'. It is Sarkin Rafi, Chief of Well-Watered Land, who is summoned to smash this offering by performing jifa on it.

MUSIC. The excerpt of the song in Example 11 below, is part of one used to call Sarkin Rafi to the dance area in front of the musicians after he has possessed his medium. He remains sitting in his resting posture in the middle of some muddy place while more senior spirits ride ahead of him. When his song begins he rises into action, stamping on to the dance area and greeting the onlookers with more of his leaps. During this relatively slow music he can be directed to the edges of the crowd to move them back, all as a part of a demonstration of his madness (see Example 11).

MISCELLANEOUS. Sarkin Rafi and his brother, Barade (title for a mounted warrior), travel together, and when one has caused an affliction it can reasonably be expected he has been aided by the other. For this reason cult-adepts who consider Sarkin Rafi a part of their lives are frequently mediums for Barade too.

Barade, also known as Sarkin Yaki (Chief of War)

PERSONALIA. His personal names are *Sumba*, *Safiyanu*, and *Sufi*, and although he is resident in House 2 he spends a great deal of time in House 1 because of his responsibilities as a royal warrior. He has a reputation for particular enthusiasm in battle, but if everything is not just right for him he sulks.

a.   *Sumba aganar yaki fasa gari ba tuya.*
     Sumba furious war, rout the town and burn it down.

b.   *Sufi dan baiwar Alla, idan da yaki a yi yaki,*
     Sufi son of Allah's gift, if there is a war fight in it,

     in babu kayan yaki a huta.
     if there are no weapons then rest.

AFFLICTIONS. He is responsible for two principal sicknesses, each of them identified by some form of bleeding. In one the victim appears to have been stabbed with a spear. Informants were particularly vague about how this might happen, saying simply that it was the kind of thing Barade would do. It is not clear how this might be understood in western terms and though we may surmise haemophilic disorders this is pure speculation since no sufferers were observed. The second and more common affliction appears due to internal bleeding, particularly in the stomach.[10] The sufferer complains that his insides feel 'hot' and also of heartburn. Even if he takes food he grows progressively weaker. He becomes dehydrated, regularly vomits blood and if not taken to the children of the bori soon after blood appears he will certainly die.

SACRIFICES AND MEDICINES. He can be addressed with either of two sacrifices, a white cock or a white ram. The colour is significant for him since his clothing is white. As with all sacrifices for spirits the animal's blood must be collected in one place on the ground, preferably near a tree which is known to be its resting place. Spirits depend upon sacrificial blood for their sustenance and such an offering is the quickest way of obtaining their attention and enlisting their support. The meat, as mentioned previously, must be distributed as alms to those in a social position to receive them and thus validate the sacrifice.

In addition to the white, handwoven cloth which Barade's medium wraps around himself prior to and during his possession-trance, a correctly adorned horse must wear at least one of his medicine belts, an empty sword-sling and hold a short spear or stick.

As Sarkin Rafi's younger brother he must wait for his kinsman to introduce himself first when both are present at the same event. When together they may be expected to combine their dances for part of the time, both jumping and falling to the ground as they perform jifa. (See *Miscellaneous* in previous section on Sarkin Rafi.)

MUSIC. When it is time for Barade to dance alone he is called with his special song, part of which is given in Example 12 below. It is one of the few songs which has two separate melodies. The lute player changes from one to the other each seven 'measures', one measure equalling once through the pattern (see Example 12).

FORMULA FOR CURING SUFFERERS AFFLICTED WITH MADNESS BY SARKIN RAFI. The illness for which this treatment is intended is described as one in which the sufferer has lost all contact with reality. Typically he has no memory nor any idea of his own identity. On occasion he may be expected to be violent, a condition which alternates with total withdrawal. He usually spends most of his treatment confined in stocks both to prevent him harming anyone, including himself, and his wandering away. It is not known whether this cure as it was related was ever used in a treatment, but since the source was considered an authority on Sarkin Rafi probably much if not all had been followed.

The treatment begins with the patient being forced to drink an infusion of *gwano* (unclassified), *malmo (Eugenia owariensis)*, and *rukuki* (unclassified) woods each day for a week. If he shows no sign of improvement a second, more powerful solution is prepared from *tsintsiyar maharba* (unclassified; the plant's root is used to cure gonorrhoea), *mazarin tsofuwa* (unclassified), *bakim makarho* (the hard wood, *Burkea africana)*, *farim makarho* (the hard wood, *Afrormosia laxiflora*), and *sanya uwar magani* (an Asclepiad plant with milky sap). The solution is again administered for seven days.

If the patient remains sick the treatment must proceed to its third phase. Pounding roots gathered from sanya uwar magani (as above), *zogali* the horse-radish tree, *Moringa pterygosperma)*, *kulkuniya* (unclassified), *barkono* (red-pepper plant), and *zakami* (Hairy Thorn Apple, *Datura metel)* together with a bit of monkey brain, the mash should be put into the patient's nostrils to be sniffed. He should then be tested to determine if Sarkin Rafi's hold over him has been weakened: he should be able to communicate with the outside world.

In the fourth week the next step may be necessary. An infusion of *mado-biya* (African rosewood, *Pterocarpus erinaceus*) wood, *gaude* (shrub with yellow fruit, *Gardenia erubescens*) roots, *tsada* (a tree bearing small yellow fruit, *Ximenia americana*) wood, *jan yaro* (Euphorbia tree, *Hymenocardia acida*) wood, which must be subsequently boiled with medicinal potash, is administered to the patient who is forced to drink three mouthfuls and is then washed with it from head to foot.

The final attempt to cure the madness begins after a month and is repeated for many (unspecified) months in combination with other cures. This consists of both esoteric ingredients and a special method of preparation. The roots, wood, or leaves from nine plants[11] are put in water to soak in a new gourd which must rest on a ring woven from a *sabara* plant (*Guiera senegalensis*)[12] and covered with a new woven grass lid. While the ingredients are soaking the following procedures are essential. A red cock, killed precisely at twelve noon offered as sacrifice to ensure the solution will achieve the desired potency; the place where it bled to be covered. A chicken, one with ruffled feathers, carefully plucked (while still alive) between midnight and one a.m. when an ant-hill must be dug up and the chicken, still living, buried. The feathers, having been burnt to ashes, are then added to the soaking plants. On the following morning the completed infusion is administered, the patient both drinking and being washed in it. Perhaps the most difficult part of this phase is that after seven days the chicken must be disinterred. If it is still alive—something hard to imagine—the patient will recover. If it is either dead or missing from its burial place, the patient has no chance of recovery.

In view of the somewhat bizarre conclusion of this phase of treatment, the informant was asked whether in his experience it had ever been successful. He avoided a direct reply, only insisting that if it was possible to cure the patient the chicken would hop out of its grave alive. Privately, he suggested that it was rare for a successful treatment to go this far and that the chicken, if dead, would only demonstrate that the sickness was incorrectly diagnosed in the beginning. If the madness was due to the work of spirits, he said, the patient would have been cured at an earlier stage of treatment.

House 3: Zauren Malamai (head of house, Malam Alhaji; the Pilgrim)

The house of the malamai (s. malam: Quranic teacher-scholar) can be explained only as an addition to the spirit world after contact with Islam. As Greenberg states, 'the existence of such a character among the iskoki as Malam Alhaji is impossible without an intimate acquaintance with Moslem ways and practices' (1946: 63).

Malam Alhaji

PERSONALIA AND OTHER OCCUPANTS. He has either two wives or one wife and one concubine. Informants say his first wife is *Kuri* and has borne him three sons, the eldest of whom is *Nakada* (Causer of Downfall). He turned out quite opposite in character to his father, and because of his evil ways was sent to live with the Pagans (House 9). Malam Alhaji's concubine or other wife is *Arziki* (Prosperity), also known as *Bagwariya* (the Gwari Woman). Since she is from the house of the Pagans informants consider it likely that she was responsible for the way in which her co-wife's eldest son was raised.

AFFLICTION. The only illness Malam Alhaji seems to be responsible for is chronic coughing, both because he is an old man and thus prone to coughing and because it seems to be an occupational malady.

SACRIFICES AND MEDICINES. Cult-adepts emphasize that animals to be sacrificed to him must be entirely white and without blemish. A ram is favoured, but a cock may be substituted. All the residents of Jangare except him have medicine belts (s. *damara*) prepared specifically for them; but his medicinal formulae are verses from the Qur'an. Their power is activated by writing them on a wooden slate from which they are washed into a cup and drunk.

MEDIUM'S BEHAVIOUR AND DRESS. As the medium sits in trance he writes verses from the Qur'an with a native pen on a slate, reads and prays, and 'pulls' the beads of his rosary. So far as could be ascertained through observation and interview Malam Alhaji does not dance. The image of him as a holy man is repeated in his praise-epithets.

a.   *Malam Alhaji na Annabi gonar salla; karanta allamu;*
Malam Alhaji of the Prophet [his] farm is prayer; well-versed with the prayerboard;

Imamu gatan salla, Imamu gatan gawa.
Imam supporter of prayer, Imam supporter of the corpse.[13]

b.   *Garin da babu malamai mushe ne.*
A town with no malams is carrion.

During a possession-trance ceremony his medium should be dressed in a white cape, gown, turban, jumper, trousers and wrapper, a red fez, and native shoes and sit on a ram-skin mat. In fact, few cult-adepts are wealthy enough to own all of these.

MUSIC. Only one song is used to address Malam Alhaji, and an excerpt of it is given in Example 13. As in many previous examples, when Malam Shu'aibu, the lute player, both plays and sings the first song for a spirit he limits his intricate finger-work to occasions when he is not also singing. When singing he strums rather absent-mindedly, keeping the tempo on his instrument's open strings but reducing the melodic pattern to its barest essentials (see Example 13).

Bagwariya

PERSONALIA. Malam Alhaji's concubine or second wife is thought not to be the kind of woman a Quranic scholar might ordinarily choose as a wife, and most informants are anxious to explain how it may happen that such a marriage could exist. Some say, after all he is an iska or jinn, and spirits sometimes do strange things, including marrying unusual partners; others that it was because Bagwariya's father gave her to the Chief of the Spirits who, in turn, gave her to Malam Alhaji in a 'marriage of alms'. This means that Sulemanu (House 1) paid her bride-price but did not marry her himself.

Cult-adepts, themselves Hausa, view the Gwari Woman in the stereotyped way in which they regard Gwari people in general. They are described as pagans, and for the Muslim Hausa this conception generates elaborate ideas about what they eat. Bagwariya is classified as a black spirit, not because of the illnesses she is said to cause, but because of the belief that as a pagan she neither prays to Allah nor observes Muslim dietary restrictions. She eats constantly, but dislikes food containing peppers. More importantly, she eats dogs and bush animals and is not particular about how they are slaughtered, furthermore she is believed actually to prefer carrion—meat either putrid or improperly slaughtered.[14] It is recorded in one of her praise-spithets,

> *Gwari uwar Mamman ina aka sam mushe aka dauko.*
> Gwari [Woman] mother of Mamman (the Prince), wherever carrion can be found it is taken.

AFFLICTIONS. She is thought to be responsible for goitre and humpback, these being part of her own physical appearance. Only rarely does she strike a victim as a primary spirit, preferring to join with her friends and kin once the victim has been afflicted. She has considerable influence over her husband and his brother's son Dan Galadima, and her help can be enlisted in persuading them to abandon the symptoms of those afflictions for which they are responsible.

SACRIFICES. As a black spirit she may be addressed only with the sacrifice of black animals, specifically, a black chicken or black goat. She prefers their blood for her sustenance, but it is also proper to distribute cooked beans as an offering to her.

MUSIC. Bagwariya's song is played just after her husband's (the end of Malam Alhaji's song is seen at the beginning of the example below) and is meant to be slightly disjointed to match her gait. The song proclaims her preference for 'unclean' foods and describes her appearance (see Example 14).

House 4: Zauren Kutare (The House of the Lepers, Head of House, Kuturu; The Leper)

The house of the lepers contains a major subsection for snakes, and *Danko*, the leader of the snake subsection, is sometimes said to be the Leper's classificatory brother, but this is nothing more than a restatement of their common residence and pseudo-kinship.

Kuturu

PERSONALIA. He is recognized as Jangare's Madaki (senior councillor) a title given to him by the Chief of the Spirits, and is believed to spend a considerable part of his time at the main gate to the palace (House 1).[15] The Hausa term, Madaki, generates three other praise-names, *Uban Dawaki* (lit. Father of the Horses; leader of horsemen), *Goje*, and *Kaura* and he may be referred to by any one of them; additionally *Kyadi* (Dried Body) and *Sautau* are two other names for him but he will be referred to here as Kuturu.

He has one wife, *Almajira*, but is believed to participate in an adulterous relationship with one of the Chief of the Spirits' wives—the Black Tall-Woman (Inna; Bakar Doguwa, see House 1). He is said to dislike appearing at a ceremony at which *Kure* (the Hyena) is also present because they are jealous of each other and compete for her favours.

The praise-epithets for Kuturu indicate two facets of his character—one fearsome the other amusing. Of the fearsome Kuturu as senior councillor it is said,

Goje akurkin dundu,[16]*wawa ka zura hannu rami.*
Goje, fowl-pen made of a thorny bush, only a fool would try to put
his hand into its opening (the barbs would catch the flesh, trying to
pull it out).

Combining the grotesque sight of a market built by lepers for lepers with
the power of the senior councillor, the following is given,

Na Hawwa dakurakon kashi maki nika maki shiga,
Of Hawwa (his wife) with [leg and knee joints] calcified so that
they cannot be softened nor moved,

wandaka wanda yai ci kasuwar Dakiro ya tsaya
lavish spender who visits the Dakiro market,[17]he stops

ya yi dake-dake dandandana, gonar gujiya na duhu
and builds the mud huts, [having a difficult time slapping the mud
on the walls with his cup-shaped hands], a farm of thickly planted
Bambarra ground-nuts

babu gurim buya.
there is no place to hide oneself.

The most sober devotees can appreciate the picture of nasal-voiced, impatient
Kuturu, crawling and sweating while trying to build a mud market-shack. Considering his appearance and behaviour at a possession-trance event (see below),
the scene is comical. But as you laugh Kuturu is watching; there is no place to
hide. When he moves out of sight it is impossible to tell which way he has gone
even if you are able to find his footprints.

Na Dakila[18] *masu sasun gado, gaba aka yi ko baya?*
Of Dakila one with a footprint like a bed's[19]have you gone up the
trail or down it?

Another of his praises suggests why his followers are dedicated to him. He
takes anything given to him as alms, but when it is time to distribute gifts or
show favours he is not a miser.

Dakunkun dakusara dan dakwa mai naso, kana ruwa
Invincible warrior, son of 'something large and round'.[20] one whose
gown is always wet, you are wet

kana gumi, da ku kuke rabo da kowa ya samu.
you are sweating;[21] if it is you[22] who is sharing out everyone will
receive something.

Kuturu is a most important character in Jangare, as a senior member of the
Chief of the Spirits' court he is both feared and respected. I have never seen him
ride any but the most proficient mediums, all men, and consequently his appearance during a possession-trance ceremony creates excitement and awe in the
spectators.

AFFLICTION. Leprosy is obviously the illness ascribed to him. When he
strikes his victim's eyes turn red, his mouth resembles a 'broken fragment of a

calabash' and his fingers curl onto his palms so that his hands resemble a 'city dweller's spoon'. Leprosy first affects the extremities of the body—fingers, toes, nose, etc.—and its appearance is frightening. Informants say Kuturu's warning signs are fever and headache and then the victim's face begins to swell. After his flesh 'begins to spoil' he becomes extremely foul-smelling.

SACRIFICES AND MEDICINES. In an attempt to arrest the illness during its earliest stages, a chicken with ruffled feathers (one unpleasant to look at) or a particular type of red-and-white goat may be sacrificed. Kuturu likes the thorny dundu as a resting place, a fowl-pen made from its branches symbolically refers to him in one of his praise-epithets (see above), and its leaves and roots are the first ingredients for an infusion administered to a patient afflicted by him.

I have wondered whether it is possible to arrest leprosy by the bori method and was repeatedly told by cult-adepts that Kuturu's cure is effective. Their claim is supported by examples of his mediums who seem to have been relieved of all the symptoms and deformities (where they were not too far advanced) of the sickness. An occasional case may be pointed to where the cure was temporarily effective but failed when the medium abandoned the cult by refusing to participate in its activities. The most impressive example of such 'back-sliding' was that of a man who admitted attempting to leave the cult and in so doing was reafflicted by Kuturu; he now bears physical evidence of his error. He has returned to the bori fold and participates in cult ceremonies but only to prevent his disease developing further. His case provides concrete evidence for other devotees who might fail to appreciate the power of angered iskoki.

MEDIUM'S BEHAVIOUR AND DRESS. A medium ridden by Kuturu acts as a leper and compulsively begs for alms. As his trance state begins his fingers close on his palms; it is important that an attendant removes any rings the medium may be wearing before the fingers become 'frozen' as the spirit might harm his mount when he rides if anything is under or on his fingers. The medium's nose runs, his distorted mouth opens far to one side of his face. He cannot walk but crawls with his feet bent under him, his toes curl downward and joints below the ankles are immovable.

Fully in charge of his horse Kuturu dominates the trance area unless his superior, the Chief of the Spirits, is also present. He vigorously rubs the ground with his elbows and slaps it and parts of his body and head with his deformed hands. This action, along with vain attempts to wipe his running nose, gives the impression of one suffering spells of intolerable itching. This, however, is not the case; the flailing of arms is interpreted as a sign of Kuturu's considerable power.

A medium possessed by him is not taken from the trance induction area as are many other mediums. When he travels it is as the Leper, but without his special paraphernalia (objects attached to mediums after having been led away from the trance-dance site) he is immovable. One of his praise-epithets alludes to this

Abba mazan gudu ba mazan kaiwa ba.
Abba (praise-name) a man[23] who runs, not a man who is carried.

Therefore, Kuturu is given his possessions for all to see. He manages his red fez without difficulty; but the knots for his leather apron are too complicated for someone without fingers, and an attendant must help him. He drags around a bag of woven grass containing his food and a small warty gourd to collect alms. Over one arm he carries a horsehair switch to beat away flies and over the other a dum-palm (*Hyphoene Thebaica*) nut string which leper's use as a formidable weapon.

MUSIC. According to Malam Shu'aibu (the senior garaya player in Kano), there are four songs for Kuturu but it is rare for more than two to be played. His first song is heard immediately after the 'door of the performance' is opened (with music for the Chief of Drummers, see below, House 6). Unlike the transitions between songs for many spirits which require one to end and an entirely new tempo to begin the next, that between a commonly heard song for the Chief of Drummers and one for Kuturu is accomplished smoothly. The former is organized into musical phrases four beats long with each beat subdivided by three eighth-notes: $\frac{6}{8}+\frac{6}{8}$ ♪♪♪ ♪♪♪ ¦ ♪♪♪ ♪♪♪ . The Leper's song is organized into musical phrases three beats long with each beat subdivided by two eighth-notes: $\frac{3}{4}$ ♫ ♫ ♫ | ♫ ♫ ♫ . Keeping the pace of the underlying eighth-notes the same, a rhythmic modulation is performed using what might be described as a type of hemiola. That is, ONE-two-three FOUR-five-six . . . becomes ONE-two THREE-four FIVE-six. To help illustrate this unusual phenomenon the end of a song for the Chief of Drummers is given as a reference in the excerpt before the first song for the Leper begins (see Example 15).

The second song for the Leper (shown in Example 16) is actually an extension of the first. In it the garaya 'speaks', playing the phonemic (tonal and rhythmic) outline of an underlying text. The gourd-playing chorus softly chants this text as the lute is played. Why this particular text should be associated with Kuturu is not altogether clear except that it is assumed he is somewhat preoccupied with its lesson; his affair with the Black Tall-Woman is cited as support for this assumption (see Example 16).

Snakes' subsection: head—Danko

PERSONALIA. Danko is also known as *Dan Musa* (lit. Son of Musa; Small Musa), *Samami* (Sudden Visitor), and *Majaciki* (Drawer of the Belly[24]). He lives in water, either rivers or wells, and visitors to such places must beware of meeting him. It is uncertain whether Danko is young or middle-aged, proponents of the former pointing out that no marriages or offspring are mentioned in his praise-epithets and those of the latter that it would be unlikely that a young spirit would hold his social position. The latter claim that other information given in the oral tradition places him as husband of *Kwakiya* (Black-Hooded Cobra), father of *Damatsiri* (type of harmless, green snake), and adopted father of *Masharuwa* (Drinker of Water[25]).

An evening tale about Danko described him as the possessor and provider of great wealth. Near a hill in Kano (the site of a reservoir for the city's water-supply) a certain unmarried woman met a strange man. Her initial impulse to run away having passed, the woman was tempted by his proposal that in exchange for a special room in her compound—to be furnished according to his specifications—she would be provided with unlimited wealth. Knowing or not who the man actually was (here the story was delayed while, to the humming of mosquitoes in the darkness, the audience argued the case for or against her naivety) she accepted this arrangement. She enjoyed her new wealth for some time, while not drastically changing her life-style she nevertheless had everything she had ever wanted. However, she found it difficult to explain how she came by her new wealth to her friends. They turned away from her until she found herself alone except for the resident of the special room whom no one saw enter or leave. Depressed and frail despite her wealth, she sought to annul her agreement with 'the strange man'. She failed (or some thought, succeeded) and died in her unhappy state. The bori people knew without doubt that the stranger was Danko.

> *Kai da kyau mata da kwadayi abin rantsuwar mutanen Haskiya*
> You are fine, women are greedy, a thing to take an oath on by the people of Haskiya[26]
>
> *da Gadas; kai ba Alla ba kana saka ciwon ciki Dam Musa.*
> and Gadas[27] you are not Allah, [but] you cause stomach trouble Small Musa.

In his praises he is shown as powerful and dangerous; being a snake he cannot be visualized otherwise.

a. *Samami biya kora nama koran nama.*
    Sudden Visitor follow driving; meat, driver of meat.[28]

b. *Carki mai adan baka, dam makodi ka fi gaban aljihun.*
    [As a] rhinoceros-bird's red mouth; a small sharpening stone is greater than the carrying capacity of any pocket.[29]

c. *Mai ido ya tagulla mai harshe ya dam buda.*
    The owner of eyes like copper, the owner of a tongue slightly split.

Finally, because he is not specifically a 'pagan' Danko is said to be a white spirit.

AFFLICTIONS. Two or three illnesses are ascribed to Danko, and one, stomach ailments, has already been mentioned. In the opinion of many informants his most serious affliction is infertility in women. The Hausa conform to the well-documented belief (cf. Lévi-Strauss 1962) in a symbolic connection between snakes and infertility. It is for this reason that women who draw water must be especially careful not to talk to strangers and to avoid any possibility of coming into contact with Danko. A third affliction ascribed to him—the ability to cause blindness by spitting into the eyes of his victims—is not widely recognized, but some informants maintain its truth. The Black-Hooded Cobra (Danko's wife), adopts this method of attack and it is thought he acquired the technique from her.

SACRIFICES. Although as we have seen, he is a white spirit, yet since his clothing must include a wrapper and turban in black or indigo only black animals may be sacrificed to him. A black male goat or a black cock are given as appropriate.

MEDIUM'S BEHAVIOUR (SEE ABOVE FOR DRESS). Possessed by Danko his medium imitates the movements of a snake, either crawling on his stomach or rising up into the striking position of a spitting cobra. He shows insatiable hunger for raw eggs, eating a dozen or more if they are given him, and an almost equal craving for raw liver. Both are symbolic of his afflictions, infertility in women and internal disorders. He possesses his mediums easily, occasionally confirming his description as Sudden Visitor by riding a medium without special invitation. All such capricious behaviour on the part of spirits is viewed with alarm and usually an attempt is made to induce the spirit to leave his mount and return when adequate preparations can be made for his arrival.

MUSIC. So far as could be determined Danko has only one song (possibly by reason of the ease with which his medium is possessed, see above). His music is slightly unusual in the bori repertoire. The common pattern of the chorus either repeating the leader's statement or singing one of a number of possible answering phrases (selection being determined by the chorus' leadership) is set aside. Instead, the chorus sings one or two set 'refrains' or provides a prearranged response to a particular statement by the ensemble leader. While slight variations may be heard in the responses sung by the chorus, the over-all impression of Danko's music is that pairs of statements and answers are more firmly fixed than in the rest of the repertoire (see Example 17).

House 5: Zaurem Filani (Sarkin Filani, Chief of the Fulani)

The Fulani House seems to be over-crowded with spirits in the senior generation. In fact no third generation at all is given in the house census. Social stratification among Fulani spirits is largely a matter of birth order, but informants list all the males of the household head's generation before any female spirits.

OCCUPANTS. The Chief of the Fulani is said to have three younger brothers, but all except one have left to take places in other houses. *Zurkalene*, the eldest, heads House 6 (see below) and has appointed the third brother as his senior councillor. *Baidu*, the youngest of all, remains in the house and little is known of his activities. Seven sisters were born here but because of residence changes demanded by marriage, all but one has left. The most notable among the sisters are Bakar Doguwa (the Black Tall-Woman; see above, House 1) and *Barhaza* (see below, House 8). A common marriage preference among the Pastoral Fulani is for a woman to marry her father's brother's son. Since (relatively considered) the sisters are thought to be so young, this system has been transformed with some Fulani spirits to include brother's son marriages. The brothers involved are the senior generation of House 6, and all the sons have been adopted by them. *Hawa'u* (also known as *Gurgunya* (Lame Woman)) married *Kure* (Hyena) and *Labuda* married *Zaki* (Lion). In exchange one of the Chief of the Fulani's brother's daughters has married a Fulani man in his house (see fig. 4).

FIGURE 4. Endogamous Fulani Marriages

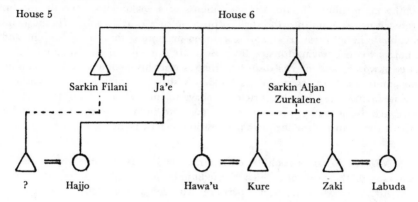

Sarkin Filani

PERSONALIA. He is also known as *Mai Ruga Dukko* (Owner of the Cattle-Encampment Dukko) or his personal name *Hardo*, and has four wives and ten children (see *Miscellaneous* below for further information on children).

The Chief of Fulani is responsible for the welfare and fertility of the herd, and according to his praise-epithets is expert in this

a.   *Sarkin Filani Mai Ruga Dukko, shekara goma zamani goma;*
     Chief of the Fulani, Owner of the Cattle-Encampment Dukko,
     ten years [and] ten places;[30]

     shanu goma shekara goma; dangwali goma
     ten cattle [in] ten years;[31] ten tether-ropes for new-born calves

     shekara goma.
     [in] ten years.[32]

b.   *Hardo mai dubun nagge.*
     Hardo, owner of a thousand cows.

He contracts with other Fulani to interbreed stock, a service for which he pays. If he considers the results successful the payment is generous; if not it is a mere token. A praise-epithet describes this practice but in a different idiom.

Taro na ba ki ban ji dadi ba, Sarkin Filani Mai Ruga Dukko.
I am giving you threepence because it was not pleasurable,[33]
Chief of the Fulani, Owner of the Cattle-Encampment Dukko.

AFFLICTION. Like many other male Fulani spirits Sarkin Filani causes his victims to abandon a sedentary existence and roam about the countryside. The wanderer finds a stick similar to that used by herders and carries it around at all times, refusing to put it down. It is said to be difficult to feed such sufferers; they will not sit down and their food preferences are limited to cassava and small fried cakes made from the residue of ground-nuts after the oil has been expressed. Though not subject to wide agreement, the one other affliction for which he is said to be responsible is scrotal hernia.

SACRIFICES AND MEDICINES. He prefers the sacrifice of white animals and, because he is a chief, only the best ram or cock is appropriate. Usually nothing more than a sacrifice is necessary in order to approach him since he rarely afflicts anyone, leaving such work to other members of his household. However, if extended treatment should be necessary an infusion is available. Among its ingredients are those associated with the Fulani—fibre used to make calf tethers, milk from a black cow;[34] one horn from a dead cow, and a type of grass called *farar bafilatana* (lit. white Fulani woman; otherwise unclassified).

MUSIC. Only one song is played for the Chief of the Fulani and an excerpt is shown in Example 18. The garaya player makes extensive use of 'double stops', strumming on both strings of his instrument, and the underlying rhythmic organization is extremely complex. Its complexity may be judged, in part, by the time it takes the gourd-playing chorus to settle into a pattern before beginning to sing. The song begins slowly (♩· =80) with four-beat phrases subdivided into twelve eighth-notes, three to a beat. By the end of the leader's first sung phrase the gourd players have changed the fourth beat of their pattern to a rhythmical-

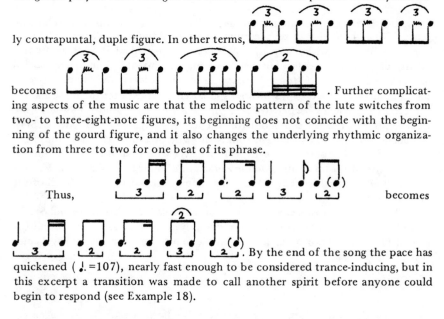

ly contrapuntal, duple figure. In other terms,

becomes   . Further complicating aspects of the music are that the melodic pattern of the lute switches from two- to three-eight-note figures, its beginning does not coincide with the beginning of the gourd figure, and it also changes the underlying rhythmic organization from three to two for one beat of its phrase.

Thus,   becomes

. By the end of the song the pace has quickened (♩· =107), nearly fast enough to be considered trance-inducing, but in this excerpt a transition was made to call another spirit before anyone could begin to respond (see Example 18).

MISCELLANEOUS. The most popular of Sarkin Filani's children are *Sambo, Mai Gizo* (Owner of Matted Hair), *Na Matuwa* (One of the She-Asses), and *Buba.*

Sambo appears regularly in possession-trance rituals held in small urban areas and is believed to be responsible for aimless wandering into the bush.

Mai Gizo was sent out of his father's house for the same reason that Malam Alhaji (House 3) had to exile his son, Nakada (House 9): both have renounced Islam.

Na Matuwa, Mai Gizo's full brother has the reputation of seducing any woman he finds alone. His character is 'difficult' but Sarkin Filani presumably thinks it reparable or he too would be living with the pagans of House 9.

Buba, the youngest child of the Fulani house, is treated more as grandson than son. His father indulges and jokes with him rather than avoiding him, and this is believed to be the reason for his emotional immaturity (cf. Besmer 1973*a*). When Buba rides he either weeps if he cannot find his parents or runs away. He is technically not a demanding horseman, so many newly initiated devotees 'practice' trance skills by being possessed by him.

House 6: Zauren Sarkin Aljan Zurkalene

Chief of the Spirits Zurkalene is a terrifying figure with one horn in the middle of his head. Although he has never been known to possess anyone, and consequently nothing can be said about the illnesses ascribed to him or his cures, a few isolated fragments of information have been preserved.

Zurkalene is believed to be Sarkin Filani's younger 'brother'[35] who, being displeased with prospects in his older brother's house left to set up his own house, taking his younger brother *Ja'e* with him to serve as his Madaki.

OCCUPANTS. The house census is filled with spirits born there but no longer living there and those presently living there but born elsewhere. Consequently it has links with many other houses in Jangare. In addition there are two major subsections—one for butchers and one for maroka. Zurkalene married Sarkin Fagan's (head of House 7) sister, *Kasa* (Puff-adder), and adopted two of his children[36] and two of his brother's children. Of the latter, one left and became Dan Galadima's second wife[37], one is a sorcerer[38] and the other, *Kure* (Hyena), is leader of the subsection for butchers. Kwakiya (Black-Hooded Cobra), Zurkalene's daughter, as we have seen is the wife of Danko (head of the snake subsection in the house of the Leper) and lives with him in House 4. Finally, although maroka form a subsection in Zurkalene's house, its leader Sarkin Makada (Chief of Drummers), spends most of his time in the palace of the Chief of the Spirits' house (1).

Two of the most active spirits in Zurkalene's house are Kure and Sarkin Makada. Both visit Sulemanu's house regularly, the Hyena lurking around the gate at night and Sarkin Makada going inside to perform his duties as royal courtier.

Kure (Hyena)

PERSONALIA. Born as we have seen in the house of Sarkin Fagan (7) and adopted by Zurkalene he first married his adopted father's sister, Hawa'u (a Fulani woman), and then *Maimuna* and *Amina*, daughters of the Chief of Butchers. When the Chief of Butchers 'retired' he recommended his son-in-law Kure for the position. This was accepted by Sarkin Aljan Sulemanu who appointed him the new Sarkin *Fawa*.

Kure has three children, but only his daughter, *Zainaba 'Yar Mahauta* (Zainaba, Daughter of Butchers), still lives with him. His sons, *Bako Mashi* (Guest Spear)[39] and *Masharuwa* (Drinker of Water) have been adopted by Danko (House 4).

Hyenas are feared in Hausa folklore, and Kure fits the stereotype. Many of his praise-epithets testify to his irascible character.

a.   *Daggu, Daggu ba hargowa, Kure dabbar Alla, Burungu*
Daggu, Daggu[40] cause uproar, Hyena beast of Allah, Burungu[41]

aljanad dare, da rabo garar warwasun[42]*kowa yai dare*
spirit of night, [your] sharing-out is excessive, anyone who goes out at night

da rabon ka.
will be shared out.

b.   *Kure mai suna Dauda, karas-karas*[43]*maye, hadiya da*
Hyena whose name is Dauda, crunch a sorcerer[44] swallow [him] while

sauran kwana.
he is still alive.

c.   *Fasa makaranta bakon limami.*
Break up the school, guest of the officiating Muslim priest.

The most likely time to encounter Kure is at night; the most likely place is the palace gate of any king. As a praise-singer testified

kowa yai dare kofar fada zai gamu da Kure; ni da nai
anyone who is at the palace gate at night will meet the Hyena; I myself went

dare kofar fada Gazau na samu.
at night to the palace gate and met him.

Kure is often said to be the patron spirit of butchers, but as one of his epithets describes, not all butchers hold this view:

Tamburan gidan Bungari, ba duka ba sai dai dai dai.
The royal drums of the house of meat-sellers, not all of them just selected ones.[45]

AFFLICTION. Headache, strangulation,[46] or nose-bleed are the sicknesses ascribed to Kure.

SACRIFICES AND MEDICINES. The sacrifice of either a red cock or a red male goat is appropriate. Should this prove ineffective (and Kure is diagnosed as the cause of the malady) an extended treatment may be required at the hands of competent bori initiates which includes medicines for drinking and washing. Central among the ingredients in the separate infusions, are dirt gathered from a place close to the local palace gate, and roots taken from a tree known to provide shade for his afternoon nap.[47]

MEDIUM'S BEHAVIOUR. The first and third of the three songs known for Kure in Kano, which may be used to invoke his presence, have purely instrumental sections which may be used after he has already possessed his medium and seeks to dance. However, dancing is not of particular interest to him. He prefers to rage around in front of the musicians, snapping at anyone who comes close to his horse's drooling, snarling mouth. During such a demonstration the role of his attendant becomes unusually important, since if he was to loose the leash tied to the Hyena the audience might panic.

MUSIC. Example 19 below includes two songs for Kure and the transition between them. The first song, which was short on the occasion of this particular recording, is given in its entirety, the chorus singing only two responses before the lute player began the transition. It will also be noted that the text sung by the chorus was muddled; the description of what it 'should have been' was given during a follow-up interview with a buta (gourd-rattle) player. All of the sections marked 'obscured' in the lute line consisted of rhythm-keeping on one string, and no particular melodic material occurred. The transition between the songs consisted of a short lute statement with an underlying text. The text was a praise-epithet for the Hyena, and the chorus 'translated' its second half as it was played. The full kirari (praise-epithet) was given as follows (cf. above):

> *kowa yai dare kofar fada zai tad da Kure.*
> anyone who is at the palace gate at night will overtake the Hyena.

The second song is given in excerpted form, but it can be seen that it sounds more 'open' than the first, using fewer sixteenth-notes in both the sung and lute melodies (see Example 19).

Sarkim Makada (Chief of Drummers)

PERSONALIA. He is also known as *Dafau* (lit. very poor quality meat cooked and sold in small pieces; a praise-name), *Madi* = *Mahadi* (the Mahdi or Revealed One), *Abdullahi* (personal name) and various other personal names and is considered by some writers to be the most important spirit in Jangare (Ames 1973; King 1967: 3 n). However, native critics say this must be due either to (a) a confusion of 'first' in a performance with 'greatest'; (b) a personal statement by a musician that as far as his craft is concerned Sarkim Makada is most important; or (c) a simple error in fact or interpretation. Cult-adepts emphatically deny that the Chief of Drummers is the principal spirit of Jangare. They admit that he comes first in a performance, 'opening the door', since in any procession maroka should precede their leaders, clearing the way and announcing their praises. They also believe that members of any craft group should show proper respect towards the craft's patron spirit, and for musicians this is Sarkim Makada, but this should not be confused with Jangare's social hierarchy. Finally, the initiated simply deny Sarkim Makada his primacy saying that everyone should know it is Sarkin Aljan, Sulemanu, who is King and thus Jangare's most important spirit.

Sarkim Makada is believed to be the son of *Abamu* and the grandson of *Karbo* (from *karba*, to receive). He has one wife, *Zabiya* (Woman Praise-Singer), and five children, one of whom is Dan Galadima's senior wife. He is described as a spirit with too many responsibilities.

> *Bulum-bulum bai makada gawas sangali gawo kore,*
> Bulum-bulum[48] give the drummer[49] an old shin-bone and an old

calabash[49]

irin akwiya ta mutu, ta bara fata dadi—kowa ya ce
a type of goat died and left her skin to pleasure—everyone says

wuya—ta kare, a kansa am mutu am ba shi da cima-zaune
to suffer[50]—she is finished; for him there was a death, he was given stepchildren[51]

guda goma sha bakawi!
numbering seventeen!

With all his difficulties, however, he is an expert musician, drumming, strumming, blowing, or singing with equal facility. These things are easy for him, and no one, spirit or mortal, is his match.

dan Abamu jikan Karbo, kada-kada ba baran gida, kowa yai
son of Abamu grandson of Karbo, drumming for money is not something to be done at home; anyone who is [to be as]

gwaninka sai yai yawo; gwaninka ba ya danga, ko ya yi
expert as you must walk around; your expertise cannot be fenced in, or if it is

ma ba zai tanki ba.
the fence will have no cross-piece (be incomplete).

A person who has committed his life to music (the maroka craft which includes 'begging' and panegyrizing), and to the Chief of Drummers, is in almost a worse position than a habitual thief.

Na Sasana ka fi sata ciwo, sai dai sata ta fi
Of Sasana[52] you are a worse illness than thievery, except that thievery exceeds

ka yawan jeji.
you in [forcing the afflicted one] to walk in the bush.

When times are bad a musician must resort to other pastimes.

Dagwami babban ciniki idan am bari 'ina wani aiki';
The drink dangwami[53] is an important trade[54] when one stops 'is there work';

in da saye da biya, ba saye ba biya ba bauta.
if it is wanted it is paid for [but] when none is desired there is no income, no slavery.[55]

AFFLICTION. The illnesses ascribed to Sarkim Makada are all related to his craft as a musician, and those afflicted by him may complain of chronic soreness in the shoulders, or of throat ailments, e.g. laryngitis, tonsilitis, tracheitis, etc.

SACRIFICES. He may be addressed with the offering either of a red-and-white goat or a red cock. The choice depends upon the affluence of the person afflicted and his family. In contrast to offerings for other spirits which are graded—goats being more significant than chickens—the sacrificial value of the alternative offerings for Sarkim Makada are considered to be equal. Apparently he understands genuine poverty (not meanness) and is accordingly sympathetic.

MEDIUM'S BEHAVIOUR. A specific example of one extreme case was witnessed during which a woman tried to strangle herself with her own hands while in a state of possession-trance. She had fallen into trance 'normally' but suddenly fell to the ground with her hands locked around her own throat. Thinking she was suffering a relapse of the illness which had led to her initiation, her attendants tried desperately to pry her hands loose. Kuturu, who was also present at the ceremony crawled to her and directed Sarkim Makada to immediately release his mare. He declared that as the Chief of the Spirits' representative at the ceremony he could not allow any spirit to maltreat his mount. The rebukes of his superior were heard and Sarkim Makada released his mare's hands. Bystanders were unable to guess what had caused his anger but agreed it was exceptionally ill-mannered of him to vent his anger on his own mount.

MUSIC. Sarkim Makada may be called with any one of his five songs, but it is not uncommon for him to ride in advance of other spirits called either with their own music or that for Magajiyar Jangare. In Example 20 an excerpt of one of his songs is given. He rarely arrives during the playing of this song, probably because it is usually the first song played by Malam Shu'aibu Mai Garaya at a possession-trance event and not enough people are ready for trance demonstrations, and its tempo does not reach the pace necessary to induce a medium's altered state of consciousness. Once possessed by Sarkim Makada his medium imitates the playing of one instrument after another, frequently appearing to manage two at a time. It is also common for him to sing songs for each of the other spirits present or expected for the event. An interesting facet of the Chief of Drummers' preferences is that he appears to favour female adepts. Many men are described as offering sacrifices to him, but they are all musicians, not cult-members who would be expected to demonstrate possession. In Kano, its surrounding hamlets, and Ningi all the active mediums for him are women (see Example 20).

House 7: Zauren Sarkin Aljan Shekaratafe

PERSONALIA. Shekaratafe is also called Sarkin Fagan and is the head of this house. Because of his inactivity very little is known about him and what can be recorded can be pieced together only with difficulty.

Informants maintain that he still occasionally possesses people but so rarely that no one can think of any examples. Although one song is known for him I have never heard it. Supposedly when he rides, his medium is shielded with a canopy and merely sits, abstaining from any dancing.

OCCUPANTS. According to informants who recognize Sarkin Fagan's existence and are willing to describe the membership of his house, he lives in water, has one wife (*Harakwai*), and at least eight children including Frog, Turtle, and 'Son of Water'. The only active member is his classificatory brother Duna, a black spirit.

Duna

PERSONALIA. He is also called *Baleri*[56] (Black-Skinned One), has one wife, *Ladi Mayya* (Ladi the Sorceress) or *Zakoma*, and three children. Kure (Hyena), his eldest son, lives in House 6 (head of subsection for butchers; see above). Ciwo Babu Magani (Illness With No Medicine), his youngest child, who left her father's house to become Dan Galadima's second wife (House 1), and the remaining child is called Manzo Maye (see p. 110 n. 114). Part of the picture presented for Duna is complex to the point of confusion. Although he is said to be an excellent bowman, specializing in shooting women so that they are unable to give birth to live children, he is not classed with other archers. He is also said to appear late at night, frequently in his victim's dreams, standing like a hyena with long black monkey hair hanging over his face. But he is not a hyena, even though one of his sons is, and he is probably not a monkey since he acts like a man.

However, there is no ambiguity regarding his colour, marksmanship, and danger. Regarding his colour it is said:

Duna dunhu ba ka sofane sai a hakori; rigarka baka,
Duna, a very black person, there is no patch of colour different from the rest of you except [your] teeth; your gown is black

wandonka baki Duna.
your trousers are black Duna.

The same theme, blackness, describes his theology:

Duna . . . kai kafiri ne, ba za a hada ka da Alla ba Duna.
Duna . . . you are a non-Muslim, you will not be joined with Allah, Duna.

AFFLICTION. Duna rarely takes full possession of his victims though he has affected many lives. He visits them in nightmares or shoots at them from out of the darkness.

Dum mai ran da ke duniya im ba a taba taba dansa ba, an taba
For everyone alive in the world if his son has never been touched

tabawa iyayensa ko kakaninsa; ba ka harbi a ketare.
his parents or grandparents have been; you do not shoot then miss.

Cult-adepts say it is not Duna's blackness which is terrifying, unless one also includes his black character. His colour hides him in the night; both he and it are feared.

Baleri Aljan, Baleri Dodo; tsakar dare mai ban tsoro,
Black-Skinned One, an aljan, Black-Skinned One, an evil spirit; the middle of the night is to be feared,

tsakar dare marecan kura.
the middle of the night is [merely] the late evening for a hyena.

MEDIUM'S BEHAVIOUR. A devotee possessed by Duna is said to perform much like other bowmen, moving in a crouched position with a miniature bow and arrow held ready for a shot. However, for many years he has not appeared among the initiates in the towns included for this study.

MUSIC. Musicians said they knew his music but had seen no reason to play it in recent memory.

House 8: Zauren Maharba (leader of house, Mai Dawa (Owner of the Bush))

Maharba (s. *maharbi*; lit. person who shoots) are archers and hunters in Jangare. They live in the bush and have some affinity with Fulani spirits from whom a few of them have obtained wives. This house also has a subsection for *buzaye* (Tuareg serfs) who use their skill with the bow to harass and rob travellers.

OCCUPANTS. The organization of Mai Dawa's house is not entirely explained in the present data; many questions generated by a comparison of the genealogical information and spirits' praise-epithets were not adequately answered. For example, Mai Dawa—also known as *Mai Baka* (lit. Owner of a Bow; the Bowman), *Adamu* (Adam), or *Gajere* (Short Man)—is listed in the genealogical data as the son of *Baleri*.[57] In his praise-epithets he is also described as a 'son' of Inna (see House 1). Since she and this particular Baleri are either sister and brother or sister- and brother-in-law no conflict arises. However, Mai Dawa's senior wife is given as *Barhaza*[58], who is one of Inna's younger sisters. Most informants find it difficult to imagine even a spirit marrying his 'mother's' younger sister and a careful examination of his praise-epithets does not solve the problem; in those his wives are *Iyani* and *Awali* and Barhaza is not mentioned, though in genealogical data all three appear. Some informants say her husband is Kure (the Hyena) and others that it is Mai Gizo (Owner of Matted Hair). However, the important point is that Barhaza is the acknowledged mother of Wanzami, who (as we have noted) holds an important position in House 1, and it is because of this that the question of whether or not Mai Dawa is his father is of particular interest to cult-adepts. As far as this study is concerned Barhaza's relationships are far from settled as informant's statements did not withstand rigorous cross-checking.

A further problem in Mai Dawa's house relates to his father, Baleri, and one of his father's brothers, a spirit known as *Duna Rage Iri*.[59] Except that the Duna of Sarkin Fagan's house is said to stand like a hyena and has long black hair over his face, it seems significant that all three are archers and in that sense belong together. However, despite the resemblance in their names they probably are not the same spirit though there is little doubt that cult-adepts who are not specifically affected by these houses in Jangare find it confusing.

To dispel any impression that Mai Dawa's house is organized on an *ad hoc* basis, one comment on an external measure of its validity should be made. The information, both for genealogical statements and praise-epithets, was collected from garaya players and cult-adepts who had been afflicted by Mai Dawa and his kinsmen. Many lute players described themselves as 'Fulani' and still more as archers. Their information about the archers' house must therefore be accepted as the best available, their own health depending on a clear understanding of the identities of the divine horsemen whom they recognize as patrons.

Mai Dawa

PERSONALIA. Despite the ambiguity in his relationships, there is general agreement about his characteristics. He is an expert hunter, afraid of neither man nor beast. Inside his hut he is tall, but when he leaves it he appears short because he walks in a crouching posture.

> *'Yan gwiyangu[60]masifa, kyashari ba kyakyari ba,*
> Small one misfortune, screaming is not [the same as] snoring,
>
> *rufa ciki[61] zara dauka saba dauka; tara makangari,[62]*
> bent over; far-away prey killed, close prey killed [with one shot] ;[63]
> hide near the trail,
>
> *dama daji kuran na daure,[64]ya hau tudu yai daidai,[65]*
> agitate the bush, shoot anything, he climbs hills to hunt,
>
> *ya je gangara yai daidai; kai da garaje, ka ki mai nawa,*
> he descends into the valley to hunt; you go with haste, you refuse
> to be slow,
>
> *dab da ruwa kusa da ruwa, tsakiya sarautar Alla dan Inna.*
> close to water near to water, in the midst a title given by Allah, son
> of Inna.

His praises also include those of hunting animals. For example:

> *Sannu Kilikinju[66] mai kunan kashi na kin jim magana.*
> Greetings Wild Hunting Dog, one whose ears are bone and refuse
> to hear speech.

AFFLICTION. The illness ascribed to Mai Dawa is unexplained bleeding. Whereas Barade causes the same affliction with a spear, Mai Dawa does it with an arrow. Typically the sickness begins with a head or bronchial cold and catarrh, but those seriously afflicted cough up blood.

a.   *'Yan gwiyangu masifa, mura masomin cuta.*
     Small one misfortune, a cold is the beginning of illness.

b.   *Dab da kasa, nesa ga rishe; Alla na marka da ruwa,*
     Close to the ground, far from tree branches; Allah controls the
     rain of the wet season,

     kai kana marka da jini, dan Inna.
     you control the flow of blood, son of Inna.

SACRIFICES. Stricken thus, a victim may attempt to appease Mai Dawa with an offering of a short-legged cock or a black-and-brown male goat. If neither sacrifices nor initiation result in a cure it is known that the arrow was tipped with poison, and although this is rare, since the poison has no antedote the victim may be expected to die.

MEDIUM'S BEHAVIOUR AND DRESS. His medium aims the bow and arrow or chops at imaginary undergrowth or slain animals as his music is played. His dancing stylizes these basic movements which are all performed from a

crouching position. He is dressed in black. The gown requires no further comment, but the hat has a long top which falls to the back of his neck. Additionally, the medium is usually given a broad axe with a long point, and a small bow
and arrow—experienced mediums using arrows tipped with poison. His leather
apron, worn to protect the lower part of his body as he stalks through thorny
undergrowth, is identical to that worn by Fulani spirits.

MUSIC. Garaya players in Kano and Ningi say there are as many as five
different songs for Mai Dawa, whom they describe as a black spirit because of
the colour of his clothing.[67] However, initiates serving as mounts for him say
that only one of these (cf. Example 21) is specifically for him and the others are
for his close male relatives who occasionally share his horses.

An unusual aspect of his music is that Kano lute players especially, use it
to relate stories about outstanding mediums for the spirit they have known. If
the occasion is informal enough and no serious attempt to induce the trance of
a Mai Dawa medium is necessary, the musicians also use the music to joke with
one another, the metaphor of his shooting providing the framework for an allusion to the conquest of women. Near the end of the transcription given in Example 21, the soloist, in this case the principal member of the gourd-playing
chorus, begins a story about the ensemble's experience with a generous Mai
Dawa medium in Ringin. First he announces to the ensemble's leader (the
lute player) that he wishes to add his own comments, then he receives the leader's
approval from the ensemble's praise-shouter[68] (see Example 21).

Barhaza (wife to Mai Dawa; see page 99)

AFFLICTION. Like her elder sister Inna, she is responsible for paralysis
in her victims. Usually afflicting women, but at least one case was observed
in which she was served by a male medium. The opinion of one healer was that
she strikes the left side of the body, but another said left-side paralysis belonged
to Inna. Such refinements are certainly the result of local interpretation. Her
praise-epithets suggest general immobility.

Dungu[69] *uwar shanu,*[70] *tafiya ba taki ba.*
Stump-of-maimed-arm mother of cattle, travelling is not for you.

According to one informant she is responsible for a number of other illnesses.
She causes those she afflicts to roam aimlessly about, or in milder cases, to walk
in their sleep.

Barhaza yini dawa kwana daji; Barhaza ku gyara gida
Barhaza spend the day in the forest, sleep in the bush; Barhaza you
fix up your house

ku kwana a daji.
[but] you sleep in the bush.[71]

She can be accused of causing stomach and headaches, and when she strikes a
man she renders him impotent. Many of these illnesses can be attributed to
other spirits, but when they occur in these combinations and are accompanied

by a subsequent paralysis or numbness on one side of the body, the diagnosis points to Barhaza.

SACRIFICES AND MEDICINES. The colour of her clothing (see below) is reflected in that of her favourite sacrificial animal—a white sheep. Her medicinal formulae include milk taken from a white cow and a white goat as ingredients and as mixing agents.

MEDIUM'S BEHAVIOUR AND DRESS. During possession-trance this Fulani woman's medium imitates milking and churning gestures to the accompaniment of her music.

> *Mai kada nono da hannun gashi.*
> One who churns milk with a hand with hair on it.[72]

She acts shyly in the presence of crowds—behaviour expected by the Hausa of a Pastoral Fulani woman—and must be restrained from running away if startled. She does not speak unless spoken to and when she replies it is in strongly Fulfulde-influenced Hausa speech. She is thought to be helpful in indirect dealings with younger members of her family (the Fulani side), all of them calling her their 'mother'.

> *Barhaza, innar Mamman, innar Sambo, innar Buba, innar Muhubbare,*
> Barhaza, mother of[73] Mamman,[74] mother of Sambo, mother of Buba, mother of Muhubbare,
>
> *innar Haro; kaza uwar iyali.*
> mother of Haro; the hen is the mother of [a large] family.

Unlike her black sister (Inna) Barhaza is believed to be a 'white' spirit, but this is a statement about the colour of her clothing. She wears a white wrapper, a white head-tie ring with strings of cowrie shells dangling from it, and thin silver bracelets.

MUSIC. Example 22 below contains an excerpt from one of Barhaza's songs, the one most commonly used to accompany her dancing.

House 9: Zauren Sarkin Arna (Chief of the Pagans)

Sarkin Arna presides over a house of black spirits. Black, it is said, because none of them observes Muslim customs and prayer and they all live in the bush, and black because that is the usual colour of their clothing. He is known to have at least three wives, two of whom are the foster mothers for two of his most famous 'children'. Nakada (Causer of Downfall),[75] the son of Malam Alhaji (see House 3), was sent to the house of the Pagans because, it is said, his character was too difficult for the Pilgrim to cope with. Similarly, Mai Gizo (Owner of Matted Hair) was given to the Chief of Pagans because he was too troublesome for his father, the Chief of the Fulani (see House 5). Both have flourished in their adopted father's house where they are free to express their anti-Muslim personalities.

Sarkin Arna

AFFLICTION. The Chief of Pagan's problem is that he can think of nothing to do but drink home-made beer. This sickness which he visits liberally on mortals[76]is aggravated by a total antipathy towards Islam.

Kai ba Kafiri ba ka fi Kafiri kafirci
Your name is not Kafiri [but] you exceed Kafiri[77]in non-Muslim ways.

Those afflicted by him are addicted to drink and turn their backs on Islam, a particularly unfortunate pair of characteristics among a Muslim population.

MEDIUM'S BEHAVIOUR. His drunkenness is supposedly revealed in the demonstration of his possession. His horse dances disconnectedly, jerking about and falling to the ground in a stupor.[78]

Nakada

PERSONALIA. He is a confusing character, both for his behaviour and adepts' reactions to it. Because of his parentage he is described by some as a white spirit, but black because of his work and place of residence. As the son of Quranic scholar he might be expected to be pious, but he is not. According to one of his praise-epithets he is an aberration:

Rago da wutsiyar kare, dam malam ka ki halim malam.
A ram with a dog's tail,[79] son of a malam[80]you refuse the character of a malam.

Thus, whatever Muslim virtues might be expected of the son of a Holy Man Nakada lacks them. If there were only this to fear from him he would be merely a curiosity, but there is more; he also has a very bad temper.

Butsatsa[81] *kayan kaba, gaba tsini baya tsini.*[82]
Pugnacious One, a load of young dum-palm fronds, a sharp point in front of a sharp point in back.

As in his song (Example 23 below) his bad manners include not offering a drink of water to a stranger and manifesting his pugnacity—or perhaps his insanity—by using fire to show his displeasure. When a stranger once asked him for a drink of water he replied by burning the man's village with one match. In his own compound his wife was cooking *tuwo* (the staple food made from corn or rice flour), and he insisted on cooking beans.[83] When fire broke out in his compound he did all he could to ensure it would consume everything.

AFFLICTION AND MEDIUM'S BEHAVIOUR AND DRESS. Afflicted by Nakada his victim may reveal similar madness, but usually another characteristic appears in that he causes his mount to eat faeces and become sexually hyperactive. His sexual activity is a particular theme of his dancing which informants describe as lewd but in some way admirable. Only a madman would welcome possession by Nakada, but because of his preoccupation with sex it is frequently said everyone is his horse. When he arrives his mount is dressed in a 'gown' made from a fish-net and monkey skins. A 'tail' is tied to him and he holds a long stick between his legs.

MUSIC. Nakada is an important figure in any possession-trance event, since he is said to close the door of the performance. Thus, the first spirit called is the Chief of Drummers and the last Nakada, the Causer of Downfall (cf. Besmer 1975). He may be called with the music given in Example 23. When he is not present his music accompanies the dancing of cult-adepts and interested bystanders as the ceremony winds down (see Example 23).

Mai Gizo (Owner of the Matted Hair)

PERSONALIA. He is also known as *Yero,*[84] Sarkin Arna's other adopted son, and as already noted came from the house of the Fulani. It is said of him,

Guntsari mugun nono, ko a ruga kare a kam baiwa.
Sour milk with lumpy curds[85] [is] bad milk, even in the cattle camp[86] it is given to the dog.[87]

To a Muslim he is a model of uncleanliness. His hair is a tangled mess, whereas the Muslim Hausa believe one should be clean-shaven; he refuses to wash, his teeth are black or missing, and he smells. His praise-epithets describe his appearance in most graphic terms.

a.   *Mai Gizan Yero kuram Maje na Doguwa, ka rau da gizan ka.*
Owner of Matted Hair Yero assistant of Maje[88] of the Tall-Woman,[89] you shake your matted hair [while dancing].

b.   *Nukan Baban Gida*[90] *idan an dama watca ta shekara ba wanke;*
The ripening of Baban Gida, even if a year passes he does not wash;

Mai baya ya turmin jima, mai jiki kadanya kadanya,
[Mai Gizo's] back is like [the texture of] a wooden board for tanning, his body is as rough as the bark of a shea-tree,

mai wari ya mushen doki, mai baki kamar cirnaka.
his smell is as [bad as] a rotting horse carcass, his mouth is [black] like that of a biting ant.

There can be no doubt that Mai Gizo is a black spirit both from the perspective of being non-town and non-Muslim. A spirit with his personal habits would not be allowed near a mosque, and from what is recorded in his praise-epithets that is quite satisfying to him.

a.   *Ba ya wanka ba ya aske, ba ya salla; da shi da gabas*
He doesn't wash he doesn't shave, he doesn't pray; between him and eastwards

sai gwalo sai tafiya dole in ta kama shi.
there is only grimmacing, only imperative fleeing when [this direction] catches him.

b.   *Ba ya ratsar gonar malam, shi ko ba ya ratsar*
He doesn't cross a malam's farm, he doesn't even cross

gonar mai salla.
the farm of someone who prays.

AFFLICTION.   In addition to the obvious afflictions—uncleanliness and a
rejection of Islam—he may also be responsible for headache and insanity. His victim's appearance is the key to the recognition of his mark.

SACRIFICES.   A black male goat or a black cock may be sacrificed to
him, the blood for his food and the meat given away as alms. It is thought to be
extremely difficult to appease him and his untreated victims can be seen wandering the streets of most cities.

MEDIUM'S DRESS AND BEHAVIOUR. Possessed by him, his medium is
dressed in skins and carries three or four metal hatchets (s. *barandami*) which he
swings over his head and slaps on his back. The hatchets are particularly mena-
cing, and while there are no recorded instances of bystanders being hurt by them,
the fear of such an accident demands that Mai Gizo be humoured when he is
present at a possession-trance event.

The most spectacular appearance by him recorded in the present data
occurred in Maiduguri when a touring medium—a stranger to the local cult—
was possessed near the end of a possession-trance event.[91] The musicians[92] and
audience wished to adjourn until the following morning, but Mai Gizo threatened
to use his weapons on them if they stopped playing. Since the medium was
unknown to them, the musicians were uncertain what would happen if they
disobeyed his demands. Taking the safest course they continued to play until
Mai Gizo himself decided he had had enough and would depart, but not before
he had secured their promise to resume the event the following day.[93]

MUSIC.   In Kano Mai Gizo may be praised or invoked with the plucked-
lute music given in Example 24. The tempo of his first song increases rapidly,
going from ♩ =144 to ♩ =160 after only a few verses sung by the leader. In Example 25 the transition between the first and second songs is shown. With a
final burst of speed the tempo moves to ♩ =200 and begins to shift from a three
quarter-note pattern (| ♩ ♩ ♩ |) to a two dotted-quarter-note one (| ♩. ♩. |).
This new orientation in the second song is accompanied by an altered gourd
rhythm and if played for three to five minutes is effective in inducing the trance
of Mai Gizo's mount (see Examples 24 and 25).

House 10: Zauren Sarkin Gwari (head of house, Sarkin Gwari)

Immediately adjacent to the Pagans' house is that of the Gwari people who are
also non-Muslim. One informant said there can be no doubt that there are no
Muslims among them since for the purpose of urinating the men adopt a standing position whereas Muslims squat down. In fact, he continued, such an abnormality is a common indication of any Gwari affliction.

The Chief of the Gwari has eight sisters and three brothers. Five of his sisters left to become the wives of *Turawa* (North Africans; see below, House 11);

one has her husband (a Pagan, youngest brother of the Chief of the Pagans, who refused to farm) living with her; one (Bagwariya) became the wife of Malam Alhaji (see House 3); and the eighth is unmarried, living with her brother. Sarkin Gwari's daughter, *Galla*, also married into the North Africans' house, continuing the pattern established in her father's generation. These marriages in successive Gwari generations have served to outline the relationship between the *Gwarawa* (pl.) and the Turawa as wife-givers/wife-receivers. The children of these Gwari women have been adopted by their mother's brother (the Chief of Gwari), and he in turn, has given his children to the North Africans either as wives or as adopted sons.

The relationship between these two houses is similar to that for Houses 1 and 2. For Sarkin Aljan Sulemanu (House 1) and Sarkin Aljan Biddarene (House 2) the tie is consanguineal—Sulemanu and Biddarene are brothers. For the Gwari and the North Africans the tie is affinal; the Chief of the Gwari and the North African men involved are brothers-in-law. From the Chief of the Gwari's angle the adoption of his sisters' children and their avunculocal residence suggests matrilineal descent, a subject to which we will return later.

Sarkin Gwari

PERSONALIA. The Chief of the Gwari is thought to consider himself a bow hunter, but this is a subject for humour among cult-adepts—those not possessed by him. One informant related how Sarkin Gwari once shot a hedge-hog—a notoriously slow-moving and timid creature. When asked what skill this feat had required he said the famous Gwari hunter had been able to kill it before it could run away. One of his praise-epithets recounts in similar terms his skill in shooting an owl.

> *Sarkin Gwari mai farar maka, yaya kai ka harbu mujiya;*
> Chief of the Gwari, owner of a white thumb-ring [worn by archers],[94]
> how[95] [is it] you shot an owl;
>
> *harbi a tsuli kumburi a ka.*
> [he said he] shot it in the anus and it swelled up at [its] head.[96]

It is also reported that he plays the garaya, as any hunter should. However, no one would comment in precise terms on his proficiency as a musician for fear of being overheard by him.

Similar to other non-Muslim spirits, his character is frequently described in terms of food preferences.

> *Ran Sarki ya dade; kafiri idan ya cika kafiri a tad da*
> May the days of the Chief be prolonged; a non-Muslim if he is fully non-Muslim [eats]
>
> *mushen doki, a tad da mushen kare, a tad da mushen rakumi,*
> horse carrion, [he eats] dog carrion, [he eats] camel carrion,
>
> *a tad da mushen kaza; kafiri in ya cika kifiri ya ci*
> [he eats] chicken carrion; a non-Muslim if he is fully non-Muslim eats

gwazarma, ya ci kwaran makankari . . . ya sha giya.
the white grubs of dung hills, he eats the insects which live in mussel-
shells . . . and he drinks beer.

AFFLICTION. Sarkin Gwari is described as a black spirit, one who does
not pray in the Muslim fashion and whose afflictions are particularly unfortunate.

SACRIFICE. To attempt to quiet his wrath his victim must sacrifice either
a black male goat or a young black dog. The latter represents something of a
problem for the Hausa since killing a puppy is not viewed with any enthusiasm,
and the meat cannot be given away as alms. Generally, it is thought that nearly
any common vegetable will serve as a suitable substitute, with the exception of
peppers which Gwari spirits are convinced are a madness of the market.

MEDIUM'S BEHAVIOUR AND DRESS. Invoked by the music given in
Example 26, he dances while attempting to blow a *kaho* (roan antelope horn) or
strum a garaya. His playing is not regarded seriously; it is simply another example of his backwardness. Everyone knows that chiefs do not play their own
instruments. His medium, when demonstrating possession-trance, is dressed in a
black gown and turban. He wears an archer's thumb-ring and carries a small
bundle of *kuli-kuli* (small fried cakes made from the residue after the oil has
been expressed from ground-nuts) which is called his 'rosary'.

MUSIC. An important characteristic of trance-inducing music is shown
near the end of Sarkin Gwari's song. Not only does the tempo increase but the
rhythm changes from a three-beat pattern to a subdivided two-beat one and back
again. Thus, the rhythm of the lute melody changes from $\frac{3}{4}$ [musical notation]
to $\frac{3}{4}$ [musical notation] or $\frac{2}{4}$ [musical notation] . Following the lute player's lead, the
gourd players adjust their accompaniment to match the lute rhythm:
$\frac{3}{4}$ [musical notation] or $\frac{2}{4}$ [musical notation] . The entire transcription retains
the ¾ time signature, since the intention of these rhythmic changes, according to
the musicians, is to create excitement but not to change the total pattern[97] (see
Example 26).

**House 11: Zauren Turawa house of North African Spirits (head of house, Bar-
kono—Pepper, or Bature—White Man)**

Barkono, four of his brothers, and one of his brothers' sons married Gwari women; three other brothers married *Buzu* (Tuareg serf) women from the house of
the Hunters (8). These North African men have chosen Buzu women since they
are said to be expert with a bow, and North African spirits enjoy warfare.
The problem of describing who cult-adepts think the Turawa spirits are has
been increased by combining two distinct groups of people in Hausa history,
both of which have 'white' skins. Originally bature meant a man from the land
of *Ture*, that is, North Africa. Arab travellers, merchants, and clerics have fre-
quented northern Nigeria for many hundreds of years, and the Hausa are well

acquainted with their expertise in a wide variety of affairs. With the coming of the British another light-skinned group was classified with the original Turawa. Recognition of the proficiency of both Europeans and Arabs in matters of warfare, learning and government, reinforced the single categorization. The primary meaning of the term bature must have been 'an Arab', although currently both Arab and European are designated meanings.[98]

It appears that the characteristics of both Arabs and Europeans have been attributed to the North African spirits. Some of them acting as Arabs while others imitate what must be considered European behaviour. Some of Barkono's praises illustrate this:

a. *Bature zaki alfanda babban dodo mai ban tsoro*
   White Man, lion, chief, great evil spirit, one who causes fear

   masu jirgi da mota.
   owner of the 'engine' and the automobile.

b. *Shi ya ci yaki da gaskiya, ya ci yaki da wayo,*
   He won the war[99] completely, he won the war with cunning,

   ya ci yaki da loga.
   he won the war at its very roots.

c. *Bature ka fi bakar fata ilimi; Bature ka fi bakar fata*
   White Man, you exceed [those with] black skin in education;
   White Man, you exceed [those with] black skin in

   dabara; Bature ka fi bakar fata wayo.
   planning; White Man you exceed [those with] black skin in cunning.

Barkono is not the only fierce and successful soldier among the North Africans. His brothers assist him as lieutenants. All are easily incited to warfare, but it is not clear whether this is due to the fact that they are North Africans, non-Muslims or simply spirits. *Dam Mama* (Son of Breast) is a case in point.

a. *Kwatangiri Dam Mama; Kafiri Dam Mama; Arne ka tura*
   Powerful One, Dam Mama; Non-Muslim, Dam Mama; Pagan, you push

   hannu kogo, ko da macijiya ta rike ma.
   a hand into a tree-cavity, [even if] a snake [is there] to grab it.

b. *Sannu Birgimar Hankaka, kowa ya ga farinku, zai ga bakinku.*
   Greetings, Rolling Flight of the Black-and-White Crow, anyone who sees your whiteness will also see your blackness.[100]

c. *Yaro kama tsamiya ka yi lilo, in ka kama tawatsa*
   Boy, catch [the branch of] a tamarind tree to swing on; if you catch [the branch of] a tawatsa[101]

   ta karye.
   it will break.[102]

Individually they are strong, but the North Africans do not fight as individuals;

their strength lies in their superior organization and as an army they are unbeat-
able. A praise-epithet for another of Barkono's 'brothers' alludes to this.

> *Kafaran mai nasara*[103]*mai 'yan soja; babbaku iyalin gwamna na*
> Kafaran the Christian (or European) the leader of soldiers; black
> ones,[104] family of the governor's
>
> *gwamna shanun gwamna; a sha wuta a sha bulala, gwanin*
> governor, cattle (i.e. soldiers) of the governor; undergo fire undergo
> beatings, a certain expert
>
> *wani ya sha wuta jiki ya kone, gwani na ya sha*
> underwent fire and his body burned, my expert underwent
>
> *wuta kamar bai sha ba.*
> fire [and came out of it] as though it was never undergone.

As non-Muslims (some are said to be 'people of the Book', i.e. Christians) they
eat the wrong foods as, for example, Sarkin Bicci (Chief of a Large Horse), of
whom it is said:

> *Kyan kafiri ko ya toba sau dubu in ya ga mushe ya taba.*
> The delight of a non-Muslim, even if he swears it off a thousand
> times when he sees carrion he will touch it.

Or display a naivety about food such as is attributed to *Halima* (the Tuareg-
serf wife of Dan Mama), below. She is reported to entertain men (for a price)
when her husband is away fighting and has organized this into a business of
which she is the 'Madam'. It is both sung and said of her:

> *Halima 'yar buzaye matar kafiri Dam Mama; don sun gan ta*
> Halima, daughter of Tuareg serfs, wife of non-Muslim Dam Mama;
> because they[105]saw her
>
> *ba ta da wayo, sai suka ba ta naman jaki sai suka ce*
> and she didn't have any sense, they gave her donkey meat and said
>
> *na dan akwiya ne, sannu madan.*
> it was goat meat, greetings madam.

North African spirits simply fail to understand the nuances of Hausa life.

> *Gwaurau Mai Kwalabe wasa ba fada ba, arne ya ce fada ne.*
> Witch-doctor with glass bottles, playing is not fighting, the pagan
> [does not understand this and] will say it is fighting.

Despite this they have good doctors among them.

> *Magori Mai Magani koya mana magani, a koya mana*
> Magori, Owner of Medicine, teach me medicine, teach me
>
> *dibam magani, a ba mu maganin duniya na lahira sai Alla.*
> how to mix medicines, give me the medicine of the world, of heaven
> there is only Allah.

Umaru Sanda Ba Buga (Umaru, Stick for Beating)

PERSONALIA. Umaru is one of the North Africans who is particularly distinguished, not by his position in Jangare, but because he seems to be the patron spirit of Ningi. Cult members are diffident about acknowledging him, but his importance to the town is not only in the imagination of non-Ningi initiates. He frequently visits possession-trance events in Ningi and was never seen visiting any other town.

It is said by non-Ningi informants that some time in the past Umaru was roaming about when he came upon Old Ningi town (about 40 kilometres from the town's present site). He liked it and decided to stay, but first he had to defeat the unnamed spirits already living there; this he accomplished through trickery and illusion added to his strong magic. Although believed not to be a Muslim he is described in his praises as having subjugated pagans.

a.   *Umaru*[106]*Sanda gagaran*[107]*gabasawa, mai kafan*[108]*karo*
Umaru Sanda test the strength of easterners,[109] owner of horns for colliding,

rago mai kafan karo.
ram, owner of horns for colliding,

b.   *Im ban da Umaru, wa yai za shi lahira ya gani;*
If it weren't for Umaru who would be able to go to the hereafter and see [it] ;[110]

mai shirim fada, arna ba su zo ba.
one who prepares for fighting, the pagans did not come.

c.   *Shegiya ido a kashi sai ka ce biri a yama, Sanda Umaru*
Bastard! Eyes in excrement [make] you say it is a monkey in the grass,[111] Sanda Umaru

Mai Ningi.
Owner of Ningi.

MEDIUM'S BEHAVIOUR AND DRESS. His usual practice in Ningi is to wait until the Chief of Drummers has arrived and thus 'opened the door', and who, immediately after he has been greeted by the assemblage and sung his own songs, calls Umaru to come.[112] He appears without delay and as soon as his mount is fully possessed he is led away to an adjacent hut to be dressed. After a few minutes during which other spirits begin to reveal themselves on the necks of their favourite horses, Umaru returns. He carries a pen and pad on which he can never quite bring himself to write, looks at the world through sun-glasses, and smokes cigarettes, usually two at a time, with the burning end in his mouth. While not dancing (which resembles marching more than anything else) he sits on his special chair, which is prominently placed to one side of the musicians draped with a red scarf. In addition to sun-glasses he wears a red shirt and trousers and western-type hat and shoes.

MUSIC. The song transcribed in Example 27 was recorded in Kano. Umaru has never been observed there but the musicians claim the song would be effective in calling him if necessary. Since no medium possessed by Umaru has been to Kano in recent memory there has been little demand for his music. Kano musicians still praise him in song, however, as it is important to acknowledge influential spirits in any house. As might be expected, iskoki are easily offended if they feel they or their relatives have not received proper respect from their horses. Thus, although it seems Umaru does not appear in Kano there is no doubt in the minds of cult followers that he is lurking in the background, waiting for an excuse to beat someone or otherwise wreak havoc (see Example 27).

House 12: Zauren Mayu. (house of the sorcerers: head of house, Batoyi[113])

Although their work is unquestionably black the occupants of House 12 are classified as 'white' spirits, since presumably they are Muslims, but very little is spoken of them—either their origins or ethnicity. Batoyi, the head of the house, is an old man whose wife is said to be *Lashe-Lashe* (Continual Licking). Their daughter Ladi Maya (Ladi the Sorceress), is the wife of Duna and lives with him in House 7 (see above). Her son[114] has been returned to his maternal grandparents, one of the few cases of grandchild adoption in Jangare.

AFFLICTION. It is certain that they eat the souls of their victims and the sign of this is delirium.

SACRIFICE AND MEDICINES. Little could be learned about their sacrifices—except (as above) that they include human souls—and nothing about their medicines. Some say that only their mounts—covert witches—know the secrets, but no one wants to be identified as a witch.

MEDIUM'S BEHAVIOUR. The sorcerer's mounts are said to sacrifice human souls to their riders by casting spells over their victims. When a sorcerer visits a possession-trance site it is warned that care must be taken to hide the eyes of the spirit to prevent anyone being gazed upon and eaten.

SYMBOLISM

Thus far in this chapter we have been looking at iskoki as characters—potential actors in possession-trance dramas and the causers of mortals' afflictions. Each of them may be examined as primary symbolic clusters, in Turner's terms, symbols which have three properties. The first of these is condensation and identifies the fact that many things and actions may be represented by a single formation. The second is unification of disparate *significata* and states that symbols commonly contain interconnected themes. The third property, polarization of meaning, has two aspects. One is that symbolic clusters frequently describe items which refer to components of the moral and social order, principles of social organization, kinds of corporate grouping, or norms and values inherent in structural relationships. The second is that clusters may, simultaneous with the first aspect, describe natural and physiological phenomena and processes which are related to the outward form of the symbol and which arouse desires and feelings (Turner 1967: 28).

Sarkim Makada (House 6) may be used as an example. An initiate's idea of the Chief of Drummers is not limited to a description of him as a spirit with a certain personality. It assumes a set of praises, music (melody and rhythm), illnesses, remedies, sacrifices, and ceremonial paraphernalia all specifically associated with him. Basically all of these things are condensed and are properties of a single, multi-faceted symbol.

Some of the things Sarkim Makada represents which appear to be entirely unrelated to each other, are in fact related because they intersect at one point: the social category occupied by maroka (musicians, praise-shouters, praise-singers, etc.). Parade or performance order, throat and shoulder ailments, musical expertise, and the colour red are seemingly disparate items; however, they share an association with 'musicians' in general, and the Chief of Drummers in particular. It will be recalled that two closely related accounts of bori concluded that because his songs and praises were performed first at possession-trance events Sarkin Makada was the most important spirit in Jangare (Ames 1973: 141; King 1967: 3 n.). This was an incorrect conclusion, since the statement of his place in a performance is generated by his social role as a maroki. In fact Sarkim Makada symbolizes greatness only in terms of 'musician-ness'; in terms of the leadership of Jangare he symbolizes clientship. Similarly, throat and shoulder ailments are not simply spirit-caused afflictions; they are the occupational maladies of maroka. The colour red is an attribute which may take on other meanings in conjunction with other bori symbols, but for the Chief of Drummers it symbolizes both his musician status and his clientship in the Chief's court. In a Hausa parade the people who precede the emir and his retainers are a group of musicians and a guard with muskets. All over Hausaland they are dressed in red.

Turner defines the third property of dominant ritual symbols as 'polarization of meaning'. One pole is ideological and refers, among other things, to principles of social organization, kinds of corporate grouping, and norms and values inherent in structural relationships. The other, sensory, pole 'the meaning content is closely related to the outward form of the symbol' (Turner 1967: 28). Perhaps the Chief of Drummers' most obvious attribute is that he is a chief— chief, that is, of a particular craft group. Any craft group needs a central authority and responsibility, a title or office passed on from father to son. Sarkim Makada's title which was confirmed by the Chief of the Spirits is a model of that pattern. As a musician, however, his title carries with it a depressed structural position in the Jangare social order. He is a professional musician, and therefore a professional witness. When alms are given he and his mortal representatives are common recipients. Hence, sacrifices made to the Chief of Drummers are not rigidly prescribed. Their content is less important than the fact of making a sacrifice. In terms of the sensory pole the Chief of Drummers represents musicianship, the patronage of cult musicians, and ritual process. It would be an unusual possession-trance event which did not begin with a call to him to 'open the door'. Thus, a most important sensory meaning attaches to Sarkim Makada; the feeling that his invocation provides an orderly beginning for any cult performance.

Behand any analysis of ritual symbols is a search for meaning; meaning which is clear to informants, either initiates, laymen, or both, and meaning which is concealed from native commentators but implied by their testimony. Concerning the latter, for example, it would be unreasonable to expect any informant to declare that cult notions about Gwari or Fulani spirits may be reduced to a few stereotypes which sedentary, Muslim agriculturalists have about people they believe are 'different' from themselves. But it is precisely these stereotypes of existing ethnic groups which provide the foundation for a description of divine horsemen of the same ethnicity.

To take a different approach from Turner, who might examine each spirit in the manner illustrated above for Sarkim Makada (that is, as a 'dominant' symbol), attention is drawn to general themes which appear repeatedly in the descriptions of spirits' personalities and behaviour. The focus is on the basic idea that ritual symbols, in this case as embodied in the shared knowledge of the spirits' identities, are 'storage units' for concepts the Hausa have about themselves and the people around them.

The amount of material in a description of Jangare and its inhabitants which outlines social organization, ties of kinship and marriage, and even norms for social behaviour is considerable. At the most basic level it can be noted that all cult-adepts attempt to provide a social order to accomodate iskoki. Accordingly, as we have seen, Jangare is divided into twelve houses, each house has its leadership, chains of responsibility or dependent offices, particular characteristics due to the ethnicity or profession of the occupants, and shorthand list of illnesses, sacrifices, and medicinal ingredients. Hausa cities bear a striking resemblance to Jangare and the 'rules' which generate their respective forms are similar. The houses of Jangare are wards in wordly cities. Generally, wards are defined by a membership of one ethnic group or sub-group, and often this group is craft-specialized. Since occupations or crafts are traditionally ascribed at birth, the ward may actually be a large extended family. Even when it is not, the model for terms of address and reference make it resemble an extended family when viewed from the outside. Finally, each house in Jangare has its own leadership, and where there are sub-groups in the house their leadership is under the authority of the house head. Wards have the same organization, responsibility for individual members being left to compound (sub section) heads. However, not all initiates view the hierarchy in the same way. Those who live in highly centralized cities such as Kano emphasize the primary leadership of one spirit in Jangare over all house heads. The same data in Ningi are interpreted to mean that the Jangare king acts as a spokesman for the houses, but they are virtually independent of him.

Many informants' accounts of Jangare family patterns (house membership lists) contain numerous references to spirits 'born elsewhere but living here' and spirits 'born here but living elsewhere'. Except for residence changes on the part of female iskoki who live with their husbands, and the occasional 'deviant' male who leaves his natal house to live with his in-laws, many spirits live with what might be called foster parents. Although adoptive parents and children employ the same terminology in addressing each other[115] as would 'real' parents and children, it should be noted that they would do so even if adoption and subsequent co-residence had not taken place. In other words foster child and foster parent are already relatives ('nephew'/'niece' and 'uncle'/'aunt') before an adoption is arranged. Typically, a spirit and his brother simply exchange children; this is the pattern which occurs in houses known to be specifically populated with Hausa spirits. And frequently the exchange is repeated in the following generation.

My first question when this practice was described to me was, why? The answer came quickly and easily: spirits, like people, must avoid their children (or parents) out of fear for their well-being or out of respect. This avoidance factor is defined most strongly in terms of real parents and children but only mildly in terms of foster parents and children. It is completely absent from the relationship between grandparents and grandchildren where total familiarity prevails. Anthropologists recognize these relationships as those of 'avoidance' and 'joking'.

We can now see what results when the rule of adoption is applied to two generations of children; it is that houses contain spirits who can live with each other either without strain (foster parents/foster children) or with complete familiarity (real grandparents/real grandchildren).

The exchange symbolically accomplishes another goal. The giving and receiving of children underlines both the solidarity and the autonomy of the respective groups involved. Children are given to *patrilineal* relatives so that their change in residence causes no problems in a larger social group membership pattern, but since they are given the 'gift' demands reciprocity which can only exist in terms of separateness.

In the house of the Gwari spirits a slight variation of this practice achieves a similar goal. The Chief of Gwari adopts his *sister's* children and it is obvious that this avunculocal residence can be explained only in terms of *matrilineal* descent. The Chief of Gwari's obligation to reciprocate his brother-in-law's gift is discharged, according to genealogical data, by giving his daughter as wife for the North Africans, his brother-in-law's group.

A curious aspect of the patrilineality of Hausa spirits and the matrilineality of Gwari spirits is that neither pattern reflects the real world of the Hausa or the Gwari. The Hausa are unmistakably bilateral, except in the case of ruling groups which emphasize patrilineal descent, and the Gwari are either patrilineal or bilateral. Either bori information provides an incorrect analysis of Hausa and Gwari social formations; this analysis of the meaning of adoption is inaccurate; or some time period other than the present supplies the context for cult knowledge.

The last proposition contains the answer, and there is good reason to believe that Jangare social patterns reflect archaic situations which have not been allowed to change. The Maguzawa or Hausa-speaking animists with whom the cult of the iskoki originated were (or are, in so far as they can still be found) rural agriculturalists with patrilineal descent groups. With the coming of Islam their clans became more endogamous and less exogamous. As the large rural gandu farming pattern was replaced by smaller farms with fewer members the clans became increasingly dispersed, setting the stage for increased bilaterality. In the cities the conditions favouring bilateral descent were even more pronounced although the fiction and preference for patrilineal affiliation remained strong in craft-group organization. For spirits believed to be Hausa, therefore, it might be suggested that their patrilineality is based either on a Maguzawa pattern or on that found among urban emirs and aristocracy who are models for their communities.

The same outline of events may be used for the Gwari. According to Murdock, the Nigerian plateau, of which the Gwari are a part, was originally the site of 'matrilineal descent . . . avunculocal residence and avuncuclans' (1959: 96). Leaving aside the conditions which led to a shift to patrilocal residence and, in the Gwari case, patrilineal (or bilateral) descent, the resemblance between bori descriptions of the Gwari and Murdock's account of their 'reconstructed' social organization is impressive.

We may conclude from this that informants' statements about the social organization of Hausa and Gwari spirit houses are a reflection of historical reality. Given the conservative nature of ritual knowledge, it is perhaps not surprising that the timeless world of Jangare should have ignored the relatively recent changes in these two groups.

Not everything known about Jangare can be linked to historical reality, however. Stereotypes are good examples of statements revealing more about those who make them than those to whom they refer. The image created for Gwari spirits illustrates this point. The Gwari are 'pagans' (which once they were) and the two symbols instrumental in amplifying the stereotype of them are dogs and non-Muslim foods. In terms of symbolic clusters pagans and dogs or pagans and 'carrion' occur together, one being associated with the other. Pagans are believed to keep dogs for food and eat improperly slaughtered animals. Whether they actually do or not is irrelevant. What is important is the social distance many cult members try to put between themselves (Muslims, in the widest sense of the term) and certain spirits believed to live in the bush.

Gwari as pagans are indistinguishable from Maguzawa as pagans in one respect: they both eat the wrong foods. But in other ways the groups are separate. Gwari spirits either have or cause goitre and hunch back and are *non*-Muslim ; Maguzawa spirits cause drunkenness and are *anti*-Muslim.

Fulani spirits provide an additional aspect to stereotyping. The illness most male Fulani cause is wandering. The Pastoral Fulani do wander; they are transhumants. Viewed from their perspective, moving about with one's cattle is the best way of life. Anyone who chose to live in one place month after month, year after year would be considered insane. The affliction as cult-adepts interpret it implies an element of aimlessness, and this is an example of the mechanism of stereotyping. More than anything else, the affliction ascribed to male Fulani spirits is a symbolic statement about the undesirability of being anything other than sedentary. It says something about how people who have an agricultural tradition should behave and describes a social category which outlines one boundary of the group.

Changing the focus somewhat, we may examine the ways in which bori ritual symbols combine with each other. When a divine horseman rides, the behaviour of his medium generally includes an illustration of the ailments for which he may be held responsible. The possession-trance itself is evidence of a spiritual presence, and the medium's actions symbolic of the spirit's identity. These elements form the basis for symbolic healing. That is, when a person admits that his affliction is spirit-caused he may be relieved of its symptoms by dedicating his life to the possession-trance cult, demonstrating his commitment by serving as a medium. The medium is 'cured', but in his altered state of consciousness he is hopelessly afflicted.

Many of the ingredients for the medicinal infusions used to treat spirits' victims are, as we have seen, symbolically identified with the offended iska. Parts of trees which commonly grow in or near Pastoral Fulani cattle camps are proper ingredients for medicines to ease the suffering of those afflicted by Fulani spirits. Dirt collected from outside the gate of any royal palace is used to treat patients marked by Kure because he is believed to lurk in such places. The roots of a dundu tree are effective in preparations for Kuturu because he uses the thorny tree as a resting place. On and on the list continues with parts of plants or other items associated with the haunts and sleeping places of this or that spirit.

The ingredients need not be collected specifically for any single application but may be stock piled for eventual use or sale. Some initiates make a business of organizing small quantities of the right ingredients into packages. Each item is wrapped in a piece of cotton and then sewn into a damara made from handwoven cloth of the type and colour symbolically identified with the spirit for which it was prepared. It is rare for a healer to open a medicine belt for its contents, since the quantity of the individual items is not usually considered adequate for an extended treatment. Belts are used symbolically *after* the patient has been cured to represent the entire treatment, that is, initiation. They are symbols of symbols. Protecting their wearer from the dangers involved when he enters possession-trance, they serve to notify a spirit (and the audience) that an emergency cure is ready at hand.

The selection of sacrificial animals follows a similar pattern. Most spirits can be addressed with the offering of a chicken. The sex, colour, type, and physical characteristics of the bird depend upon the spirit for whom the sacrifice is intended. A short-legged cock for Mai Baka, because it resembles his crouched stance. A red cock for Sarkim Makada, as red is the colour of his clothing. For the black spirit, Inna, a black hen is needed. For others the association between the chicken and the spirit for which it is intended is unexplained. Dan Galadima, for example, requires a white cock with a brown saddle-shaped design on its back, but why is not clear. Ducks may be substituted for chickens in the case of spirits who live in or near water. Some pagan spirits are thought to demand dogs. In most cases the fact or thought that an animal possesses attributes analogous to a spirit marks it as a proper sacrifice.

More serious sacrifices or those to be offered by affluent sufferers demand large animals rather than chickens or ducks. Goats, sheep, and cattle may all be grouped according to the spirits for which their colour patterns or other characteristics make them appropriate. Sufferers believed to be afflicted by title-holders in Jangare are required to limit their sacrifices to such animals. As has been noted about the kind of offering appropriate for the Chief of the Spirits, it is said 'As the ostrich is too large to land on a branch, so too the Chief exceeds the sacrifice of a ram'.

The act of sacrificing an animal symbolizes a pact between victim and afflictor. The 'rules' state that the spirit should accept the blood of the animal in place of human blood. The animal thus stands both for the giver and the receiver of the sacrifice. But sacrifice is often only one part of the contract. To ensure the offended iska will not revisit his victim in anger the victim must become a 'child of the bori', a horse of the gods. He must participate in cult ritual and demonstrate skill in possession-trance. It is to an examination of these two topics that we now turn.

NOTES

[1] Adamu reigned from 1923 to 1955. This incident was reported to have taken place early in his reign (cf. Patton 1975).

[2]It should be noted that male spirits do not confine their selections to men but may possess women too.

[3]Songs which may have texts are extremely variable. This is because their rules of order are based on such things as language-music relationships, semantic content, type of vocal ensemble, and rhythmic patterns rather than on a special sequence of textual items. Thus, they are either long or short in duration, depending upon the specific situation in which they are sung.

[4]Music with an underlying text is commonly found in the repertoires of court musicians, but also occurs with musicians who play the kalangu (double-membrane, stick-struck, hourglass pressure drum) either for butchers or entertainment. With royal musicians their instruments are described as reproducing a limited set of special texts according to a system which recognizes both phonemic tone (in its chanted version) and vowel-length. The special texts may be described as 'underlying' in that they are not spoken, merely understood (cf. Ames 1971: Besmer 1971).

[5]Tremearne records *Mai-Inna* (Inna) and *Doguwa* as being the same spirit (1914: 269-70). He describes her as a 'somewhat incomprehensible' spirit, consisting of two halves (1914: 332-3) one urban and the other from the bush. Greenberg notes the same for Inna in his study (1946: 39-40) but this distinction seems to have been lost to modern devotees.

[6]Reuke lists Dan Galadima as the real son of Sarkin Aljan and Inna (1969: 115). This conforms fairly well with the present data except that he is an adopted, not real son, of his parents. Reuke's diagrams make no distinction between real and adopted children.

[7]*dan na gode* (son of I give thanks) is usually taken to be the praise-epithet of a strong, short man. Informants explain that here it means that Dan Galadima will take anything from anyone, saying 'thanks' and lose it in gambling.

[8]The Hausa title, Magajiya, is sex-specific and refers to a woman. The same title for a man would be given as *Magaji*.

[9]Essentially the same praise-epithet is recorded by Tremearne (1914: 360)

[10]If this affliction is a bleeding ulcer it is interesting to compare part of the bori cure with some western treatments. The patient is required to drink large quantities of milk (in this case it must be taken from a black goat) which serves as the vehicle for special leaves added to it.

[11]These include *buruku* roots (a small unclassified shrub), *duman rafi* roots (the convolvulus *Ipomoea repens*), *tawatsa* buds (the tree *Entada sudanica*), *farad dorawa* wood (locust-bean tree *Parkia filicoidea*), *marga* wood (a tree also known as *gama fada*; unclassified), *sarkakkiya* leaves (from a dense thicket), *duhuwa* roots (a thickly wooded place in otherwise open country, *sarkin itatuwa* (unclassified) or *sansami* wood (the tree *Stereospermum kunthianum*), and *mashayi* roots (hollow-branched shrub *Clerodendron capitatum*).

[12]This plant's pounded, dried leaves are used for piles, and its wood-smoke keeps flies off cattle. From its roots is obtained a decoction for nursing-mothers and infants.

[13]He prays over it as it is buried.

[14]Any animal which is not killed by having its jugular vein cut and bled to death is termed *mushe* (carrion). If the animal is inappropriate the meat is still carrion even though this slaughtering procedure is observed.

[15]There is some dispute as to whether he is Sarkin Aljan Sulemanu's senior councillor or his brother's official. Informants agree it was on the authority of Sulemanu that he was given his title, but some say he serves Sarkin Aljan Biddarene's court and not his senior brother's. This opinion is supported with the praise-epithet: *Kuge na kofar fada, Madawakin Nasara, Madawakin Sarkin Aljan Biddarene* (Kuge [a praise-name for the Leper] of the palace gate; senior councillor to the Victorious One, senior councillor to the Chief of the Spirits Biddarene).

16Dundu (acacia-like shrub with thorns *Dichrostachys nutans*) is believed to be the favourite resting place for Kuturu.

17The Sudan Interior Mission (SIM) leprosarium market to the west of Kano City.

18Probably means Dakiro, SIM's leprosarium.

19The Leper's toes are as functional as those of a bed leg; the print is round.

20This implies wetness. The 'something large and round' could be an abbreviation for the harvest rain which falls in large drops.

21The wetness is caused by his leprosy which is still active and not yet dried up.

22In the text the plural 'ku' is used but refers to a single individual.

23The usage is plural but the reference is singular.

24An epithet for any snake.

25The water he drinks is rain; he appears in the sky as a rainbow.

26Haskiya: Danko's mythical town near Jangare.

27Gadas: a small village north of Zaria, North Central State where Danko is said to be particularly active.

28He causes his enemies to flee, and when they do he continues to chase them.

29Danko may appear slight in stature, but his power exceeds that of any mortal.

30Each year the camp may be found in a different place.

31The herd increases every year so that at the end of ten years it is ten times its original size.

32Each cow produces one calf every year.

33Said to a prostitute.

34The colour reversal was unexplained.

35Probably a patrilateral parallel cousin (father's brother's son), judging from the genealogical data.

36One of these is Zaki (Lion) who married Zurkalene's sister, Labuda a Fulani woman.

37Ciwo Babu Magani (Illness with No Medicine), daughter of *Duna.*

38*Manzo Maye* (Manzo the Sorcerer), son of Duna. Informants could not decide if Manzo still lived in Zurkalene's house or whether he had returned to his mother's father's house (12). The census lists him in both places (see below).

39This translation is uncertain but may refer to *bikwam mashi,* a conquered area and its inhabitants.

40Praise-name for the Hyena, actually the name of his father-in-law.

41Burungu: epithet for a hyena.

42*Garar warwasu:* meaning uncertain; translated here as 'is excessive'.

43*Karas-karas:* the sound heard when a person eats raw kola nut, potato, ground-nuts, etc.

44The sorcerer's power is ineffective against the Hyena.

45That is, the Hyena is a special symbol for meat-sellers, though not all of them.

46He holds his victim's throat, causing him to choke.

47The *doka (Isoberlinia doka)* shade tree is his favourite resting place.

48The sound of drumming.

49Plural usage, but denotes a single individual or item.

50This refers to the use of the skin as a drum-head. It makes pleasant sounds but gets beaten in the process.

51It is a thankless job to feed them, hence'*cima-zaune*' (food-eaters sitting down).

52Sasana: some obscure member of the Chief of Drummers' ancestry.

53Dangwami is made from the pulp of locust bean pods and tamarind 'water'.

54It is not clear whether he sells it or gets drunk on it.

55Musicians are expected to debase themselves in front of their patrons, hence the allusion to slavery.

56Not to be confused with another *Baleri* who is the father of *Mai Baka* (the Bowman; see below, House 8).

57Baleri here is said to be different from Duna (see above) whose second name is also Baleri.

58Also *Barahaza.*

59Duna Rage Iri may be literally translated, Black-Skinned One, Reducer of Seeds. I was unable to discover a more satisfactory explanation of this name and suspect my notion of it is inaccurate.

60*Yan gwiyangu*: lit. children of smallness; plural usage denoting a single individual.

61*rufa ciki*: lit. closed stomach.

62*makangari*: said to mean *gangara*, a path downwards [to a stream].

63Under normal circumstances one might say that this was phenomenal luck. For Mai Dawa it is a matter of skill.

64*kuran na daure*: lit. hyena which is tied up.

65*yai daidai*: lit. he does correctly.

66*Kilikinju = Kirikinju.*

67According to Greenberg, the original native classification divides spirits into those of the town and those of the bush (1946: 29). 'Black', therefore, is a description of his locale, the bush, and not of his religion. Modern informants agree with this, saying his colour has nothing to do with whether or not he is a Muslim which, in fact, they say he is.

68This approval is nearly automatic, since he would never ask if he thought it might be inappropriate. For the leader's part the pressure for him to allow the statement is considerable, the request having come to him publicly in song form.

69Dungu: probably from dungu (stump-of-maimed-arm).

70*Dungu uwar shanu*: also said of her sister, Inna (see above).

71A somnambulist.

72The hair is from her *coiffure.* She uses the wrong hand with which to prepare food.

73'mother of' (innar): she is actually their mother's sister.

74Mamman: the Prince (Dan Galadima: see above).

75Nakada: said by King to be derived from *na kada* (one of over-throwing that is, causer of downfall) (1967: 19 n.). Greenberg translates Nakada as 'the striker' (1946: 39).

76One of Sarkin Arna's victims is said to be Alhaji Mamman Shata, a norther Nigerian musician-entertainer of great renown. As it is sung in a song for the Chief of Pagans, *'Alhaji Shata yana zubawa; she ya sa na ce "kada wani tsinanne ya zage mai giya"* (Alhaji Shata is pouring [it down] ; it is because of him that I say 'do not let a certain accursed one abuse the owner of beer').

77 Kafiri: lit. non-Muslim; also the name of a North African spirit.

78When he is not drunk when dancing he goes through all the motions of farming. He sets out his field, plants it, and harvests it. All this work, of course, is to get grain for beer.

79The dog is a classic symbol among the Hausa, standing for a non-Muslim.

80Malam Alhaji (Malam, the Pilgrim).

81Butsatsa: a thing with neither a head nor a tail. Not knowing its front from its back it cannot be dealt with.

82This epithet for a pugnacious person is usually given as follows: *butsatsa kayan kaba, koina suka; gaba tsini baya tsini* (pugnacious one, a load of young dum-palm fronds everywhere pointy; a sharp point in front and a sharp point in back).

83Pagans are thought to prefer beans to corn or rice.

84Yero (= Dabo): said by Abraham to be the name for a fourth son (1962: 160). The genealogical data for the present study show Mai Gizo as the Chief of the Fulani's fourth son.

85Sour milk with lumpy curds (guntsari): i.e. Mai Gizo.

86cattle camp (ruga): the house of Sarkin Filani, Mai Gizo's father.

87dog (kare); euphemism for pagans who are thought to eat dogs. In other words, the house of the Chief of Pagans.

88Maje: one of his father's brothers in the Fulani house.

89Tall-Woman: the Black Tall-Woman (Bakar Doguwa) also called Inna.

90Baban Gida (lit. Father of the House): the name of one of Mai Gizo's mediums in Kano City.

91Mai Gizo's visit in Maiduguri is documented on one band of an LP recording to be released through the Centre for Nigerian Cultural Studies (Ahmadu Bello University) and Decca (Lagos) Ltd. (Besmer 1975 b).

92In Maiduguri spirits are called with music played on a goge accompanied by kwarya.

93Promises made to spirits by those not possessed by them (the musicians in this case) seem rarely to be fulfilled. Satisfied that they had given Mai Gizo a chance to ride, the cult and musicians decided not to continue the performance the next day and were confident no evil would be visited upon them for breaking their promise.

94Euphemism for a lucky shot.

95How (yaya) has a double meaning—'how was it done?' and 'why was it done?' The praise assumes the second, but Sarkin Gwari's reply is to the first.

96The tip of the arrow came out of its head.

97A new pattern is described as *juya kida* (lit. 'change drumming'). To 'change drumming' in any performance is to abandon the previous song and begin a new one.

98Bargery's dictionary, compiled between 1928 and 1933, gives the first meaning of bature as 'an Arab', and the second as 'European or other "white man"' (1934: 95). Abraham's dictionary, the second edition of which appeared nearly thirty years after Bargery's, gives a definition which has not changed for current usage: 'white man, European (including Arab or Syrian)' (1962: 90).

99The conquest of northern Nigeria by the British in the early 1900s.

100Epithet for a quick-tempered person.

101The tree *Entada sudanica.*

102In other words, 'don't lean on a broken reed!' (Abraham 1962: 863). The epithet does not make it plain whether Dam Mama is the strong branch or the weak one, but it might be inferred from other of his praises that he is *not* dependable.

103Christian or European. Not to be confused with *nasara* (victory).

104From the colour of their veils and gowns, and perhaps evil.

105Exactly who is not certain.

106*Umaru*: the same as Umaru.

107*gagaran*: probably the same as *gagaran*, 'to test the strength of'.

108*kafan*: (= *kaho + n*) '[animal] horn of'.

109easterners: residents of 'eastern' places, e.g. Ningi.

110Umaru is said to have been buried by his enemies who thought he was dead. He returned very much alive.

111An illusion created by Umaru.

112Both the Chief of Drummers and Umaru ride female mediums in Ningi.

113Batoyi is perhaps the same spirit as *Bagiro* (Fetishism) whose epithet is *Bagiro kakan tsafi* (Bagiro, grandfather of fetishes) or as *Magiro* (cf. Greenberg 1946: 31; Tremearne 1914: 262-4).

114Her son is Manzo Maye (Manzo the Sorcerer). There seems to be some problem with his residence, since some say he has been adopted by his father's classificatory brother, Sarkin Aljan Zurkalene (House 6, see above) and lives there.

115While terms of address are the same, terms of reference are, of course, different.

Chapter 5 · Ritual and Possession-Trance

The primary aim of this chapter is to reach an understanding of the social dynamics, processual structure, and symbolism of bori ritual performances. A conspicuous feature of most bori rituals is possession-trance, an altered state of consciousness, and close attention will be paid to the techniques used to induce it, its development as a skill, and its use by the bori cult. The investigation of cult rituals follows two levels each of which is dependent upon data collected through observation and interview. At one level an attempt is made to understand what bori performances mean to the adepts themselves. At the other their statements are augmented with explanations which adepts seem only dimly aware of but are nonetheless relevant to an understanding of bori ritual behaviour. It should be emphasized that this second level is not a product of the anthropologist's imagination. It is similar to the 'underlying' or 'deep structure' of language as viewed by transformational linguists. Postulating non-surface or deep structures does nothing more than attempt to account for the ogranizational principles actors must have in mind when they say, for example, that performance A equals performance B despite the phenomenological fact that the two are in an important sense unique. Whether the actors are aware of deep-structure organization is beside the point. When two performances are described by cult-adepts as having the same 'meaning' their underlying structures must be the same; conflicting meanings cannot be explained with a single underlying structure.

Two kinds of ritual are found in cult practice. One of these is the healing or initiation rite, *girka*,[1] and shares the characteristics of rites of passage observed by Van Gennep (1960). After a candidate has been accepted into the cult he is required to participate in the periodic rituals (the second type) which serve both the internal purposes of the cult and the external requests of the community. It should be added that the requirement to submit oneself to these performances is not legislated by the cult. Adepts are motivated by a fear of being revisited in a harmful way by the spirits which necessitated their initiation in the first place, as it is believed that any hint of scorn on the part of an adept could result in provoking the anger of those iskoki for ever on his head. Periodic rituals known as *wasam bori* (lit. 'play of bori') or *wasa* (play) do not generally involve any demonstration of possession-trance and to be absent from these is safe. Those rituals described simply as bori, unless they are totally staged, are *de rigueur* for most adepts, particularly those who have been especially invited to attend, and the full force of their obligation to the residents of Jangare can be called upon.

The fact that possession-trance is such an important aspect of bori rituals coupled with the recognition of a considerable recent interest in altered states of consciousness[2] has led to a somewhat extended treatment of the topic here. Cult-adepts' explanations of the meaning of possession-trance—even where statements could be recorded which related to such purely technical matters as induction, perfection of the skill, and subjective impressions of what was happening—did not seem to answer all the questions. In the case of musicians, for example, they considered as adequate an explanation or prediction of what a medium would be expected to do when a particular piece of music was played. Our standards of adequacy did not always match, and I found myself seeking some hidden clue, some physiological or psychological reason why such behaviour could be elicited. Thus, the reader's indulgence is asked for those purely speculative sections which attempt some deeper understanding of possession-trance, particularly the induction phase.

SOCIAL DYNAMICS AND CULT RITUAL

It would be convenient if bori rituals were a part of a larger social mechanism to maintain the general morality of Hausa society. For those involved in bori this is the case, but the fact remains that only a small percentage of the population has been accepted or marked for membership in the cult. Certainly the shared cultural knowledge about bori activities, music, praise-epithets, and lore is large, but most Hausa Muslims joke about the efficacy of bori spirits and the unenlightened people associated with them.

Earlier in this study (cf. Chapter II) Lewis's work on 'spirit-possession' cults in north-eastern Africa was mentioned. It was observed that Lewis maintains a useful distinction can be made between 'main morality cults' and 'peripheral cults'. While it seems inaccurate to equate Islam with Lewis's main morality cults, much of what he describes for peripheral cults is applicable to bori. The women's cult of zar spirits, he says, 'appears to function as a compensation for their partial exclusion from full participation in the men's world of Islam' (Lewis 1971*b*: 214). What Lewis seeks is an answer to his question, 'what categories of persons most frequently succumb to spirit-possession and figure most prominently in possession cults?' (1966: 309). He suggests that people who belong to 'marginal social categories' or who are psychologically disturbed are particularly inclined to cult membership (1971*b*: 215).

Although Lewis' suggestion has much to be said for it, his implied explanation that such cults are all a part of the 'war between the sexes' drew sharp criticism. Looking at possession-trance from a different perspective, Wilson posits that such cults are 'a means to status or identity definition, and [possession-trance] arises in contexts when individual status is jeopardized or rendered ambiguous' (1967: 376-7).

One whose status identity is somewhat ambiguous, arising from some personal characteristic (homosexuality, transvestism, nymphomania, etc.), specific social condition, or regularly recurring condition associated with the life cycle (Wilson 1967: 375), can seek either to have his social identity changed or his social status regularized and defined through participation in bori rituals. Marked by 'abnormality' and accepted as a candidate for membership in the cult through an identification of iskoki as the cause of the problem, a person's behaviour becomes explainable, and simultaneously earns a degree of acceptability, after completion of the bori initiation. Symbolic transformation from a suffering outsider—outside both the society and the cult—to one whose status includes the description, horse of the gods is achieved.

For example: the data collected for this study include a case of a woman who was initiated into the bori cult after being diagnosed as suffering from a left-side paralysis caused by a female Fulani spirit, Inna[3]. In Hausa society women are customarily the wards of men—their fathers, brothers, guardians, or husbands—and any woman who would like to lead an 'independent' life finds her choices, within that context, extremely limited. The woman in the case-study mentioned above was one who had had great difficulty adjusting to her role as a ward of any of her relatives, consanguineal or affinal. She had lived with her parents in a small rural community until her first marriage when she left to live with her husband in a near-by city. Her marriage turned out badly, eventually terminating in divorce, and she returned to her father's farm. Anxious to live in the city, any city, but unwilling to accept any of her matrimonial prospects, she remained with her family, worried and unhappy. One morning she awoke and reported that the left side of her body, her hand and foot, felt numb. Her condition deteriorated even as her parents vainly sought aid first from a local malam and then from the near-by dispensary. Suspecting that her affliction was due to the work of iskoki since they themselves had been cult-adepts, her parents arranged to have her taken to a renowned cult doctor who had also been a family friend. The healer diagnosed her illness, arranged for a cure, and at the conclusion of her treatment was kind enough to allow her to live in his compound, under his care and supervision.

From the perspective of this case-history the woman's girka (curing/initiation ritual) provides a clear example of redressive and regulative institutions of the bori cult. She was said to have deviated from cult-prescribed behaviour dictating that places sacred to supernatural spirits should be treated with deference and respect. In her case she *admitted* urinating (although accidentally) in a place reserved for Inna. The spirit's displeasure at this was symbolized by her illness; it also symbolized the need to incorporate her into the bori cult as a medium for Inna and those of Inna's relatives who had assisted in aggravating the affliction. That her paralysis was treatable meant that she had been chosen for membership in the cult, not for the grave.

As implied earlier, 'proper' women are the wards of men. A woman who becomes a cult-adept usually has two options from which to choose regarding her place of residence after initiation. She may return to her relatives or live under the authority of the adept who supervised her cure. In the latter case she may accept a status as a karuwa ('harlot'), only if she has been previously married. If her initiation leader was a woman, the new initiate has successfully escaped from all but the formal requirements of being some man's ward. If her initiation leader was a man, his guardianship is substituted for the customarily restrictive supervision of either family or husband.

Consider the anomaly of this woman's status. As an unmarried individual of marriageable age she contradicted the culturally defined, 'natural' condition for adults, and refusing a new marriage after divorce generated ambiguity in her status. The solution to the problem lay in the cult girka which both validated her status as a karuwa and allowed her to leave her parents' compound without upsetting the social order. We might speculate that neither the advice offered by her family's malam nor the medicine prescribed by the local dispenser was effective in her illness, primarily because neither provided the ritual framework with which to cushion the potentially disturbing social transition the woman wished to make.

In addition to illustrating how an ambiguous status may be regularized this example may be viewed from the perspective of what Turner called 'rituals of affliction' (1967: 9). During such rituals, people with a cult status (those who have been stricken by maladies believed to have been caused by supernatural spirits and have been 'healed' by initiation into the bori cult) administer to those who seek relief from an illness or malady diagnosed to have been caused by spirits. The sufferer, judged to have been 'caught' by one or more iskoki, becomes the subject of the girka ritual which is directed towards appeasing the offended spirits through the elaborate manipulation of a variety of 'medicines', promises made on behalf of the sufferer that he will always be a faithful mount for the spirit, and sacrifice. Through healing/initiation the candidate joins the 'community of former sufferers' (Turner 1969: 14) and with the perfection of his cult skills may himself attain the status of healer. Illness is revealed as serving a dual purpose: punishment for some wrong doing, and divine selection for cult membership.

However, rituals of affliction which attempt to correct behaviour estimated as deviant by society as a whole but as appropriate by the cult, constitute only a small part of bori ritual activity. Most bori activity falls into that class of ritual devised to anticipate cult-determined deviations and conflicts. Held generally in conjunction with non-bori events (e.g. wedding ceremonies etc.) their function has been described by analysts as entertainment. While there is no doubt that adepts and wedding guests alike consider entertainment an important aspect of these rituals it must be emphasized that both wasa (which does not include a demonstration of possession-trance) and bori (which does) are held by ritual specialists whose activity is acceptable as entertainment and not by professional entertainers enacting a ritual show. The Hausa social fabric lays stress on the division of people into professional groups of one kind or another, and professionalism carries with it the implication or expectation that money will be paid for services rendered. In examining what happens to gifts and money collected during wasa or bori events the theme of the *non*-professionalism of the participants is underlined.

As each medium performs, gifts and money are given to the *musicians* on behalf of the riding spirit. It is collected in individual piles, each of which is identified by a spirit's name and separated from items given specifically to the musicians. At the close of the event, the most important musician—a professional—supervises the distribution of valuables to the mediums. He calls out a spirit's name, describing the gifts which have been collected for him, and then the elaborate rules of etiquette governing the distribution of gifts and money are applied. As noted above, spirit's gifts are kept separate from those specifically given to the musicians. This action is extremely important, describing symbolically the chief musician's rights of ownership and reallocation. The decision of how much will be reserved for the musicians and how much should be given to the spirit's representative (his horse), hardly involves the medium at all. Determined by the musicians with the approval of a senior cult representative, all but a small fraction of each pile is given to the medium if the 'take' is judged small or half or less if it is considered large. The medium does not argue about his share for to do so would be considered impolite and ill-mannered. His share is a *gift* to him, not a payment for his services.

The line between such gifts to a participating adept and a payment is exceedingly fine, but the distinction is maintained in the explanations of the actors themselves. It is said that money is given to a musician as payment for his services, since to fail to do so might result in 'his heart growing cold'. A medium's heart cannot grow cold during his dissociated state; he is (or should be if his possession-trance is 'true') unaware of the specifics of the gift-giving behaviour of those around him. The spirit may show displeasure at someone's lack of generosity, but his medium (who is, typically, amnesic about his trance) would not have grounds for expecting a minimum fee; since the money was a gift to a spirit, who is the medium to treat it as anything other? All things considered, the adept does not demonstrate possession-trance for money—although he may depend heavily on his mediumship as a source of income. He submits himself to the will of the spirits on his head, for to fail to do so would result in his own ill health, a recurrence of an old affliction. During his initiation he promised (or it was promised for him) that he would be a devoted mount for the spirits which had gathered on him, and his regular participation in cult rituals is an important part of his obligation.

Another of his responsibilities is to give gifts on behalf of those spirits left with him when he is an observer and not a participant in an event. In fact this obligation is responsible for many of the gifts given during periodic bori rituals. The exchange of gifts within the cult during performances symbolizes both the solidarity of the group and the definition of its parts. In other words, the gifts serve to link adepts together through their common affliction by specific spirits, but each separate occasion of the giving underlines and separates the respective roles of performing medium and involved observer. As the roles reverse so does the direction of the gifts, and viewed in its totality this direct exchange emphasizes the equality of cult members possessed by the same spirit.

Spirits, however, are not believed to be organized on a socially egalitarian basis, and important senior spirits may be expected to command greater generosity than their junior kinsmen. The larger gifts given to senior spirits thus take on an element of tribute, the size of the gift symbolizing the spirit's social placement in Jangare.

A related point here is the apparent, although rarely stated, stratification among cult members. To a considerable extent the rank of the spirits on an adept's head tends to reflect his social placement within the possession-trance cult, or, more concisely, senior adepts are ridden by senior spirits, junior adepts by junior ones. Actually this system of correspondences is fairly unreliable, but it would be rare for a newly initiated devotee to be ridden regularly by the 'most important' spirits on his head before having perfected his skills as an adequate mount by possession by one or more of the junior spirits which he had been left with at his initiation. The acknowledgement of a medium's expertise depends solely upon his ability to demonstrate possession-trance in a convincing way. Neither the medium's sex, age, length of time in the cult, or relative affluence seem to be considered in judging his achievement. Thus, a kind of crude map of adepts' social relationships may be seen in the identities of the spirits which ride them at any public possession-trance event.

An essential aspect of both girka (initiation or curing) and bori (periodic ritual with possession-trance) rituals is the music used to summon spirits. Without the accompaniment of some 'music', even if it is only handclapping (Greenberg 1946: 52), iskoki will not ride. The fact that musical performance is necessary in cult rituals points to lines of division and co-operation within cult organization. Cult musicians are considered to be musicians involved in cult practices, not initiated adepts with musical skill. In terms of social differentiation they are nominal outsiders, professionals, drawn into ritual performances for a specific purpose. Even when a musician has himself been a trancer, his separateness from the community of cult devotees is symbolized by the description of him as a maroki rather than as a dam bori. A maroki is never expected to fall into trance, and a dam bori, *qua* medium, is never expected to invoke spirits.[4]

The absolute distinction between those who call iskoki and those who are ridden by them exists in every cult ritual. Since callers are also usually given the responsibility of interpreting what spirits say and mean through their mediums, a curious paradox in cult social organization is revealed. The people who choose and direct the arrival of iskoki ask questions of them, interpret their answers,[5] and direct their behaviour as they ride—in short, those who lead ritual performances—commonly are not themselves initiates of the cult.

In the previous chapter a few of the praise-epithets and songs associated with some important spirits were documented. Some songs were described as significant for inducing trance; others were given as appropriate for directing the behaviour of a spirit once it had arrived. Such songs and the various praises and sayings are all a part of the ritual material entrusted to musicians. Furthermore, the determination of when and if cult music is to be played is not a matter internal to cult responsibilities and obligations. Musicians, as we have said, consider themselves to be professionals and as such expect to be paid for their services. They also require a series of prestations to obligate them first to attend a ritual performance and then to prepare their instruments for playing (cf. Besmer 1975).

With so many keys to a ritual performance held by non-initiates the potential for conflict between musicians and adepts is always present. But since there are fairly clear rules of conduct to ensure co-operation disagreement is rarely allowed to surface. The ultimate sanction or expression of dissatisfaction is withdrawal, and any musician or adept who feels a situation fails to meet his expectations has the right to withhold his services. Musicians especially can choose unemployment in situations which they fear might render them victims of cult supporters' meanness. Adepts are faced with a more limited range of choices since they must temper their actions with the knowledge of their covenant with the spirits on their heads which demands that they participate somewhere. When faced with an intolerable situation, male mediums in particular 'go on tour'.

One final point can be made about the social dynamics of cult ritual, and that includes the differentiation and integration of initiates. During the girka ritual the poles of cult leadership are symbolically separated. The candidate is described either as a *'yar fari* (lit. daughter of white) or a *dam fari* (lit. son of white) from the colour of the cloth used to cover the neophyte during the initiation. In this context the white cloth which must be devoid of any coloured design or intricately woven pattern symbolizes the social nakedness of the neophyte. The candidate is treated as a liminal person, belonging neither to any secular group nor to the cult. The initiation is conducted by a *uwar girka* (lit. mother of the initiation) or *uban girka* (lit. father of the initiation), but this senior medium represents more than initiation leadership. This role is performed by the cult's local authority, either a woman or a man, and is symbolic of the person's achievement as it is acknowledged by the membership. The initiation leader is assisted by a *mai mukuru* (lit. owner of a woman's loin-cloth) who, as the translation suggests, is always a woman. The initiation assistant's role includes a considerable number of 'domestic' responsibilities (e.g. the preparation of food and the organization of accommodations) and, accepting the general Hausa ascription of these duties to women, no man would be thought competent to manage the position. The two main categories of cult membership are hardly represented in the initiation ritual. Except when they visit the initiation leader's compound as observers, *'yam bori* are not obvious.

The girka thus outlines the highest and lowest categories of cult membership, categories which are primarily based on achievement rather than ascription. Under the rubric of a cure the potential for any neophyte to become the most senior member of the cult is affirmed, since no other qualifications are applicable than an initial affliction and a subsequent perfection of the skills of possession-trance.

The temporary focus on cult hierarchy so obvious in the initiation ritual is only dimly present in the periodic rituals of the bori cult, but the reaffirmation of distinctions based on achieved skills is continued. The cult's leader at first directs the organization of his subordinates, but as soon as the possession-trance phase of the ritual begins such leadership is submerged in the general description of him as one of the 'children of the bori'. It is often possible to identify the cult leader either by the social position of the spirit riding him or his competence as a trancer, but the complete equality of male and female mediums is symbolized by the conviction that spirits ride either stallions or mares with equal enthusiasm. The emphasis seems to be on the social unification of cult membership, the petty hierarchies of mortals counting for little with iskoki.

INITIATION

In the previous section cult initiation was viewed from the perspective of social dynamics. We may now take a closer look at girka rituals as examples of diachronic processes closely related to the structural levels described by Van Gennep for *rites de passage* (1960). Elsewhere I have discussed a specific initiation in some detail (Besmer, in press, a) so parts of this section will be in the nature of a summary of that material.

An important characteristic of rites of passage is that they are generally associated with life-crisis events in which the ritual subject moves from one ascribed status to another. Birth, puberty, marriage, and death provide the occasions for which the shared characteristics of rites of passage are most obvious. However, it is also the case that the transition between *achieved* statuses is marked with a special ritual of the same type as described by Van Gennep. The bori initiation/curing rite provides an example of this.

In the minds of cult members the primary reason for conducting a girka lies in its efficacy as a cure for a spirit-caused malady. Illnesses believed to be curable by girka are extremely varied and range from impotence, infertility, insanity, and paralysis to rashes and boils. Each specific illness or set of symptoms is symbolically linked to the actions of a specific spirit. No less important to an understanding of girka but perhaps less directly stated in the actions of participants, the ritual identifies the recruitment of a new cult-adept. This is symbolized by the definition of a successful cure as one which results in the attainment of harmony or reconciliation between the sufferer and the iskoki diagnosed to have caused his illness. The continued obligation of the former sufferer to obey the commands of the spirits on his head is expressed in the description of him as a 'horse of the gods' as well as in the denial that a cured person has been exorcized of the afflicting spirits. In other words, girka is a two-sided coin: with cure written on one side and initiation on the other.

Examining the term girka this symbolic dualism becomes clear. One meaning of girka is related to *girka* (to boil). Besides indicating a frequent method of preparation used for medicinal solutions, boiling means heat or fire and thus covers many of the other methods of preparation. In an important sense, therefore, girka symbolizes 'medicine' for the actors. This meaning can be represented as follows:

girka $\rightarrow$ boiling $\rightarrow$ heat/fire $\rightarrow$ medicine $\rightarrow$ cure.

Heat also symbolizes body temperature and constitutes the most important sign of genuine ('of truth') possession-trance. A parallel meaning of girka is thus:

girka $\rightarrow$ boiling $\rightarrow$ heat/body $\rightarrow$ trance $\rightarrow$ mediumship.

Van Gennep observed that transitional rites commonly contain three successive and distinct phases of ritual time: separation, margin (transition), and aggregation (incorporation). Separation is distinguished by the removal and isolation of the candidate from his normal social and physical surroundings. During margin or transition the status of the ritual subject is ambiguous *vis-à-vis* both his former position and his coming one. And finally, aggregation or incorporation is characterized by a stable social state in which the new initiate assumes the rights and obligations of his status as a child of the bori.

Each phase in the initiation process may be examined in terms of its associated ritual symbols. These are represented in both 'things' and special behaviour and are striking in that nearly everything stands for something other than it appears to be. Ritual 'things', for example, include an inventory of 'non-medicinal' initiation materials ordered according to venue and temporal sequence; the 'medicines' used by the initiation leader with both general and specific properties; and the paraphernalia used during possession-trance performances. The behaviour of the participants—ritual subject, initiation supervisors, and musicians—is no less complex in the meaning attributed to it. The second and third phases of the initiation in particular have their own sets of procedures, gestures, music, and expected responses, and if any set is abbreviated it is believed the initiation will fail, that is will result neither in the cure of the patient nor the recruitment of a cult-adept.

The first phase of ritual time, separation, contains 'symbolic behaviour signifying the detachment of the individual . . . either from an earlier fixed point in the social structure or a set of cultural conditions (a "state")' (Turner 1967: 94). It is not possible to become a candidate for girka and remain resident with one's kinsmen: 'out-patient' treatments are quite separate from full scale cures. The candidate, selected on the grounds that his affliction is serious enough to require girka is therefore removed from his normal residence to the initiation leader's compound. All social ties and restrictions are severed, underlining the belief that the ritual subject can never return to his previous state, though the behaviour of his sponsors seems contrary to this belief, since they anticipate his eventual cure and return home. Except in unusual circumstances, however, this never happens, or it if does it is only as a brief transition to an inevitable change.

With the candidate symbolically isolated from the outside world within the initiation leader's compound the real work of the girka may begin. This takes place during the second phase of ritual time, the transition or liminal period, during which the 'state of the ritual subject (the "passenger") is ambiguous [as] he passes through a realm that has few or none of the attributes of the past or coming state' (Turner 1967: 94). This state includes the activation of the ritual roles described in the previous section, special gestures and procedures symbolic of mediumship, behaviour symbolic of social structural ambiguity, and symbolic materials confined to the initiation ritual.

As mentioned earlier three roles predominate in the girka. The first is that of the cult-adept directing the ritual; the second that of the leader's female assistant; and the third that of the ritual subject. The 'father/mother of the initiation' is responsible for all the arrangements prior to and during the ritual. He/she appoints an assistant, supervises the collection and preparation of the medicines and girka materials, and contracts with a cult musician for him and his ensemble to perform morning, afternoon, and evening throughout the initiation/curing period. The initiation assistant administers the girka medicines, prepares the neophyte for each session, cooks his/her food, and performs the special gestures symbolic of the mediation of initiates between non-initiates and supernatural spirits when the latter are called by the bori music. The ritual subject ('son/ daughter of white') remains passive and withdrawn except when certain spirits are summoned by music and the first stages of possession-trance and then of dance are taught. At other times the neophyte is presented with the cult's esoteric knowledge about iskoki, their relationships, characteristics, medicines, songs, and praise-epithets, but except as necessary for an adequate demonstration of possession-trance no mastery of this is required.

During the liminal or transition period the neophyte is regarded as completely helpless and must be spoon-fed by the initiation assistant. From the perspective of the social structure the ritual subject is invisible, a non-person. Any personal property which might suggest rank or kinship position is forbidden and the single piece of clothing, a body wrapper, which the neophyte brings to the girka must be given to the initiation assistant at the conclusion of the ritual. Invisibility is further emphasized by removal from all social activities—for

example, conversations are conducted as though the neophyte were not present
—and the ritual subject is covered (hidden) with a blanket when the musicians
invoke the spirits.

Before the musicians begin to play, the initiation assistant prepares the site
as well as the neophyte for the session. At the initiation site she places a grass
mat upside down (the unpolluted side) with the top of the mat pointing east
(the direction of the spirit world of Jangare) and stands at the back of the candidate, holding his hands behind him. In this position the pair walk around the
mat, then across its length, and its width, each three times. With this greeting to
the spirits concluded the initiation assistant seats the candidate on the mat,
facing east, his legs outstretched, and puts into his hands a special initiation
charm (*dada* or *'ya*) consisting of secret medicines wrapped in a small piece of
white, handwoven cloth and ornamented with cowrie shells. Another, smaller,
initiation charm is tied around the neophyte's chest to ensure that the ritual will
result in a cure, and a small chicken feather is stuck in his hair over his right
temple. The initiation assistant then ties the ritual subject's big toes together and
with another piece of cloth or twine, his thumbs together. Finally, she covers
the candidate with a white, handwoven cloth, tucking it in all around, and seats
herself to the candidate's right, facing north.

The ritual subject's posture and orientation are symbolic of complete
submission to the will of the spirits which have caused the affliction. Divine
horsemen are believed to prefer to mount an 'unbroken' horse which is both
concealed[6] and hobbled, so that thus prepared, there should be no reason why
even the most sensitive spirit would decline the invitation. The slight vibration of
the chicken feather in the candidate's hair is a sign that a spirit is on his neck and
may be spoken to through him.

The liminal phase is expected to last for six days, but up to thirteen may
be required to assure that all the afflicting spirits have had a chance to indicate
their attitude towards the ritual subject. During this period the cult musicians
play three times a day, beginning each performance with the songs for Sarkim
Makada and concluding with those for Nakada, representative of public possession-trance order. For the first three days the songs in between are for pagan or
black spirits, and it is considered improper to speak when these malevolent spirits
are invoked. To do so would be to encourage one of them to possess the candidate permanently, and because of their potential for destructiveness this would
be unfortunate. Therefore, as each of these spirits' songs is completed with a
minimum of activity the initiation assistant 'buries' the spirit with the motion of
a *tumfafiya* (shrub; *Calotropis procera*) wand. The stick touches the neophyte's
head, moves down the taut cover to his feet, and then touches the ground. This
gesture is effective in coaxing the spirit off the neophyte's head and directing it
to dismount.

On the morning of the fourth day the musicians play songs for spirits
which live in the east, that is white or Muslim spirits. As each of these spirits is
called the initiation masters ask its help in making the ritual subject well, repent-
ing on his behalf for anything which may have offended it. Putting his head under the blanket covering the ritual subject, the initiation leader asks the spirit if
it is prepared to sit peacefully on the candidate. To help the spirit speak through
the candidate's mouth the initiation leader rubs the candidate's teeth with a silver ring or a hen's egg.[7] If no answer is forthcoming the initiation leader affirms

to the spirit that while it is known that mortals do not have the power to drive a spirit away they cannot be prevented from begging it to go in peace. With the questionable spirit thus appeased the movement of the tumfafiya wand down the neophyte's cover provides the signal for the musicians to change their playing and call another spirit.

There is some disagreement about who decides when the music is to be changed. Initiation masters claim they direct the change by dismissing the previous spirit with the motion of the initiation wand. Musicians, on the other hand, say they signal the change with musical cadences. The determination of the person responsible for the decision is important in understanding whether or not cult-adepts control the flow even of an initiation performance. It is probable that the decision is made jointly by initiates and non-initiates (musicians). It would be dangerous for a musician to dismiss a spirit (musically) before it had been formally honoured by the initiation leader, so in girka performances especially musicians must pay close attention to the verbal cadences of cult initiates.

If, while under the neophyte's cover, the initiation leader sees the chicken feather in his hair beginning to vibrate and his body to tremble and perspire, he knows that spirit is willing to speak through the neophyte's mouth. Such behaviour on the part of the ritual subject is, of course, early evidence of an altered state of consciousness during which the ritual subject will serve as the spirit's medium. If an answering spirit refuses to sit at peace or otherwise rejects the candidate it is not thought to be particularly serious. Its help is requested and after an appropriate interval it is 'buried'. If the spirit agrees not to harm the candidate a promise is made, before the next spirit is called, that he will always be its devoted horse.

As this liminal phase continues the spirits have agreed to sit at peace with the ritual subject and will therefore be left on his head, take greater and greater possession of him as they are called for each session. Even as the candidate first responds to efforts to induce him into a trance state his eventual cure is predicted. As the first signs of possession-trance appear the initiation leader directs that his fingers and toes are untied. Thus freed, the neophyte's hands may be expected to move suddenly from his lap and out to the ground at his sides. Even more encouraging to the participants is when the ritual subject begins to perspire and quiver and then stands and falls backwards to the mat in a seated position. These falls, which are allowed to occur in sets of three, are interpreted as the spirit's greeting to the initiation assembly and symbolize the other goal of the girka ritual, the recruitment of a cult member. The liminal phase draws to a conclusion as the candidate's skill in entering and deepening possession-trance is developed and the songs, praises, social relationships, gestures, and dances of the spirits on his head are emphasized.

It should be clear that possession-trance is one dominant symbol in girka. The other dominant symbol is healing. Between the sessions during which the musicians perform to invoke spirits the ritual subject is treated with special medicinal preparations designed to promote the relaxation of the symptoms of his affliction and reconcile him with the afflicting spirits. These medicines are believed to have three aims. The first is represented by preparations used to treat the ritual subject's primary illness and contains items symbolically associated with the spirit diagnosed to have caused it. The second is administered for protection against illnesses caused by other spirits which have selected the candidate, and these are usually kinsmen of the primary afflicting spirit. The third type is given in a general way to protect the candidate from the dangers of possession-trance and from any other spirit-caused malady. Each of these preparations is for one of four uses: to be drunk (*sha*), washed with (*wanka*), rubbed (*shafe*), or burned as incense (*turare*). The ingredients for these preparations are commonly transformed into medicines through the application of heat or fire or natural fermentation (which produces heat); a conspicuous theme of the girka ritual.

In organizing medicines aimed at treating the sufferer's primary illness it is important to identify the particular spirit causing the trouble. A vague outline of the spirit's identity can be predicted through matching the candidate's affliction with those defined by the broad vertical social structures of the spirit world, its houses. Fulani spirits, for example, cause either 'aimless wandering' if they are male or paralysis if female. Spirits from Sarkin Arna's house cause anti-Muslim behaviour and Gwari spirits non-Muslim behaviour coupled with neck or back swelling. The final determination of the name of the spirit causing the affliction is made through direct questioning by the initiation leader during girka sessions.

General medicinal preparations effective in the treatment of the affliction's broad characteristics (i.e. those which are appropriate to an entire family of spirits) are used until the specific cause (spirit) is revealed. After it is known which spirit has claimed responsibility for the illness ingredients specific to it are used. For some items no explanation could be given for their inclusion, but for others the symbolism is clear. Particularly 'meaningful' ingredients are those which stand for the spirit in one of a variety of ways: as already noted, parts of plants in which it likes to rest or which grow near its favourite sleeping places; dirt or waste material gathered from places it likes to visit; and items which have the same name as the spirit or share with it some common characteristic (colour, texture, praise-name, shape, etc.); ingredients associated with its favourite kinsmen or bond-friends in Jangare; and things associated with either its craft or social position.

Once a victim has been afflicted by one spirit others can be expected to have joined it. Ritual subjects, therefore, are treated with preparations specific to these assisting spirits as they are determined during the girka sessions. A final group of preparations is used to protect the candidate from the potentially harmful effects of possession-trance. Some divine horsemen are known to be particularly demanding of their mounts, forcing them to jump from high places,. perform an assortment of acrobatics, or submit to a variety of tests of endurance, so that specific medicines are administered to 'toughen' the candidate. Many of these are preserved in medicine belts to be worn by the ritual subject as he demonstrates possession-trance.

The final phase of a rite of passage is incorporation. As Turner observed, 'in the third phase the passage is consummated. The ritual subject . . . is in a stable state once more and, by virtue of this, has rights and obligations of a clearly defined and "structural" type, and is expected to behave in accordance with certain customary norms and ethical standards' (1967: 94). The incorporation phase of a girka ritual focuses on a public possession-trance performance described either as a *kwanan zaune* (lit. night spent sitting up) or a *wasa na hira*[8] (lit. entertainment for chatting) but also includes a final ritual washing, special

gift-giving, and a sacrifice. During the possession-trance ceremony the ritual subject is displayed as a 'cured' person and is referred to as a horse of the gods rather
than as a neophyte. To merit this description the new initiate must demonstrate
possession-trance during the event, and for the first time when the spirits on his
neck ride, the ritual paraphernalia associated with each of them are tied to him
by strong knots. Even if his altered state is shallow his status as a medium is
recognized. An interesting aspect of the performance is that mediums for the
same spirits as those on the new horse's neck dance with him, instructing him in
the finer points of their spirits' favourite dances and gestures. Lack of skill in the
new initiate's performance does not invalidate the event.

After this performance which usually takes place after the beginning of the
seventh day of the girka (nightfall of the sixth) the new initiate ritually washes
from head to toe, gives a few special gifts to the initiation assistant, and sponsors
the sacrifice of an animal prescribed for the primary spirit on his head. Of all
these the washing, which appears obviously connected with the new initiate's
non-status as a ritual subject, at first seems out of place. However, its clear placement within the incorporation phase becomes apparent with the statement that
the new initiate 'washes himself'; the action is connected with what a horse must
do upon return from an altered state of consciousness.

Then the initiate must give the wrapper, food and water bowls, and ladle
which he had been required to provide for the girka to the initiation assistant.
These objects are polluted for the initiate, symbolizing his helplessness during
the girka's liminal phase, but none the less, they are his. Giving them to the initiation assistant provides a solution to the problem of their disposal and emphasizes the conviction that they will never again be needed. This social distance
from the girka is further increased by the requirement that the new initiate shall
not enter any initiation place, which clearly accounted for the absence of any
cult-adepts except his initiation masters, at his own girka.

Finally, the initiate must provide a sacrifice to sustain the spirits who have
been instrumental in his cure, as all initiates are expected to do when the gods
have shown them special favour. This sacrifice provides a curious mixture of
Muslim and non-Muslim symbolism. The animal must be butchered according to
Muslim law (made to take a drink of water,[9] face east,[10] and its jugular vein cut
with a steel knife), but it is directed to iskoki and not Allah. The blood is
collected in a shallow hole where it is left for spirits to drink, and, as we have
noted previously, the meat must be given away as alms, the recipients[11] validat-
ing the offering by their acceptance of it, while the skin, head, and feet are given
to Sarkim Makada's mortal representatives, the cult musicians.

PERIODIC POSSESSION-TRANCE PERFORMANCES

As suggested above one of the obligations of a cult-adept is regularly to provide
his services as a mount for the spirits on his head. There, perhaps, psychological
or psychiatric reasons why a medium should feel this pressure to enter possession-
trance, but for the purposes of the cult these reasons are translated into social
terms. To maintain or increase one's status placement in the possession-trance
cult one must be a willing participant at cult performances. So far as could be
determined in the present data the occasions for possession-trance performances

which are prompted purely by cult stimuli are relatively few. In fact the only public performance described as unrelated to any external event or invitation, except for those performances which are a part of initiation/curing rituals, is a harvest ceremony called *fasa kabewa* (lit. smashing a pumpkin). Held after the harvest of pumpkins (long after the harvesting of all types of corn) and at any other time when cult solidarity is demanded, the smashing of a ceremonial pumpkin by Sarkin Rafi is said to be symbolic of an agricultural people's gratitude for a bountiful harvest and, since the pumpkin itself is believed to have special medicinal properties, of the power of cult medicines and mediumship. The only other type of performance held specifically for cult purposes is not open to the public as it takes place within the walls of an adept's secluded compound. When a spirit has turned against a devotee it may be necessary to hold a special performance in which male cult musicians play to quiet a spirit's unrest (*kidan juyi*: lit. drumming for a change of state).[12]

Of the 'external' events which are frequently used to justify public possession-trance performances the week of wedding festivities is the most common. In the case of weddings it is generally a member of the bride's family who asks cult musicians and adepts to perform for one or more of the observances during the week: the 'capture' of the bride (*kamar amarya*); the removal of the bride to the house of an older, matrilaterally related woman (usually her mother's sister), where henna is applied to her hands and feet (*kunshi*); the bringing of the bride to the groom's house on Thursday evening where guests sit up the entire night, talking, playing cards, or watching a possession-trance performance (kwanan zaune); and the distribution of gifts by the bride's family on Friday afternoon (*wuni*) (Besmer 1975: 107-8). Kwanan zaune and wuni are sometimes spoken of collectively as *biki* (feast), and when possession-trance performances are kept to a minimum may be the only two wedding-related events for which a cult performance is requested.

Two other events may also find devotees demonstrating mediumship. One is ordinary naming ceremonies (*wasan suna*), particularly for children born to devotees or cult sympathizers, and the other is for the Mulim festivals of Id al-fitr and Id al-Kabir. *Kwanan zaune na salla* and *wasar salla* are held in a semi-private section of the emir's palace or in front of the emir's mother's compound during the eight evenings marking the Festival octave. Held with the emir's tacit approval, although not at his specific request, salla performances serve the double purpose of giving Muslim spirits the chance to ride in the festival parade and of assuring non-Muslim spirits they have not been forgotten.

A story is told of a palace guard who refused to allow bori people to hold this latter series of performances, claiming that they were anti Muslim and a disgrace. Unsuccessful in their attempts to impress upon him the necessity of holding the performances, the musicians and adepts withdrew, knowing that some evil was sure to be visited upon the guard by the spirits lurking in the palace. Later that night it was reported that he had been seized by the neck, lifted into the air, and thrown to the ground, dead. His replacement was not so foolish and allowed the children of the bori to enter the gate the next night. The emir took no part in this dispute and no prosecution of any cult-adept followed. Bori people knew that the guilty ones were not mortals but palace iskoki.

For possession-trance to occur at any of these ceremonies spirits must be invoked by means of special melodies and rhythms played on one of a number of combinations of instruments. In Kano the most popular bori ensemble consists of a garaya and two or more *butoci* (s. buta). In Maiduguri an ensemble consisting of a goge and kwarya gourds is used. In some places, Ningi for example, either type of music may be heard, but in the goge ensemble a sarewa replaces the bowed lute.

These are all-male ensembles, and for the most part they perform outside compound walls, usually in a cleared place immediately in front of the sponsor's house. Kwarya gourds played by women are also used for certain possession-trance ceremonies, but since such performances take place within secluded compounds they are rarely attended by men. Kidan kwarya (lit. drumming of kwarya) or kidan amada (drumming for amada music) are not specifically included in the present study, although the underlying principles for possession, when it occurs, are the same as for performances by male musicians.

The diachronic order for possession-trance ceremonies follows one of two patterns based on the presence or absence of one song or group of closely related songs intended to induce the trance of all participating mediums simultaneously. There does not seem to be any functional difference between ceremonies which are organized with one pattern or the other, and the context for the choice appears to be based in local custom and devotee preference. Particularly susceptible mediums can have their trance state induced by playing either Magajiyar Jangare's (see above, Example 10) music or the trance-inducing music for the primary spirits on their heads. Reticent mediums must have particular pieces played for them, so ceremonies of the 'simultaneous' type have built into their structure the option that the general be changed to the particular when the situation demands it. Most branches of the cult favour one pattern of trance-induction over the other, but in Ningi the two are used interchangeably.[13]

According to musicians and trancers, cult performances—whether or not a demonstration of possession-trance is included—have a structural (which is usually also a temporal) order. Informants' statements describe elements which are obligatory for the performance to be considered meaningful and those which, based on participants' assessments of the situation or event, are optional. Their statements also describe transformations—exceptions, eliminations, alterations, and sequences—which under special conditions are either obligatory or optional (cf. Besmer 1975).

Most of the analysis presented below is relevant to performances of the 'simultaneous-induction' type which in Kano (where most of the data were collected) happen to be organized by plucked-lute and gourd-rattle cult musicians. Where 'serial-induction' structure is known to be different from simultaneous-induction' structure, mention will be made of the fact and the serial pattern explained.

Broadly viewed, public possession-trance performances contain three important divisions: preparations (*shirin* kida; lit. preparations for drumming), the performance itself (kida; drumming), and the redistribution of the gifts and money collected during the performance (*rarraba*; lit. to share out).

The preparations for a performance include both the gifts which are given to oblige the recipients to attend as actors (musicians and trancers) and an announcement to prospective guests that the event will be held. The person who calls the performance, its host, is expected to provide a small gift of kola nuts, a few small bags of hard candy, and cash (*goron kira*; lit. kolas for calling), which is given either to a member of the cult or a cult musician, depending on the giver's affinity with either group. The receiver organizes the participation of selected musicians and trancers by sharing the host's gift with them. At all levels of this formalized gift-giving the obligation to accept the gift is considerable, and once accepted there is virtually no way to avoid participating in the event.

There is one important rule of exception built into the gift-giving aspect of a ceremony's preparation. When the host or principal redistributor (a senior musician or adept) and a potential receiver have previously established some sort of social relationship, or when the redistributor and the receiver both have cult status, it is possible that the gift may be replaced by obligation. Instead of re- ceiving a portion of the calling gift, the potential participant may simply accept a verbal invitation and use his acceptance as a lever in some future transaction or for the satisfaction of a prior social debt. In the case of such exceptions the per- manence of various interlocking social relationships is emphasized, and in fact the obligation ledger is never allowed to balance.

The other part of the preparations, the invitations to the guests, falls into two categories, depending on whether or not the performance is to be part of the week of wedding festivities. If a wedding is involved the announcement for any specific performance is spread to the guests who would ordinarily be exp- pected to attend the event even if no bori was to be performed. For example, at the performance identified by the staining of the bride's hands and feet with henna it would be considered inappropriate for the friends and relatives of the groom to attend even if they were cult sympathizers.[14] Because of their leader- ship and due to the fact that the cult performances are tied to rituals identified with the bride, it is clear that the bride's representatives play a more active role in this week than those of the groom. The mai kira (caller) is usually from the bride's kin, and along with others of the bride's family, her obligation to be generous especially towards musicians is great. When both groups, represented principally by their women, are present at a performance (typically, those which take place Thursday night and Friday afternoon), they divide themselves spatial- ly, the groom's kin sitting on one side of the playing area and the bride's kin on the other.

Possession-trance performances which are not part of any wedding cere- mony still maintain the essential division between hosts and guests. The entire performance and the way in which gifts are given to third parties establishes or reaffirms a social relationship between the principal participants. Perhaps un- aware of this social undercurrent, many such performances have been described as 'entertainment' (which they certainly are), but their importance as events in which obligations are created and reciprocated cannot be overlooked.

The second broad constituent of a possession-trance performance is identi- fied by the beginning and ending of the musical accompaniment. Informants make a distinction between performances intended to include demonstrations of possession-trance (kidam bori) and those which do not (kidan wasa). It will be recalled that performances with trance are conducted so that devotees either enter trance together with the playing of one trance-inducing piece of music or enter trance one after the other with a series of separate, spirit-associated pieces.

All these performances share a number of common initial elements. Ac- cording to musicians, the kola nuts which served to call them to the event are only useful in obliging them to appear. A generous host recognizes this and

upon the musicians' arrival he approaches them with another gift as an inducement to sit down and unpack and prepare their instruments. Similar to the calling gift, when a social relationship already exists between musicians and caller
this gift may optionally be replaced with an obligation, the caller merely greeting
the musicians and providing them with a special mat on which to sit. Secondly,
when the musicians, now totally in control of event process, begin to play their
first song it is in praise of Allah. This is particularly important in urban communities in which everyone believes he is a Muslim—an attitude about which devout
Muslims are sceptical—but the practice also exists in so-called 'marginal' or rural
areas. And finally, as has already been stated, the first spirit praised or invoked
by the music is Sarkim Makada the spirit who 'opens the door'.

At this point performance divides into the three types mentioned earlier:
(a) no trance; (b) trance induced simultaneously; (c) trance induced serially.

The most conspicuous feature of a serial-trance induction performance is
that it is known very early after it starts whether or not it will include actual
possession-trance. Guests and participants may not all arrive at the performance
site together, but little time is wasted waiting for late-comers. If the first spirit
called, Sarkim Makada, does not secure a mount while his music is being played
it is fairly certain he will not come. The same conditions exist for other spirits
as they are invoked, first the most senior spirits in Jangare, then the middle-
generation ones, and, finally, the most junior ones. As each spirit possesses a
medium and the latter falls into trance, other adepts who may have hoped to be
possessed by the same spirit either interrupt their induction processes or prepare
themselves for a different spirit. It is not unusual for particularly exciting pieces
of music to result in the arrival of one or more spirits than the one actually called.

Mediums' statements imply that one of the advantages of the serial type
structure is that it allows one medium to be ridden by more than one of the
spirits on his neck. After demonstrating possession for one spirit there is time to
'recover' and then return to the trance-induction area and be possessed by
another.

Since performances which do not include possession-trance and those
which use the 'simultaneous-induction' pattern have much in common regarding
process and structure, they may be discussed together. It should be emphasized,
however, that despite similarities on the surface, 'rules' for order are distinct and
actors' expectations of what is supposed to happen differ from one type to the
other.

Both types of performances begin the same way (see above). Except in
Ningi where the town's patron spirit, Sanda Umaru, is called second, the spirit
thought to follow Sarkim Makada is Jangare's senior councillor, Kuturu[15] who in
turn is followed by Danko although by this point the specific order tends to vary
from place to place. The general principle is that Jangare's senior spirits should
be invoked before its lesser ones, but the determination of the hierarchy is a
matter of local option.

During the early stages of both wasa and bori gifts are given to the musicians and to excellent dancers (they in turn pass their gifts to the musicians),
there being no indication that anyone will fall into trance. If the caller does not
indicate to the musicians that a demonstration of trance is desired the performance continues as an accompaniment for dancing until it is too late 'to fit

trance in'. Shortly after this Nakada's music is played and 'closes the door' of the performance.

However, if the caller approaches the musicians with a tray of kola nuts, candy, and cash as *goron gwiwa* (lit. kola nuts for knees; a pre-trance gift for adepts) and says to them 'Bismilla' (Please begin), there can be no doubt that the presence of spirits at the performance is requested. After the caller places the tray in front of the musicians and then retires, interested mediums come over one by one to accept a portion of the gift. By accepting a part of the goron gwiwa a medium obligates himself to participation in trance demonstration. With this gift the atmosphere of the performance is transformed from 'play' to the serious work of accommodating the arrival of spirits.

The participating trancers (who have accepted the 'gifts for their knees') organize themselves immediately in front of the musicians and the process of inducing their altered states of consciousness begins. The song described as appropriate is that for Magajiyar Jangare, and shortly after it starts all the devotees should have entered the first phase of possession-trance, each ridden by a different spirit. In exceptional cases other music or special procedures[16] are necessary to induce the trance of inexperienced or 'difficult' mediums, but everything possible is done to avoid this.

A few general comments about the observed behaviour of possessed mediums can be made at this point. Hausa possession-trance is reported to occur at two levels, mediums describing the first as the arrival of the spirit and the second as its actual ride. As their spirits arrive many mediums show signs of catalepsy or epileptoid seizure. Perspiring profusely, their bodies seemingly racked with convulsions, they cough or vomit and froth at the mouth and nose. Very quickly their trance states are stabilized, and they begin to gesture or move in a manner consistent with the character of the spirits on their necks. When a spirit is said to be in control of his horse's behaviour his medium is appropriately attired either at the trance-induction site or, if the materials are elaborate or numerous, at one side of the site or in a changing room close by. Consistent with their image of themselves as horses, possessed mediums must be backed by their 'grooms' through narrow passageways or door openings to confined places (e.g. changing rooms).

When the horse returns to the performance area it is ready first to greet (and be greeted by) the musicians and important guests and then to dance or otherwise demonstrate the spirit's ride. Some spirits treat their mounts roughly, causing them to beat their bodies, throw themselves to the ground, or crash violently through the spectators. Others ride quietly, and when not dancing their horses roam around as though in a somnambulistic state.

If a spirit wishes to leave it obtains the attention of the musicians by thanking them for their music and seats its mount on the ground. The musicians bid it farewell and then play a short, fast piece for it. Its medium sneezes or otherwise returns to himself: the divine horseman has departed. When all the spirits have gone and Nakada's song is played, the ceremony is over. All that remains is the sharing out of the gifts and money collected during the event (see above).

It will be seen that an important part of periodic possession-trance cermonies is related to its context as a gift-giving event. Without the necessity to exchange gifts or create social obligations a cult performance is totally artificial and lacks emotive power. 'Staged' performances on a fee basis are an example of, this. The participants regard them as nothing more than entertainment, a mere sketch of the social ceremony. There is no separation between guests and hosts which the event can mediate. Musicians and praise-singers consider it inappropriate to announce gifts in any detail, since there is no 'other side' expected to match the giver's generosity.

Possession-trance ceremonies held for weddings, namings, or for cult purposes have an entirely different tone. Social values are reinforced, and, as was discussed earlier (Chapter II), gift-giving is laden with the symbolism of individual and group interaction. Many gifts presented at a cult performance imply a three-sided structure. The givers appear to compete with each other in demonstration of generosity, a central Hausa value. But givers who are divided into groups of guests and hosts do not present their *gifts* to each other; they present their generosity, and it is generosity which demands reciprocation. Such gifts are given to musicians who share them with event participants. A 'restricted' exchange system exists between guests and hosts who consider themselves equals, but between any one of them and the musicians an asymmetrical system is revealed. The musicians are permitted to reciprocate gifts only with their service as witnesses and their acceptance of a low status. Thus, with each gift the donor proclaims both his position in his group and his group's position with respect to his gift-giving opponents (equals) and musicians (inferiors).

Musicians are well aware of the significance attached to gift-giving. Indeed, they use it to their advantage in the belief that low social status need not be translated into low economic status. Part of their strategy is to attempt to drive a wedge between hosts and guests, hoping to stimulate their respective gift-giving impulses with their demand for social equality. For example when a guest presents a gift to a musician at a cult performance the music stops and spectators are urged to hear a praise-shouter's public announcement of it. The gift as well as the identity of the giver are described in most elaborate detail, and the gift's positive attributes are maximized to the fullest extent (see above, Chapter III). With the presentation publicly witnessed it is not the musicians who feel the pressure to reciprocate, but the hosts who may be observed in discomfort.

As has been noted, many gifts are given by cult sympathizers from either side of the spectators in order to reaffirm a pact with a spirit. In this respect they are similar to individual commitments in alms-giving. Although alms descend in the social hierarchy in so far as it is 'beggars' or musicians (alms-receiving specialists) who witness and receive them, they are given as tribute to the Almighty or, for those affiliated with the bori cult, to spirits. As implied in an earlier discussion of exchange (see above, p. 32), social stratification is a necessary element in alms-giving since a recipient of alms is not expected to reciprocate in the future, but to validate the gift by acknowledging the purpose for which it was given. That it is inappropriate for them to reciprocate is translated into social inequality in that recipients of alms are thereby placed in a depressed social position in respect to givers of alms.

Since gifts to spirits represent an individual commitment for givers, generosity is not really involved and no competition exists. Whether musicians and praise-shouters are aware of the social implications of gifts for spirits may be open to debate, but their behaviour in such instances is striking. Such gifts are received quietly and without any interruption of event process. They are set aside in piles according to the names of the spirits for whom they were given,

with the intention of dividing them among the 'poor', i.e. musicians and participating mediums (see p. 29).

POSSESSION-TRANCE: AN ALTERED STATE OF CONSCIOUSNESS

Altered states of consciousness (ASCs) range from ordinary sleep to hypnotic
states, trance, and drug-induced hallucination. Possession-trance differs from
trance in terms of its cultural definition. When a medium enters possession-trance
he is believed to be inhabited—in Hausa terms, ridden—by a supernatural being,
and this is evidenced by one or more of the following: talking and acting like
the possessing spirit; lapsing into a comatose state; speaking unintelligibly to the
observer though subject to translation by adepts or musicians; exhibiting such
physical symptoms as twitching, wild dancing, acrobatic displays, frothing at the
mouth and nose, and heavy perspiring. During this time the medium's own identity is 'invisible', and everything he does or says is attributed to the possessing
identity, and, as we have noted, typically, when he returns to himself he is
amnesic about the activity of the spirit which possessed him.

Some aspects of Hausa possession-trance also appear in other societies
in which trance states occur and they are related to the psysiological and psychological characteristics of the altered state. But bori possession-trance is rendered
uniquely Hausa by the cultural patterning of a medium's gestures while in the
dissociated state. When a person is prepared for mediumship (initiated into the
bori cult), he is taught both how to respond or identify induction cues and how
to act when being ridden by this or that spirit. This learning process takes place
in and out of the person's 'alert waking consciousness', and continues even after
he has been formally accepted as an adept.

The implication of this learning process is that possession-trance is a skill.
Some mediums are more proficient at demonstrating this skill than are others.
We have already stated that within the context of the event it rarely matters
whether an individual's possession-trance is real or faked. If his intentions are
good other mediums consider his demonstration acceptable. Critics from neighbouring cult groups, however, are not as generous, are quick to characterize an
entire performance as worthless, and may stereotype all participants in the area
as quacks and charlatans. Thus, an adept from Kano is likely to describe bori in
Katsina as a sham even if he is also convinced that medicine belts prepared in
Kaita (one of its hamlets), are the best to be had.

In his study of the Moroccan Hamadsha, Crapanzano lists a number of
factors distilled from a variety of sources which are relevant to trance induction
in this religious brotherhood (1973: 231-5). In an effort to reach an understanding of what is happening when a bori adept enters an altered state of consciousness some of Crapanzano's factors are explored here. These are (1) sensory
overloading; (2) changes in motor activity; (3) suggestion; (4) special breathing
techniques; and (5) drugs.[17]

Sensory Overloading

Both auditory and visual overloading are used in the induction of bori possession-
trance. As reported in earlier sections of this study, mediums are insistent that

no spirit can be called (that is, possession-trance cannot be induced) without some kind of musical or rhythmic accompaniment. The content of this accompaniment is culturally defined so that devotees fall into trance state only when certain kinds of music or specific songs are performed. For devotees with a sufficiently generalized response pattern the playing of Magajiyar Jangare's music is effective, but when dissociation is complete each adept is possessed by a different spirit. For other adepts, particularly inexperienced ones or strangers to the area in which the event is taking place, only the trance-inducing music for each of their particular spirits is effective in accomplishing dissociation.

Each of these pieces described by musicians and devotees conforms to common pattern. All follow a relatively slow piece of music which has an organizing pulse of around 120 beats per minute, which seems to set a basic pattern on which sensory overloading is to occur. The trance-inducing piece itself often has two phases, one which establishes a relatively quick and increasing tempo (pulse=160+ to 200) and another which sustains the fastest pace (pulse= 200+) but implies an ambiguity in metric organization. As the tempo increases the volume and density of sound also increases so that auditory overloading takes place both in terms of the number of musical cues being given and their acoustic strength. In other words musical phrases at the fastest tempo occur at short intervals and with the highest intensity. Within each phrase the distinction between duple and triple rhythmic organization is blurred; typically, the melodic instruments (lutes or flutes) outlining the former and the rhythmic instruments (gourds) stating the latter. Auditory over-stimulation is also assisted by the excited, forceful exclamations of praise-singers and -shouters who may either encourage a spirit to finish his preparations and mount his horse or proclaim the greatness of the spirit or his medium.

Clearly cult musicians are aware of the efficacy of auditory over-stimulation in particular since a common technique used in encouraging dissociation is to walk among the mediums, shaking and beating the loudest cult instrument, the gourd-rattle is unmatched in its intensity and usually provides sufficient stimulation to push even an inexperienced medium into an altered state of consciousness. No decibel readings were made for this instrument, but at a distance of two feet or less it can safely be said its intensity approaches the threshold of pain.

For performances held at night visual overloading may also facilitate possession-trance, particularly when the brilliant white light of a pressurized kerosene lamp within a few feet of the participating devotees provides a sharp contrast to the darkness of the surroundings. Many adepts stare into the light, eventually seeming to focus on some spot well beyond it.

Changes in Motor Activity

Continuing to follow the pattern of variation from some previously established level, both the limitation and heightening of motor activity may facilitate a medium's ASC. In places where a pattern of 'simultaneous' induction is used such as Kano, prospective mediums frequently dance to the music played during the pre-induction phase of a ceremony. Even when not dancing the pounding of other dancers' feet immediately in front of the musicians draws the attention of waiting adepts. In contrast, adepts preparing to fall into trance sit unmoving and introspective as the music for Magajiyar Jangare begins.

In Maiduguri adepts waiting to enter possession-trance sit quietly at the edges of the crowd. Expected to fall into trance one by one (serially), each waits until it is time to be possessed before beginning to dance. As the lute plays the trance-inducing music for a particular spirit his devotee comes forward and dances, slowly at first, then with increasing speed and energy.

The onset of dissociation is usually marked by some type of explosive physical activity, jerking, twitching, or spinning around on the ground. Some adepts reach this first stage of possession-trance, defined by informants as evidence of the spirit's efforts to get settled on his horse's neck, through total immobility prepared with dancing. Others achieve the same results with frenzied dancing and foot-pounding prepared with immobility.

Ningi adepts fall into trance simultaneously or serially depending upon the nature of the event and individual circumstances. Events which appear to be motivated by reason internal to cult practice, e.g. incorporation rituals after initiation/curing and harvest rituals, are frequently characterized by serial induction while periodic possession-trance events such as those held because neighbouring adepts have gathered for market day use the simultaneous pattern. The distinction between the two methods of trance induction is not always clear, and it is not unusual for an event which has started out with the serial pattern also to include the simultaneous one, some adepts dissociating 'out of order', two or more at a time. Non-sequential possession during a serial-induction event is not considered a caprice as when a spirit takes possession of someone unexpected, uninvited, and unwanted. Devotees account for it by explaining that the medium was supposed to fall into trance; the spirit simply could not wait and secured his mount in the midst of the excitement.

Suggestion

The suggestion received by a devotee to enter an ASC occurs at a variety of levels, ranging from the general to the specific. At the general level the mechanism of suggestion begins when a medium accepts part of the 'calling gift' before the event. Since this gift is given as much as two days before a possession-trance performance the medium may have a lot of time in which to anticipate his participation as a horse. The suggestion is reinforced with the distribution of the 'gift for the knees' just before the trance-inducing phase of the performance begins. The medium's obligation to attempt to enter possession-trance is now greatest having publicly accepted a share of the two gifts requiring reciprocation with an altered state.

With the onset of the trance-inducing phase of an event where a number of mediums dissociate simultaneously suggestion becomes specific. The musicians call spirits using melody, rhythm, and text, praise-shouters declare the impending arrival of the divine horsemen, and fellow mediums begin to thrash about, perspiring and frothing at the mouth and nose. Cult leadership also plays a role in suggestion, the senior medium—acknowledged for his proficiency in demonstrating possession-trance—sitting or walking among the participants and encouraging each of them to dissociate.

Suggestion is not confined to the activities of people but has a spatial dimension. Possession-trance occurs in a carefully organized physical space in which musicians face a small open area surrounded by spectators. The culturally-defined, 'best' place in which to enter an ASC is within this area not more than approximately fifteen feet from the musicians. The distance from the musicians is reduced to around six feet if heavy dancing precedes the onset of the ASC. Mediums who minimize their motor activity to induce trance sit in one of two positions, either reclining on the ground and leaning on one elbow, or seated with their legs outstretched as in the initiation/curing ritual.

Special Breathing Techniques

Both hyperventilation and hypoventilation are employed to induce trance. Hyperventilation overoxygenates the blood reducing its carbon dioxide level. Mediums who use this technique begin their induction with frenetic, heavily accented dancing to music played specifically for the spirit to possess them.

Hypoventilation reduces the blood oxygen level, increasing its carbon dioxide content and is less dramatic in its effect than hyperventilation, because it is coupled with a reduction in motor activity. Mediums who employ this technique appear to sit quietly, occasionally yawning. In the case of dissociating devotees yawning is not the result of boredom but an indication of a high carbon dioxide level in the blood caused by under-breathing.

Possibly one of the functions of the cloth used to cover an initiation candidate is to reduce the oxygen level of the air he breathes. According to ritual practice, the cloth must be tucked securely around the candidate who is thus forced to recycle his own breath, its oxygen content decreasing as its carbon dioxide content increases. Thus, the cult statement that a horse must learn to be covered before a spirit will ride may be translated into a training device to develop the technique of hypoventilation.

Drugs

It was reported that some devotees prepare themselves for possession-trance ceremonies by drinking certain infusions said to give them 'power'. This was never confirmed in the present data, the mediums interviewed claiming neither to eat or drink anything special. They also said that the medicinal preparations used by devotees are clearly distinguishable from what are known as 'pills' (amphetamines) and hallucinogenic drugs.[18] It must be concluded from observation and the statements of participating cult-adepts that possession-trance events are not characterized by drug-taking.

The same may not be said of participating musicians; although contrary to popular opinions Hausa musicians generally are not habitual drug-takers. A few cult members admit to taking amphetamines before a potentially lengthy ceremony. This, they say, is to give them the endurance needed to play continuously for as long as six hours. Unquestionably such drugs create 'playing machines'—of the lute players especially. An important side effect of 'pills' is that they reduce the patience and otherwise good humour of those using them. An ensemble leader under the effect of amphetamines makes everyone work at his pace—fast and tireless.

No psychological tests were administered to dissociating adepts; it is unlikely that any such tests have ever been given to mediums during possession-trance rituals. Based on observation and interview, however, it is possible to understand at least a small part of what mediums feel during and after their ASCs.

During all phases of possession-trance mediums show an inward shift in attention, 'turning off' much of the outside world. It is extremely difficult to hold a conversation with an adept in an ASC, many such conversations resulting in simultaneous monologues involving the possessing spirit and some external person. In Ludwig's terms a person in a state of trance is 'less able to "be aware of being aware" ' (1968: 77). One mental process of which ceases to function is memory; as previously indicated, mediums have no recollection of what they said or did during trance state. In cult terms the explanation is given that the medium's personality ceased to exist while being ridden by a divine horseman. It was the spirit who was present, not the adept.

Mediums relinquish conscious control of many of their 'normal' behavioural patterns, taking on the character of the possessing spirit and serving as its mouth-piece. Thus the practice of using pronouns and forms of address appropriate to the spirit and not to the medium can be understood.

All gestures and emotions displayed by a possessed medium are elaborately exaggerated. Large hand, arm, or leg motions are common, and dissociating adepts seem incapable of dealing with small things (such as knots) and even mildly complex directional gestures. Gradual changes of emotional states are unknown, adepts seeming to leap from one extreme to another. Interestingly enough, the range of expression seems never to include humour.

Such bodily discomforts as numbness, tingling, itching and bodily distortions characteristic of paralysis and leprosy are often a feature of trance behaviour. Nothing the medium does can relieve these symptoms while dissociation continues. Mediums also enjoy an immunity from the appropriate discomforts for punishing activities. Such feats as jumping from high places, burning the skin with a flaming torch, beatings with iron tools, and wildly acrobatic displays do not result in any physical injury, and consistent with the general amnesia described earlier, nothing can be remembered of their occurrence or discomfort when the ASC is over.

Unquestionably related to the value of possession-trance as a therapeutic activity, mediums who have returned from being ridden by the spirits for ever on their necks report that they 'feel much better' for having participated in a bori ritual. The best way to relieve feelings of depression, anxiety, or frustration they say, is to turn themselves over to the divine horsemen of Jangare. Indeed, such feelings are interpreted as a sign that the spirits think it is time for an adept to renew his dedication to them. Thus, while bori activities may be condemned by the population as a whole every adept knows his obligation. Only a madman or a corpse can ignore it.

NOTES

[1]Girka (initiation) is most certainly derived from girka (to boil), symbolic of the heat a person must experience to come in contact with supernatural spirits, that is, fall into a state of possession-trance.

[2]See, especially, Beattie and Middleton (1969); Bourguignon (1973); Crapanzano (1973); Goodman (1972); Goodman, Henney, and Pressel (1974); Lewis (1971 a); and Monfouga-Nicolas (1972).

[3]This case provided the basis for a paper on initiation into the possession-trance cult in Ningi (cf. Besmer, in press, a).

[4]Greenberg describes a situation in which an adept summoned spirits by rhythmic hand-clapping. No musician was available for the event, so the role was filled by an adept. However, acting as the 'caller', the adept was probably insulated from even involuntary, uninduced possession-trance.

[5]During an initiation/curing ritual it is the initiation leader—usually a senior cult-adept—who communicates directly with the spirits after the musicians have summoned them.

[6]The covering blanket may have a function in teaching hypoventilation (see below).

[7]It was never possible to discover the symbolism of these objects. No apparent connection could be found between speaking or teeth and silver rings or hens' eggs, the participants insisting that the objects were simply successful in 'opening the neophyte's mouth'.

[8]Despite the inclusion of the term wasa (play), which is normally reserved for performances which do not contain a demonstration of trance, this event is a true possession-trance ceremony.

[9]Let it not die of thirst.

[10]Towards Mecca or Jangare.

[11]The recipients are usually socially sanctioned 'alms-receivers', e.g. beggars of all types (including musicians), Quranic pupils, and malams.

[12]Kida is the generic Hausa term for drumming, bowing, plucking, or shaking a musical instrument. Kidan garaya, for example, may be translated as 'plucking of the two-stringed lute' or 'plucked-lute music'. Kidan juyi, therefore, means either 'drumming for a change of state' or 'music to change a state'. For consistency, kida is rendered as 'drumming', even when the context implies 'music for' or 'plucking of'.

[13]The Ningi case illustrates another point. The trance-induction pattern is not tied to the presence of a particular type of ensemble (garaya, goge, or sarewa) nor to a particular group of musicians. The same musicians play for 'simultaneous' induction as play for 'serial' induction.

[14]If any of the groom's friends or relatives is also a maroki (praise-singer, -shouter, or musician) who is affiliated with the cult it is possible for him to appear in that role.

[15]King's liturgy from a Katsina women's performance lists Gangu as following the Chief of Drummers (King 1967: 3; 20-3). There can be no doubt that this is another name for Kuturu, since the spirit is described as a leper and as the 'father of courtiers' (a euphemism for any senior councillor). Further, his nickname is *Goje* which is a praise-name for any Madaki.

[16]One such procedure is called *karo da kai* (lit. banging heads together). I saw only one instance of its use, and that was when a young medium was unable to fall into trance after the others had. The musician-leader held the boy by his ears, banged foreheads with him, and forced him to the ground. Holding him there with a foot on his neck, the musician then played the song for the boy's special spirit. Within ten minutes the boy had fallen into trance and was able to rejoin the ceremony.

[17]It is recognized that limiting the induction factors to these five when there are, undoubtably, many more aspects which should be examined is something of an injustice. I can only ask the reader's patience for this sketchy treatment and suggest he begin with Ludwig(1968) and Crapanzano (1973) should he be interested in further information on trance induction.

[18]Monfouga-Nicolas, however, reports the use of a hallucinogenic plant, *babba juji* (Hairy Thorn Apple; *Datura metel*), by adepts in Maradi (1972: 177).

Chapter 6 · Summary and Conclusions

The possession-trance cult in its true perspective is just one aspect of a comprehensive pre-Islamic Maguzawa religious system centred around the worship of
iskoki (s. iska). Supernatural spirits are believed to be infinite in number, although only some are known by name and have definite personalities and powers.
According to Greenberg, the worship of these spirits by non-Muslim Hausa took
the following forms: (a) domestic sacrifices which were performed semi-annually
before the sowing season and after the harvest during which the head of each
Maguzawa compound acted as a family priest; (b) certain kinds of rites which
were thought to be beneficial to the entire Maguzawa community; (c) individual
sacrifices in compounds which were considered private rituals; and (d) the possession cult which combined the religious and the dramatic (1941: 56-7).

In Muslim Hausa communities most of these practices have been replaced
by Islamic ones, but the cult of possession-trance still finds considerable expression. At a superficial level possession-trance performances may be viewed as entertainment for such life-crisis events as marriage and naming ceremonies; but at
a deeper level they provide a framework for the diagnosis and cure of sickness
and misfortune believed to have been caused by spirits, a context for behaviour
which would otherwise be considered as culturally inappropriate, a social organization for persons seeking self-help in socially stressful situations and who are
considered to be deviants by the society as a whole, and a context for the expression of the social relationships within and between Hausa groups.

While the cult of possession-trance is officially condemned by devout Muslims, this attitude is not universally shared by the populace. Greenberg observes,
'Mohammedan learned men, through the identification of the spirits worshipped
by the pagan Hausa with the unbelieving, or pagan jinn postulated by Moslem
religious doctrine, entertain a belief in the actual existence of and power of these
spirits, and thus create a condition which permits considerable survivals of the
iskoki cult among the mass of Moslem Hausa' (1946: 69-70).

As was mentioned above the belief in the efficacy of the curative powers of the cult is an important reason for its popular support. However, possession-trance as a diagnosis of many physical and mental illnesses as well as misfortune is only one type of explanation available to Hausa people. As Muslims, relief may be sought through prayers and offerings to Allah and the wide assortment of Muslim prophylactics. These include the wearing of amulets containing passages from the Qur'an written on small pieces of paper sewn into leather covers, and the drinking of an infusion of the ink used to write a particular Quranic passage and/or 'cure' on a wooden writing slate, and the water with which it is washed off. Particularly in urban or semi-urban areas treatment for illness is also sought within the context of modern medicine, in clinics, dispensaries, or hospitals.

In the case of a bori cure we have seen that the illness is diagnosed by either the local leader of the cult or, where cult leadership is ineffective or diffused, the leader of the musician-group used to invoke spirits during possession-trance events. The diagnosis is based both on the context of the first symptoms as well as the symptoms themselves, and is used to formulate a hypothesis about the identity of the specific spirits believed to be the cause of the illness. Thus, the malady is described as a sign that the afflicted person is wanted by the spirits as a 'horse' or medium. The person is 'possessed', but not having been initiated into the cult does not know how to respond.

This negative aspect of possession is transformed with trance into a positive one, thought to benefit both the spirit and the medium, through initiation into the bori cult. Initiation is spoken of as girka, and if successful, results in the patient's cure. It also marks the recruitment of a new member to the cult, since it is thought that spirits cannot be exorcized from their victim and that he must accept their power and authority. In accepting a cure—always organized by someone who has suffered a spirit-caused illness and cured by initiation into the cult—the patient's own initiation is similar to that which Turner has described for the Ndembu of Zambia as a ritual of affliction 'performed *by* associations of the formerly afflicted, who have the status of cult-adepts, *for* the presently afflicted' (italics in the original) (1968: 53).

Hausa possession-trance in the context of the bori cult may be considered from the perspective of recent thinking on altered states of consciousness (ASCs) in general. In Ludwig's words, ASCs are 'those mental states, induced by various physiological, psychological, or pharmacological maneuvers or agents . . . as representing a sufficient deviation, in terms of subjective experience or psychological functioning, from certain general norms as determined by the subjective experience and psychological functioning of that individual during alert waking consciousness' (1968: 69-70). An important aspect of ASCs which has been considered in this study is the factors which may play a role in the induction of possession-trance.

FACTORS FOR THE INDUCTION OF POSSESSION-TRANCE

Sensory Overloading

As far as could be determined, sensory overloading, particularly of the audio type, is crucial in the induction process. The Hausa themselves say that spirits cannot be 'called' without the performance of some kind of musical instrument or ensemble. But auditory over-stimulation is not based solely on the rhythmic playing of special musical instruments, nor on the restricted songs and epithets sung or spoken for individual spirits. It is deeply connected with musical *variation*. Specific musical patterns are established and then broken, musically, so that contrast becomes a key element in the auditory dimension. When performances occur at night an element of visual overstimulation may also be employed. This takes the form of the intense energy of a pressurized kerosene lamp whose stark, naked light is a brilliant contrast to the dark surroundings. The light seems to act as a focal point for the eyes of bori mediums entering trance.

Changes in Motor Activity

Both the limitation and heightening of motor activity are used in possession-trance induction. In Kano where adepts commonly fall into trance together the usual pattern involves complete immobility in which trancers recline on the ground at the feet of the musicians. During this physical immobility the medium's attention appears to become directed solely upon falling into trance. In Maidurguri where adepts enter trance serially the emphasis is on heightened motor activity which takes the form of frenzied dancing just before the onset of dissociation. The Ningi situation reveals a combination of the two approaches, one being selected by some cult-adepts and the opposite by others, the two methods sometimes occurring within the same event.

Suggestion

Suggestion may be as general as the expectations of the audience and participants or as specific as the remarks or songs of the musicians, praise-singers, and other dissociating devotees. Once it has been determined that a demonstration of trance is expected of a cult-adept the social pressure operating to force him to fall into an ASC is considerable. As members of the cult fall into trance they may join the musicians and praise-singers in consciously or unconsciously encouraging reluctant devotees to follow their lead. Suggestion also has a spatial dimension. If a devotee can be seated in the correct place (immediately in front of the musicians) and in the correct position (reclining on the ground, leaning on one elbow) or persuaded to dance in front of the musicians during music appropriate to the spirit 'on his head', other trance-inducing factors may operate to produce dissociation.

Special Breathing Techniques

Hyperventilation which leads to an abnormal loss of carbon dioxide from the blood is a common technique used to induce possession-trance among cult-adepts. It is most conspicuous during 'serial-induction' type events when it is coupled with heightened motor activity. In such situations dissociation follows energetic dancing and leaping.

Hypoventilation, the increase of carbon dioxide in the blood due to under breathing, is less obvious in its use by mediums. It is most certainly a part of the preparation for an ASC by mediums whose other techniques include bodily limitation as in 'simultaneous-induction' type events. Cult-adepts who expect to be ridden by spirits believed to be responsible for paralysis, itching, and leprosy most often begin their preparations while seated on the ground and use hypo-ventilation techniques to induce possession-trance.

Drugs

Except for the use of amphetamines by some musicians who claim that they are needed for endurance, cult performances are not occasions for drug-taking. In fact, mediums generally do not use even mildly hallucinogenic drugs (such as marihuana) even when possession-trance rituals are not anticipated.

SOCIAL AND CULTURAL CONTEXTS

At one level the social function of bori performances is to direct attention to such events as marriage and naming ceremonies, occasions when they are frequently held. Considered in this way possession-trance is a satisfaction of curiosity or an interest in novelty. As Beattie and Middleton have noted for 'spirit-possession' cults in general, they may be a means of 'letting off steam'—a drama, theatrical performance, 'providing lively entertainment and a means of catharsis' (1969: xxviii). However, the essential character of the bori cult is probably not simply that of a purely dramatic spectacle in which audiences watch a performance by cult-adepts in trance on a stage.

Viewed by Hausa participants, the utility of cult activities lies in their explanation of disease and its cure. Informants' statements are filled with reports of often spectacular cures of chronic mental and physical illnesses. While a bori 'cure' may do little more than provide a means whereby repressed needs and desires can be expressed in a socially sanctioned way, symbolically restated in the notion of healing as an achievement of harmony with the inflicting cause rather than as its elimination, the fact remains that it allows formerly 'maladjusted' individuals to lead an 'acceptable' social life. Physical ailments are another matter. Some of them are psychosomatic and are treated identically to mental illnesses. Where organic causes (from the observer's point of view) are at the root of a physical ailment, the sufferer either recovers because of some kind of curative power of the mind properly harnessed—as in the cures reported to me of patients suffering the early signs of leprosy—or is pronounced 'incurable' by bori means. Even in hopeless cases the sufferer is encouraged to participate in the cult and derives some measure of group support and understanding for his affliction.

An important social aspect of bori cult emerges when considering the status of cult-adepts and cult musicians. Lewis (1966: 1969: 1971b) and Beattie and Middleton (1969) comment on what has been termed the cult of deprivation. Mediums who in everyday life occupy positions of relatively low status and who might be said to attain an element of social redress or an increase of prestige through cult involvement are not uncommon, particularly in Somaliland. Where there is a high degree of participation by women in cult activities, a corresponding association between male homosexuality with transvestism and possession-trance may be evident (Beattie and Middleton 1969: xxv).

The Hausa case affords a good example of both deprivation and deviation.

In a Muslim social fabric which stratifies society into horizontally separate groups, cult-adepts are almost outside the pale. Even when farming is their major source of income, mediums are viewed by the society as a whole as somehow 'different' from other farmers whose occupation is respectable enough if not highly placed. Female participants in the cult are stereotyped as prostitutes, women who should be married according to the tenets of Hausa society and Islam but who choose to remain single for personal or economic reasons, and are recruited from the lowest social stratum of their society. While all women in traditional Hausa society are treated as second-class citizens, female mediums are viewed with particular suspicion by non-cult people because of their refusal to accept their 'proper' social role. Some male participants are clearly homosexuals and not a small percentage of these are transvestites. All are considered as deviants from 'normal' social behaviour.

Musicians and praise-singers are also placed at the bottom of the social hierarchy. All musicians share this low social placement, royal musicians and popular performers included, but bori musicians seem to have an unusually low position and, except for artistic considerations based on creativity and virtuosity, are rarely ranked above any other type of musical group. If their status is low at least they may attain social recognition based on musical excellence.

All of these people—prostitutes, homosexuals, transvestites, musicians, and, it should be generally added, people possessed by supernatural spirits—deviate in one way or another from what is considered socially acceptable. Within the bori cult they are able to attain a measure of social prestige not possible in Hausa society as a whole.

Another aspect of the possession-trance cult which was examined in this study is the way in which individual and group bondedness and separateness are revealed during public performances. Far from merely providing 'entertainment' for such non-cult events as weddings and naming ceremonies the structure of possession-trance activities provides an occasion for the realignment and reaffirmation of the elements of the Hausa social fabric. Indeed, the absence of this type of context from performances arranged on a 'fee' or 'contract' basis, including bori ceremonies held for private audiences and the growing number of folk arts festivals (in other words, staged demonstrations), has sometimes led to an evaluation of bori as a form of Hausa drama at best or even a sham. Participants clearly distinguish between socially meaningful and artificial performances, but when the possession-trance component of the event is considered authentic even a staged demonstration does not invalidate the concept of supernatural involvement in the lives of mortals.

When a possession-trance performance is also the occasion for significant gift-giving[1] by non-adepts (typically, when it may be described as 'public') individuals state their separateness through prostations. Making a claim to the evaluation of his character as generous, an individual both fulfils the expectation that he give a required number of gifts prior to and during the event to ensure its orderly progress when he is its host, and 'spontaneously' gives gifts not directly associated with event structure. Musicians receive the gifts and witness their giving, but they do not reciprocate with gifts of their own. The burden of that obligation falls on other guests (or hosts) who, similar to the first giver, make prestations to assert their generosity. This asymmetrical exchange binds opposing givers together, underlining their social relationship as affines or as people serving the same spirit. It also results in the public acknowledgement of an individual giver's claim to being a person with *kirki* (lit. excellence; kindness and generosity) (cf. Barkow 1974). Failure to give or reciprocate or an inadequate prestation leads to a depreciation of a person's prestige and, by extension, of the social position of the group he represents.

RITUAL AND SYMBOLISM

Part of the task of this study has been to examine bori from the point of entry provided by its ritual and symbols. Accepting Turner's definitions, ritual refers to the 'prescribed formal behaviour for occasions not given over to technological routine, having reference to beliefs in mystical beings or powers', and symbol as the 'smallest unit of ritual which still retains the specific properties of ritual behavior . . . the ultimate unit of specific structure in a ritual context' (1967: 19). The ritual symbols which have been considered include objects, activities, relationships, events, gestures, and spatial units in bori activities.

As was mentioned above initiation into the bori cult is achieved through the process of a ritual of affliction. Rituals of affliction are performed on a non-automatic basis and are prompted by the diagnosis of a spiritually caused illness. During such rituals the formerly ill administer to the currently ill, and so it is that religious status in the bori cult is achieved through affliction. Thus, as Turner observes, affliction has a double meaning: it is both a punishment for some kind of neglect or transgression—for bori spirits do not possess a victim without provocation—and it is evidence of a spirit's selection of his victim as a cult member (1967: 10). But initiation also marks the transition from one social status to another, from outsider to insider, at least as far as cult membership is concerned. Most social transitions fall under the heading of life-crisis rituals (birth/naming, marriage, death) and are concerned with ascribed statuses, but the bori initiation is a ritual applied to an achieved status.

Bori rituals may also be periodic as in the performances for such life-crisis events as naming and marriage during which the performance takes on the aura of a theatrical display: or cyclical as in annual performances just after the harvest. These performances do not fall within the rubric of rituals of affliction and have been considered for their sociological or psychotherapeutic effect. In many respects they resemble what Marks has described as 'reliving the call' (1974), initiates reaffirming their pact with iskoki.

All cult performances are characterised by special instruments, music, objects, behaviour, and spatial considerations. They may be viewed from the perspective of psychological dissociation or altered states of consciousness as described earlier, but they also provide the investigator with a symbolic inventory. This inventory has been analysed with an attempt to discover its 'meaning' based on a model provided by Turner (1967). Turner describes three analytical divisions of symbolic meaning each of which is tied to a process used to obtain the data. The first of these is 'exegetical' meaning and consists of the explanations of the actors, both laymen and ritual specialists. The second is 'operational' meaning and concerns observations of the use of ritual symbols and their obtainment, and how they are prepared and manipulated in a rite. The third is 'positional' meaning, the meaning of any symbol in relation to other symbols in the system, particularly in a given set of ceremonial occasions (1967: 50-1).

Some symbols seem to be more important than others to the actors, and these are described as dominant symbols. A central feature of dominant symbols is in their polysemy or multivocality (Turner 1967: 50; 1969: 41-2), that is the unity of sometimes disparate meanings within the same symbol. Possession-trance itself is a dominant, central symbol in bori ritual. It denotes the presence of a possessing spirit, and participants behave differently towards a cult-adept when he is in trance than when he is not. A person ceases to be when in possession-trance; it is the spirit which has possessed him which becomes the centre of attention. Possession-trance also symbolizes cult membership, dividing the world into bori mediums and laymen. It is symbolic of good and proper behaviour within the bori context and of the cure which the medium enjoys. Within the ritual situation itself possession-trance is a concrete indication of time and place. It is a marker in ritual process in which the activities in an event may be positioned with reference to the onset and conclusion of dissociation.

Possession-trance also has positional meaning and depends upon other symbols, including various psychological and physiological factors, for its operation. Aural, specifically musical, symbols are central among those upon which possession-trance depends. Needham has commented on the importance of percussion and percussive effects in communicating with the spirit world (1972: 391-8), but he doubts that any other musical factors need be included in a general statement on transition ritual and shamanistic performances. However, the Hausa bori cult is a rather more specific case, and melody *is* judged to be significant both in inducing ASCs and in cueing the behaviour of the participants in possession-trance (see below). It is concluded here that music, consisting of melody, form and rhythm, is a dominant symbol in bori ritual. It also has a polysemic aspect characteristic of other dominant symbols. Music identifies cult activities in general and ritual phases in particular. It further provides a statement of the interdependence between socially marginal groups, musicians and cult-adepts. Simultaneously it underscores the separateness of these groups. Musicians themselves do not fall into trance and are not, at least in their role as musicians, initiated members of the bori cult.

Special mention can be made of the equestrian theme of the bori cult and the importance of horsemanship in Hausa society in general. Kings and commoners alike keep horses in their domestic compounds when they can afford them, and they are a most highly prized domestic animal. During the major religious festivals in Islam, Id al-Fitr and Id al-Kabir, the display of horses bedecked in colourful splendour and of expert horsemanship in the many ceremonial parades are a prominent feature. According to the statements of the actors in the bori cult, possession-trance ceremonies are symbolic of such Hausa parades. Consistent with general parade organization, the spirit who 'leads the way' is a musician, and the king of the spirit world is somewhere in the middle, preceded and followed by spirits in a ranked social hierarchy.

Cult-adepts themselves are described as horses of the gods, and supernatural spirits are said to 'mount' them at the onset of possession-trance and 'dismount' at its conclusion. Special subsidiary roles during cult performances are assumed by people described as 'grooms', and it is their responsibility to guide the actions of particularly reckless horses.

MUSIC

A significant portion of the oral tradition of the bori cult is expressed in song and chanted form, and its preservation and transmission is in the hands of musicians, non-initiated associates of the cult. The melodies, rhythms, and texts which are the constituent elements of bori songs are all identified with particular spirits and are used to praise them, invoke their presence, and direct their activity during possession-trance events. Well-known or popular spirits may be addressed with as many as five different songs but most have only one associated with them. Since it is not uncommon for proficient bori musicians to be familiar with the behaviour, relationships, and characteristics of as many as 130 divine horsemen the number of songs such musicians know is large, frequently exceeding 160 items.

For purposes of classification four types of song structures are used for the entire corpus. One of these is the solo type in which one musician, usually the leader of the ensemble but occasionally a senior member of the chorus or a pure vocalist, takes the entire responsibility for the singing. When the ensemble's leader does the singing he usually alternates sung verses of variable length with purely instrumental passages. When another member of the group does the singing verses follow one another with little delay, and only the best vocalists can avoid using repetition (which is described as an undesirable characteristic when frequently employed) to keep the song going.

A second song type follows a litany pattern. The ensemble leader and the chorus alternate singing, the chorus either repeating the leader's statement or singing its semantic complement. Particularly when the leader's and chorus' phrases are different the role of the principal member of the chorus assumes an importance in directing the choral response. There is a potential for disunity when the chorus is singing phrases textually unlike those of the leader, but chorus members are expected to yield to the direction of their section leader.

Songs of the refrain type constitute a third category in the corpus. Most of such songs use a single choral response which is repeated after every verse sung by the leader. A smaller number includes two refrains, the selection depending on the specific verse preceding it. Many verses are 'bound' to a specific refrain and reveal highly patterned, rehearsed structures. When, however, verses and refrains are not tied together, the former occurring in phrases of varying lengths, melodic and rhythmic cues are used at the end of a verse to indicate to the chorus when the primary or general refrain should be sung.

Songs of the fourth type have no sung text. Such purely instrumental pieces may, however, have an implied text identified with the spirit with which the song is associated. Songs in this category frequently have a higher musical density based on pulse and individual sounds per unit of time than vocal pieces.

The criteria which determine the selection of one form over another are based on the temporal order of possession-trance rituals, the identity of the spirit addressed, and the availability of a suitable horse for a given spirit. Specific songs for spirits are invariably sung using the same structural 'rules' from occasion to occasion. Thus, songs and forms are bound together regardless of when they are performed. Ritual structure, however, requires that spirits be addressed in parade and hierarchical order, and viewed in this way it is the spirits which are broadly ordered and not song forms. Depending on the type of trance-induction method used in the ritual, 'fast' pieces (vocal or instrumental) for each spirit which are also associated with its arrival tend to be included or excluded as the spirit is addressed. Rituals in which adepts fall into a state of possession-trance serially, one after the other in parade order, include quick-tempo pieces to assist in induction through hyperactivity prepared with inactivity. Rituals in which adepts fall into trance simultaneously at a special point in the event avoid fast pieces unless they are needed to encourage the trance of a 'difficult' medium. Simultaneous induction with a general induction piece—always the song for Magajiyar Jangare—is achieved by inactivity prepared with hyperactivity. When no mount is available for the spirit addressed all of its songs, fast and slow, vocal and instrumental, may be played with little fear of upsetting event structure. In such cases pieces which would ordinarily be used to accompany the spirit's arrival are merely danced to, and no one is expected to fall into trance. These may in fact be used to prepare the limitation of bodily acitvity characteristic of simultaneous induction.

Chanted phrases and praise-epithets consitute another part of the cult's oral tradition entrusted to musicians. These phrases which are like songs in that they are tied to specific spirits provide a storehouse for the shared cultural knowledge about who the divine horsemen are, what they do, and how they are tied to specific spirits provide a storehouse for the shared cultural knowledge about who the divine horsemen are, what they do, and how they are related to each other. Many are included in spirits' songs as sung or implied texts while others are only broadcast by praise-shouters as performing musicians invoke the residents of Jangare.

The future of the bori cult is as uncertain as any institution rooted in the past. As urban people become more 'modern' they tend to turn their backs on the ways of their parents. As long as it is believed that supernatural spirits are part of the reason why mortals suffer misfortune and illness and that the same spirits provide a source for cures the cult will be able to maintain its vitality. The number of people participating in bori rituals seems never to have been particularly large, but it is significant to note that replacements continue to appear among the ranks of the horses of the gods and the musicians who serve them. The bori cult has faced condemnation in the past, and it has survived despite the zeal of those who sought to eliminate it. Part of its solution was to include new elements with the old, an important example being the addition of Muslim cleric spirits to match the influence of Islam. Cult-adepts are not afraid of the future, facing it instead with a kind of quiet resignation. As it is said of the Sorceress, 'What does it matter if you eat my soul? If you do we will go about together.'

NOTES

[1]Gift-giving is always a part of 'meaningful' performances. The gifts may be small or merely promised as in the case of events not really open nor widely attended by the non-initiated public, but they never seem to be absent altogether. Even such highly restricted events as initiations and consultations imply sets of exchanges between adepts and spirits, adepts and musicians, or adepts themselves.

APPENDICES

Appendix A • Hausa Glossary and Index

Abamu *(Àbaamù):* a supernatural spirit in House 6, 94
Abba *(Abbà):* praise-name for Kuturu, the Leper, 86
Abdullahi *(Àbdùllaahì):* personal name for Sarkim Makada, Chief of Drummers, 94
Adamu *(Aadamù):* Adam; personal name for Mai Dawa, Owner of the Bush, 98
akayau *(akayau):* metal rattle, 52, 60 n.
Alhaji *(Àlhaajìi):* Pilgrim; title for a man who has been on the pilgrimage to Mecca, 60 n.
aljan *(àljan)* or aljani *(àljanìi);* fem. aljana *(àljanaa);* pl. aljanu *(àljànuu);* Arabic: jinn, supernatural spirit, 4
Ali *(Àli):*personal name for Kunnau, 77
alilliba *(alillìbaa):* tree, *Cordia abyssinica,* 52
Alkali *(Àlkaalìi):* Muslim Judge; title for Wanzami, the Barber, 68, 78
Alkalin Jangare *(Àlkaalin Jangare):* Muslim Judge of Jangare; title for Wanzami, 74
Almajira *(Àlmaajìra):* Female Quranic Pupil; wife of Kuturu, the Leper; a supernatural spirit in House 4, 84
almajiri *(àlmaajìrii):* Quranic pupil, 60 n.
amada *(aamadaa):* style of women's performance, 51
amale *(amaalèe):* lit. 'huge camel'; low-pitched string on the garaya lute, 61 n.
Amina *(Amiinà):* a supernatural spirit in House 6, 92
Arziki *(Arzìki):* Prosperity; a supernatural spirit in House 3, 82
Awwali *(Awwàli):* a supernatural spirit in House 8, 98
Azurfa *(Azùrfa):* Silver; a supernatural spirit in House 1, 72

Baba *(Bàaba):* Father, 38
babbar garaya *(bàbbar gàraayaa):* large plucked lute, 52, 60 n.
Babbar Salla *(Bàbbar Sallàa):* the Greater Feast; Id al-Kabir, 64
Badakuwa *(Bàadaakùwa):* a supernatural spirit in House 2, 76, 78

Throughout this Glossary and Index the transcriptions within the parentheses follow these conventions: Long vowels are indicated by double leters; single letters are used to indicate short vowels. Low tones are marked with an /`/ over the vowel to which it applies, and high tones are left unmarked. The rarer falling tone is marked with a /ˆ/. The bilabial glottalized stop is written as /ɓ/; the alveolar glottalized stop as /ɗ/; the alveolar fricative/affricate as /ts/; the glottalized semivowel as /'y/; and the velar glottalized stop as /ƙ/.

Bafilatana *(Bàfilaatàna):* Fulani Woman; descriptive name for Bakar Doguwa, the Black Tall-Woman, 70

Bagwariya *(Bàgwaarìya):* Gwari Woman; descriptive name for Arziki, Prosperity; a supernatural spirit in House 3, 82, 83, 84, 105 *(see also* Example 14)

Baidu *(Ɓaidù):* a supernatural spirit in House 5, 89

Bakar Doguwa *(Baƙar Dooguwaa):* the Black Tall-Woman; a supernatural spirit in House 1, 67, 70, 84, 89 *(see also* Inna)

Bako Mashi *(Bàakoo Maashì):* Guest Spear; a supernatural spirit in House 4, 92

Baleri *(Ɓaleerì):* Black-Skinned One; a supernatural spirit, 97, 98 *(see also* Duna)

bandiri *(bàndiirìi):* circular, frame-drum, 34, 60 n.

Barade *(Baràade):* title for a mounted warrior; a supernatural spirit in House 2, 76, 80–81, 99 *(see also* Example 12)

barandami *(bàrandamìi):* hatchet, axe, 100, 104

Barhaza *(Bàrhaazà):* a supernatural spirit in House 8, 67, 74, 89, 98, 100–101 *(see also* Example 22)

Barkono Bature *(Bàrkòono Bàtuurè):* Pepper, North African; a supernatural spirit in House 11, 106–7

Batoyi *(Bàtòyi):* a supernatural spirit in House 12, 66, 110

batsa *(baatsaa):* indecent remarks, 33

Bature *(Bàtuurèe):* European, North African, Arab, 107; a supernatural spirit *(see* Barkono)

bawa *(baawàa):* pl. bayi *(baayìi)* slave, 31

biki *(bìkii):* feast, especially for a wedding, 134

boka *(bookaa):* medicine man, 'native doctor,' 6, 48

bori *(bòorii):* Hausa cult of possession-trance; a supernatural spirit

Buba *(Buubà):* a supernatural spirit in House 5, 92

busa *(buusàa):* to blow, 35

busan sarewa *(buusàn sàreewàa):* blowing a whistle, 28

buta *(buutàa):* gourd rattle, 37, 72, 94, 135

Buzu *(Buuzuu):* pl. Buzaye *(Buuzàayee)* Tuareg serf, 65, 98

cashiya *(caashiyaa):* speeded-up tempo for dancing; instrumental display piece, 59, 73

Ci Goro *(Cìi Goorò):* Eat Kola-nuts; a supernatural spirit in House 1, 72

cim baki *(cim bàakii):* goatskin lining around the hole on a garaya lute, 53

Ciwo Babu Magani *(Ciiwòo Baabù Maagàni):* Illness with No Medicine; a supernatural spirit in House 1, 72, 97

dada *(dàadaa):* special initiation charm, 130 *(see also* 'ya)

Dafau *(Dàafau):* praise name for Sarkim Makada, Chief of Drummers, 94

Dakiro *(Dàaƙìròo):* market for lepers, 85

damara *(d̃amaràa):* pl. damaru *(d̃amàruu)* medicine belt, 50, 83, 115

Damatsiri *(Dàamàatsiirì):* a green snake; a supernatural spirit in House 4, 87

dam bori *(d̃am bòorii):* lit. 'son-of the bori'; male cult-adept, 12, 126

dam fari *(d̃am farìi):* lit. 'son-of white'; male initiate

Dam Mama *(d̃am Màama):* Son-of Breast; a supernatural spirit in House 11, 107, 108 *(see also* Kwatangiri, Dam Mama)

Dam Musa *(d̃àm Muusà):* Son-of Musa; Small Musa; a supernatural spirit, 87 *(see* Danko)

dan Daudu *(d̃àn Daudù):* pl. 'yan Daudu *('yan Daudù)* lit. 'son-of Daudu'; male homosexual/transvestite; a supernatural spirit in House 1, 18

Dan Galadima *(ɗan Gàlàadiimà):* the Prince; a supernatural spirit in House 1, 18, 25–26, 30 n., 67, 70, 72–74, 76, 78, 92, 94, 97, 115, 116 n. *(see also* Examples 6, 7, and 8)

Dan Kama *(ɗan Kaamàa)* pl. 'Yan Kama *('Yan Kaamàa):* lit. 'son-of Catching'; Hausa comedian, 32, 33, 34

Danko Dam Musa *(Dànko ɗam Muusà):* Danko, Small Musa; a snake spirit in House 4, 22, 84, 87–89 *(see also* Example 17)

Dan Mama *(see* Dam Mama)

daraja *(darajàa):* social rank, 46

Daudu *(Daudù),* 30 n. *(see also* Dan Galadima or dan Daudu)

dodo *(dòodoo):* evil spirit, 6

dogarai *(dòogàrai):* s. dogari *(dòogarìi)* bodyguards, 65

Doguwa Ta Kwance *(Dooguwaa Ta Kwànce):* Tall-Woman of Lying-Down; a supernatural spirit, 70, 116 n. *(see also* Bakar Doguwa or Inna)

doki *(dookìi):* lit. 'stallion'; male cult-adept, 12

duma *(dumaa):* gourd, 52

Duna *(Duunà):* a supernatural spirit in House 7, 96, 97–98, 110

Duna Rage Iri *(Duunàa Ràgee Irì):* a supernatural spirit in House 8, 98

dundu *(ɗunɗuu):* thorny tree *Dichrostachys nutans;* resting place for Kuturu, the Leper, 86, 114

durkusa *(durkùsaa):* bow; kneel down, 45

fadanci *(faadancii):* lit. 'court language'; obsequiousness; flattery, 45

farar bafilatana *(farar bàfilaatànaa):* type of grass, 91

fasa kabewa *(faasàa kàbeewàa):* lit. 'breaking of a pumpkin'; bori agricultural ritual, 10 n., 134

Filani *(Filaanii):* Fulani, 65

gada *(gàdaa):* crested duiker *Cephalophus grimmi,* 52

Gajere *(Gàjeere):* Short Man; praise-name for Mai Dawa, Owner of the Bush, 98

Galla *(Gallà):* a supernatural spirit in House 11, 105

gandu *(ganduu):* co-operative farm on ancestral land, 6, 113

ganga *(gàngaa):* double-membrane, cylindrical drum, 51

garaya *(gàraayàa):* two-stringed plucked lute, 35, 60 n., 69, 71, 73, 135

gidan karuwai *(gìdan kàarùuwai):* house-of prostitutes, 13

girka *(gìrkaa):* healing or initiation ritual, 121, 123–24, 127ff

giwa *(gìiwaa):* lit. 'elephant'; low-pitched string on the garaya plucked lute, 61 n.

godiya *(goodìyaa):* lit. 'mare'; female cult-adept, 12

goge *(gòogee):* single-stringed, bowed lute, 135

Goje *(Goojè):* praise-name for Kuturu, the Leper; praise-name for any Madaki, senior councillor, 84, 85

goron gwiwa *(gooron gwiiwàa):* lit. 'kola-nuts for the knee'; pre-trance gift to mediums, 138

goron kira *(gooron kiraa:)* lit. 'kola-nuts for calling'; performance preparation gift, 135

Gurgunya *(Gurgunyà):* Lame-Woman; a supernatural spirit in House 6, 89 *(see also* Hawa'u, Gurgunya)

Gwaurau Mai Kwalabe *(Gwàurau Mài Kwalàabe):* Witch-Doctor With Glass-Bottles; a supernatural spirit in House 11, 108; *(also called* Gwaro Mai Kwalabe)

habaici *(habaicii):* hurtful innuendo, 33

Hadiza *(Hàdiizà):* a supernatural spirit, 70 *(see also* Bakar Doguwa or Inna)

Hajjo *(Hajjò):* a supernatural spirit in House 5, 67, 90
Halima *(Hàliimà):* a supernatural spirit in House 11, 108
Harakwai *(Hàraakwài):* a supernatural spirit in House 7, 96
Hardo *(Hardò):* praise-name for Sarkim Filani, Chief of the Fulani, 90
hasatan akebe *(haasatàn àkèeɓee):* concealed gift, 29
Hawa'u *(Hàwa'ù):* a supernatural spirit in House 6, 89, 90, 92 *(see also* Gurgunya, Lame-Woman)

Ibirahim *(Ìbìraahìm):* personal name for Sarkin Rafi, Chief of Well-Watered Land, 78
Inna *(Innà):* Fulani: Mother; a supernatural spirit in House 1, 22, 70–72, 75, 84, 98, 99, 100, 123 *(see also* Bakar Doguwa and Examples 3, 4, and 5)
iska *(iskàa):* pl. iskoki *(iskookii)* supernatural spirit, 3, 6, 14, 63, 82, 86, 110, 121, 134
Iyani *(Iyàani):* a supernatural spirit in House 8, 98

Ja'e *(Jà'e):* a supernatural spirit in House 6, 67, 90, 92
jaki *(jàakii):* lit. 'donkey'; bridge of a garaya plucked lute, 52
jifa *(jiifàa):* lit. 'throwing'; bori jumping into the air and landing on the buttocks with legs outstretched, 73, 76, 79, 81
jigo *(jìigòo):* lit. 'pole'; sacred corner or tree in a cult person's compound, 14

kadanya *(kadânyàa):* shea tree *Butyrospermum parkii,* 71
Kafaran *(Kàfàrân):* a supernatural spirit in House 11, 108
kalangu *(kàlànguu):* double-membrane, hourglass-shaped, pressure drum, 31
kamar amarya *(kaamàr amaryaa):* lit. 'capture of the bride'; ceremonial aspect of the Hausa marriage ritual, 134
kanwa *(kanwaa):* potash, 22
kanya *(kanyàa):* African ebony tree *Diospyros mespiliformis,* 22, 71
Karamar Salla *(Kàramar Sallàa):* Small Sallah; Muslim festival of *Id al-fitr,* 29 *(see also* Babbar Salla)
karba *(kàrɓaa):* to receive, 94
Karbo *(Kàrɓo):* a supernatural spirit in House 6, 94
karuwa *(kaarùuwàa* or *kaarùwàa):* pl. karuwai *(kàarùuwai* or *kàarùwai)* formerly married, now single person; prostitute, 11, 123–24
karuwanci *(kaaruwancìi):* prostitution, 11
Kasa *(Kaasa):* Puff-Adder; a supernatural spirit in House 6, 92
kasambara *(kàsamɓaraa):* brush-like instrument made from guinea corn stalk, 54
Kaura *(Kaura):* praise-name for Kuturu, the Leper, 84
kazagin amada *(kazagin aamadaa):* small calabash in an amada group for women's performances, 51
kida *(kidàa):* to drum; rhythmic/melodic pattern; section of a possession-trance performance, 35, 69, 135
kidam bori *(kidâm bòorii):* lit. 'bori drumming'; performance with possession-trance, 28, 136
kidan amada *(kidân aamadaa):* lit. 'amada drumming'; women's amada performance, 135 *(see also* kidan kwarya)
kidan bori *(see* kidam bori)
kidan garaya *(kidân gàraayaa):* strumming (lit. 'drumming') a two-stringed garaya plucked lute, 28
kidan goge *(kidân gòogee):* bowing (lit. 'drumming') a single-stringed goge lute, 28

kidan juyi *(kidàn juuyìi):* lit. 'drumming for a change of state'; ceremony to quiet a supernatural spirit's unrest, 134

kidan kwarya *(kidàn ƙwaryaa):* drumming on large, inverted, hemispherical calabashes for women's possession-trance ceremonies, 28, 135

kidan wasa *(kidàn wàasaa):* lit. 'drumming of play'; performance without possession-trance, 136

kirari *(kiraarìi):* descriptive praise-epithet, 39, 59

komo *(koomoo):* large plucked lute, 52; *(see also* babbar garaya)

kotso *(kòotsoo):* single-membrane, hand-struck hourglass-shaped pressure drum, 60 n.

Kuge *(ƙugè):* a supernatural spirit in House 4, 65

Kukar Makau *(Kuukar Màakau):* a baobob tree known as Makau (lit. 'Slave'?) near Ningi, 63–64

kuli-kuli *(ƙulìi-ƙulìi):* ground-nut cakes, 106

Kunnau *(Kùnnau):* a supernatural spirit in House 2, 77

kunshi *(ƙunshìi):* ceremony to apply henna to bride's hands and feet, 134

Kura *(Kuura):* a supernatural spirit (male) in House 5, 67

Kure *(Kuurè):* the Hyena; a supernatural spirit in House 6, 84, 89, 90, 92–94, 97, 98, 114 *(see also* Example 19)

Kuri *(Kuri):* a supernatural spirit in House 3; wife of Malam Alhaji, the Pilgrim, 82

kutare *(kutàaree):* s. kuturu *(kuturuu)* lepers, 65

Kuturu *(Kuturu):* the Leper; a supernatural spirit in House 4, 65, 70, 84–87, 96, 114, 137 *(see also* Examples 15 and 16)

kwadayi *(kwàdàayii):* greediness, 38

Kwakiya *(ƙwaakìya):* Black-Hooded Cobra; a supernatural spirit in House 4, 87, 92

kwanan zaune *(kwaanan zàunee):* lit. 'night spent sitting up'; type of public possession-trance performance, 132, 134

kwarya *(ƙwaryaa)* pl. koruka *(ƙoorukàa):* large, hemispherical calabash, 13, 25

kwaryar goge *(ƙwaryar gòogee):* hemispherical calabash used to accompany the goge bowed lute, 56

kwaryar kidan ruwa *(ƙwaryar kidàn ruwaa):* hemispherical calabashes which are inverted and played on calabashes containing water during women's possession-trance performances, 35, 50

Kwatangiri, Dam Mama *(Kwàtangirì, dam Màama):* Kwatangiri Son-of Breast; a supernatural spirit in House 11, 107–8 *(see also* Dam Mama)

Kyadi *(ƙyaadì):* Dried Body; praise-name for Kuturu, the Leper, 84

Labuda *(Làabudà):* a supernatural spirit in House 6, 89, 90

Ladi Mayya *(Laadi Mâyya):* Lahdi the Sorceress; a supernatural spirit in House 7, 97, 110

Lashe-Lashe *(Làashe-Làashe):* Continual Licking; a supernatural spirit in House 12, 110

leda *(leedàa):* plastic or artificial cat-gut, 52

Mabuga *(Mabùuga):* Corn-Threshing Place; a supernatural spirit in House 1, 68

mabushi *(mabùushìi):* horn blower, 35

maciji *(macìijii):* pl, macizai *(màacìzai)* snake, 65

Madaki *(Mâadaakìi):* senior councillor, 65, 84, 92 *(see also* Kuturu, the Leper)

Madi *(Màadi):* Revealed One; praise-name for Sarkim Makada, Chief of Drummers, 94

Magajiyar Bori *(Magaajìyar Bòorìi):* Heiress of Bori; a female leader in the possession-trance cult, 13, 25ff

madaci *(madàacii):* African mahogany tree *Khaya ivorensis,* 71

Magajiyar Jangare *(Magaajìyar Jangare):* Heiress of Jangare; a supernatural spirit in House 2, 70, 74, 76–78, 96, 135, 138

magudiya *(maguudìyaa):* lit.'female ululator'; high-pitched string on the garaya plucked lute, 61 n. *(see also* giwa)

Mahadi *(Màhàdi):* Revealed One; praise-name for Sarkim Makada, Chief of Drummers, 94 *(see also* Madi)

maharbi *(mahàrbii):* pl. maharba *(mahàrbaa)* bowman, archer, hunter, 65, 98

mahauta *(mahàutaa):* pl. butchers, 65

Mai Babban Zane *(Mài Bàbban Zanè):* Owner of a Large Body Cloth; praise-name for Magajiyar Jangare, 77

Mai Baka *(Mài Bàka):* Owner of a Bow; a supernatural spirit in House 8, 98, 115 *(see also* Mai Dawa)

Mai Dawa *(Mài Dawà):* Owner of the Bush; a supernatural spirit in House 8, 65, 74, 98–99, 100, 115 *(see also* Example 21)

Mai Fitila *(Mài Fìtìlà):* Owner of a Lamp; a supernatural spirit in House 1, 72

mai garaya *(mài gàraayàa):* player of the double-stringed plucked lute, 36

mai gida *(mài gidaa):* lit. 'owner of the house'; compound head, 6, 14

Mai Gizo *(Mài Gìzo):* Owner of Matted Hair; a supernatural spirit in House 9, 67, 91, 98, 101, 103–04 *(see also* Examples 24 and 25)

mai goge *(mài gòogee):* player of the single-stringed bowed lute, 36

Mai Iyali *(Mài Ìyaalì):* Owner of a Family; a supernatural spirit, 77 *(see* Kunnau)

mai kira *(mài kiraa):* lit. 'owner of calling'; performance host, 136

Maimuna *(Màimunà):* a supernatural spirit in House 6, 92

Mai Ruga Dukko *(Mài Rùgaa Dukkò):* Owner of the Cattle-Encampment Dukko; praise-name for Sarkim Filani, Chief of the Fulani, 89, 90

Majaciki *(Majàacikì):* Drawer of the Belly; a supernatural spirit; praise-name for Danko, 87

mai kiwo *(mài kiiwòo):* pl. masu kiwo *(màasuu kiiwòo)* herder, groom; attendant, 12

mai magana *(mài màganàa):* lit. 'owner of the speech'; a speaker at a bori possession-trance performance, 40

mai magani *(mài maagànii):* possessor of medicine; herbalist, 7, 108

mai mukuru *(mài mùkuruu):* lit. 'owner of a woman's loin cloth'; initiation assistant, 127

mai sarauta *(mài sàrautàa):* pl. masu sarautaa *(màasuu sàrautàa)* title-holder, 11

Majidadin Kwarya *(Majìidaadìn kwaryaa):* lit. 'Majidadi of the kwarya gourd'; female musician, 36

makadi *(makàdìi):* drummer, 35

makafi *(màkàafii):* pl. blind persons, 65

makau *(màakau):* a type of grass, 75

makera *(makèeraa):* pl. blacksmiths, 65

malam *(maalàm):* pl. malamai *(màalàmai)* Quranic scholar, 11, 64, 65

Malam Alhaji *(Maalàm Àlhaajì):* Malam, the Pilgrim; a supernatural spirit in House 3, 16, 65, 68, 72, 75, 82–83, 91, 101, 105 *(see also* Example 13)

Mamman *(Mammàn):* praise-name for Dan Galadima, the Prince, 84

Manzo Maye *(Manzò Maayè):* Manzo Sorcerer; a supernatural spirit in either House 6 or House 12, 97

maratayi *(maràatàyii):* carrying strap for a garaya plucked lute, 53

maroki *(maròokii):* pl. maroka *(maròokaa)* male praise-shouter/musician, 28, 31, 35, 60 n., 65, 94, 111, 126

masakin kadawa *(masakin kadàawaa):* large calabash used for drumming, 51

Masharuwa *(Mashàaruwa):* Drinker of Water; rainbow serpent; a supernatural spirit in House 4, 87, 92

mawaki *(mawàaƙii):* pl. mawaka *(mawàaƙaa)* singer, 35, 40, 60 n.

mayu *(maayuu):* pl. sorcerers, 66

na gaskiya *(na gàskiyaa):* lit. 'of truth'; authentic (possession-trance), 24

Nakada *(Nàkaadà):* Causer of Downfall; a supernatural spirit in House 9, 82, 91, 101–3, 130, 138 *(see also* Example 23)

na karya *(na ƙàryaa):* lit. 'of lie'; fraudulent (possession-trance), 24

Na Matuwa *(Nà Maatuuwa):* One of the She-Asses; a supernatural spirit in House 5, 91

Nana'aishe *(Nànà'aishè):* a supernatural spirit in House 2; also known as Nana *(Nàana),* 76, 78, 79

rago mai tozali *(ràgoo mài toozàlii):* ram with black rings around the eyes, 73

Ramadan *(Ràmàdân):* the Muslim month of the Great Fast, 5

rarraba *(rarràbaa):* lit. 'to share out'; redistribution of gifts received at a public possession-trance performance, 135

riga *(rìigaa):* man's gown, 34

roko *(ròoƙoo):* lit. 'begging'; musician's craft, 31, 35

Sabon Gari *(Saabon Gàrii):* Strangers' Quarter (in northern cities non-northerners live here; in southern cities northerners live here), 33

sadaka *(sadakàa):* alms, charity, 27

Safiyanu *(Safiyaanù):* praise-name for Barde, 80

saki *(saaƙii):* cotton material of black and blue strands woven into a tiny check pattern, 73 *(see also* Dan Galadima)

salla *(sallàa):* lit. 'prayer'; festival, 29 *(see also* Karamar Salla)

Samami *(Samami):* Sudden Visitor; praise-name for Danko, 87

Sambo *(Sambò):* a supernatural spirit in House 5, 91

sana'a *(sàna'àa):* craft, 18, 31

Sanda Umaru *(Sandà Ùmarù):* (see Umaru Sanda Ba Buga)

sarauta *(sàrautàa):* pl. sarautu *(sàràutuu):* title or position, usually royal, 12

sarewa *(sàreewàa):* end-blown flute, 52

Sarkim Bicci *(Sarkim Biccì):* Chief of a Large Horse; a supernatural spirit in House 11, 108

Sarkim Bori *(Sarkim Bòorii):* Chief of the Bori; male cult leader, 12, 48

Sarkim Fagan *(Sarkim Fagàn):* a supernatural spirit in House 7, 92, 96, 98 *(see also* Sarkin Aljan Shekaratafe)

Sarkim Filani Dukko *(Sarkim Filàanii Dukkò):* the Chief of the Fulani, Dukko; a supernatural spirit in House 5, 65, 67, 74, 89–91 *(see also* Example 18)

Sarkim Makada *(Sarkim Makàadà):* Chief of Drummers; a supernatural spirit in House 6, 92, 94–96, 110–11; 115, 130, 133, 137 *(see also* Example 20)

Sarkin Aljan *(Sarkin Àljan):* the Chief of the Spirits; a supernatural spirit in House 1, 27, 62, 64, 65, 70 *(see also* Sarkin Aljan Sulemanu)

Sarkin Aljan Biddarene *(Sarkin Àljan Biddaareenè):* the Chief of the Spirits, Biddarene; a supernatural spirit in House 2, 65, 68, 70, 72, 76

Sarkin Aljan Shekaratafe *(Sarkin Àljan Shèekàràatàfe):* the Chief of the Spirits, Shekaratafe; a supernatural spirit in House 7, 65, 96 *(see also* Sarkim Fagan)

waka *(waakàa):* to sing; song, 35, 60 n.

wakar bori *(waakàr bòorii):* song for a bori spirit, 51

wakar kishiya *(waakàr kiishiyàa):* song for a jealous co-wife, 51

wakar nashadi *(waakàr nàshaadìi):* song of happiness, 51

wakar siyasa *(waakàr sìiyaasàa):* song for clemency, 51

wakar yabo *(waakàr yàboo):* song of praise, 51

wanka *(wankaa):* wash; medicinal application method, 132

Wanzami *(Wànzaamì):* the Barber; a supernatural spirit in House 1, 67, 68, 74–76, 78, 98
(*see also* Example 9)

wasa *(wàasaa):* lit. 'play'; performance with no possession-trance, 124

wasam bori *(wàasam bòorii):* lit. 'play of bori'; bori ceremony without a demonstration of
possession-trance, 122, 124, 135, 136, 137; (*see also* kidan wasa or wasa)

wasa na hira *(wàasaa na hìiraa):* lit. 'entertainment for chatting'; type of public possession-
trance performance, 132

wasan suna *(wàasan sunnaa):* naming ceremony, 134

wasar salla *(wàasar sallàa):* bori performances during Sallah octave usually held in or near
the Emir's palace, 134

Waziri *(Wàziirì):* Vizier; royal office-holder's title, 60 n.

Wazirin Kwarya *(Wàziirìn kwaryaa):* Vizier of the kwarya gourd, 36

wuni *(wunìi):* gift-giving ceremony on Friday afternoon following a wedding, 134

wurin kida *(wurìn kidàa):* cowrie shell plectrum for a garaya plucked lute, 53

wurin kidam buta *(wurìn kidàm buutaa):* cowrie shells fastened to the left hand and used
to play the buta gourd rattle, 54

'ya *('yaa):* special initiation charm, 130 (*see also* dada)

'yam bori *('yam bòorii):* lit. 'children of the bori'; cult adepts, trancers, 12; (*see also* dam bori
or 'yar bori)

'yan hamsin *('yan hàmsin):* lit. 'sons of fifty'; male homosexual, transvestite, 18

'yan lela *('yan leelàa):* pl. non-professional group of dancers consisting of Quranic 'pupils',
60 n.

'yar bori *('yar bòorii):* lit. 'daughter of the bori'; female cult-adept, trancer, 12

'yar fari *('yar farii):* lit. 'daughter of white'; female initiate, 127

Yariman Ruwa *(Yàriimàn Ruuwa* or *Yàriimàn Ruwa):* Yarima of Water; a supernatural spirit
in House 2, 76

'yar kwarya *('yar kwaryaa):* pl. 'yan kwarya *('yan kwaryaa)* female, hemispherical-gourd
player, 35, 51

'Yar Mairo *('Yar Mairo):* a supernatural spirit in House 1, 72

Yero *(Yerò):* personal name for Mai Gizo, Owner of Matted Hair, 103

Zabiya *(Zaabìya):* Woman Praise-Singer; a supernatural spirit in House 6, 94

zabiya *(zaabìyaa):* female praise-singer/musician, 34

Zainaba 'Yar Mahauta *(Zàinabà 'Yar Mahàuta):* Zainaba, Daughter of Butchers; a supernatural spirit in House 6, 67, 92

zakara mai sirdi *(zàkaràa mài sirdìi):* red cock with a saddle-shaped design on its back, 73

Zaki *(Zaakì):* Lion; a supernatural spirit in House 6, 89, 90

Zakoma *(Zaakòma):* praise-name for Ladi Mayya, 97

zambo *(zàmboo):* provocative speech and song, 33

zane *(zanèe):* body cloth, 50

zaure *(zaurèe):* lit. 'thatched, round entrance-porch to a compound'; house or section of the spirits' world, 65

zikiri *(zikìrii):* Muslim creed-formula, 60 n.

Zugu *(Zugu):* praise-name for Sarkin Rafi, Chief of Well-Watered Land, 78

zumbulutu *(zumbùlutùu):* type gourd, 52

Zarkalene *(Zurƙàaleenè):* personal name for Sarkin Aljan Zurkalene, 89

*Appendix **B** • Houses of Jangare*

(1) Genealogical Charts

Key

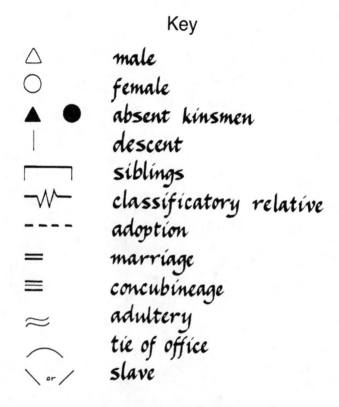

△	*male*
○	*female*
▲ ●	*absent kinsmen*
│	*descent*
⌐─┐	*siblings*
─W─	*classificatory relative*
- - - -	*adoption*
=	*marriage*
≡	*concubineage*
≈	*adultery*
⌒	*tie of office*
\ or /	*slave*

Key to Numerical Code

The first number in the code represents the spirit's residence; the second number represents the spirit's birthplace; the last number is the birthplace census number. Where it is not certain where a spirit was born, this is indicated with a "0."

I. HOUSE OF THE CHIEF OF THE SPIRITS, SULEMANU

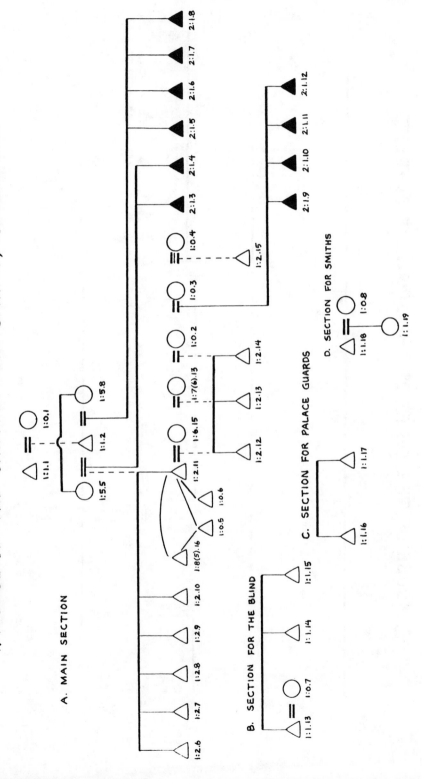

A. MAIN SECTION

B. SECTION FOR THE BLIND

C. SECTION FOR PALACE GUARDS

D. SECTION FOR SMITHS

168

2. HOUSE OF THE CHIEF OF THE SPIRITS, BIDDARENE *

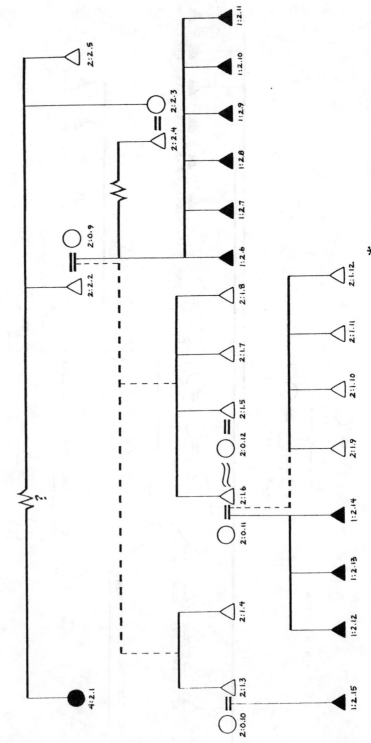

* YOUNGER BROTHER OF SULEMANU (1:1.2)

3. HOUSE OF THE MALAMS

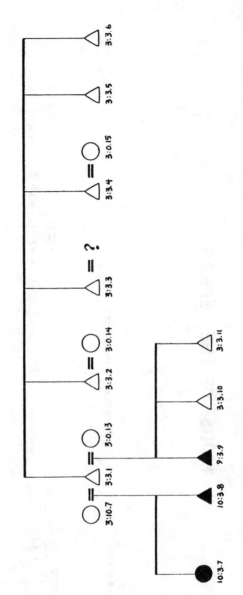

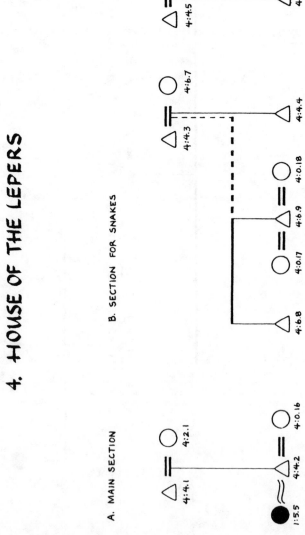

4. HOUSE OF THE LEPERS

A. MAIN SECTION

B. SECTION FOR SNAKES

5. HOUSE OF THE FULANI

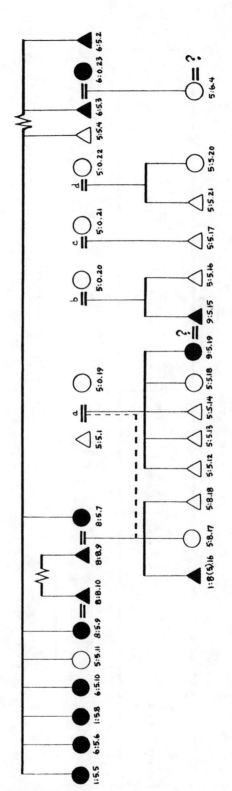

172

6. HOUSE OF THE CHIEF OF THE SPIRITS, ZURKALENE

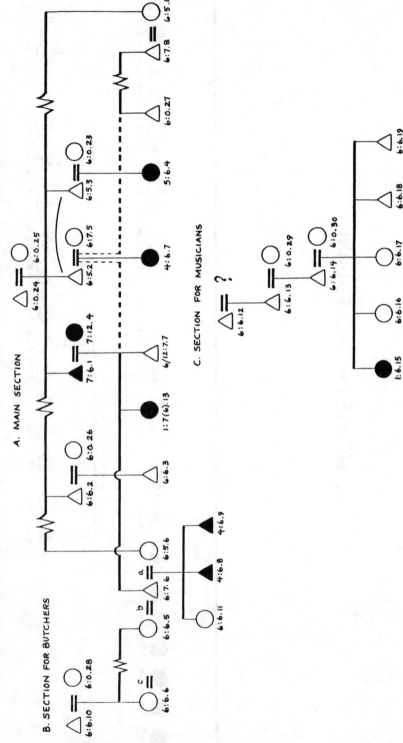

A. MAIN SECTION

B. SECTION FOR BUTCHERS

C. SECTION FOR MUSICIANS

7. HOUSE OF THE CHIEF OF THE SPIRITS, SHEKARATAFE

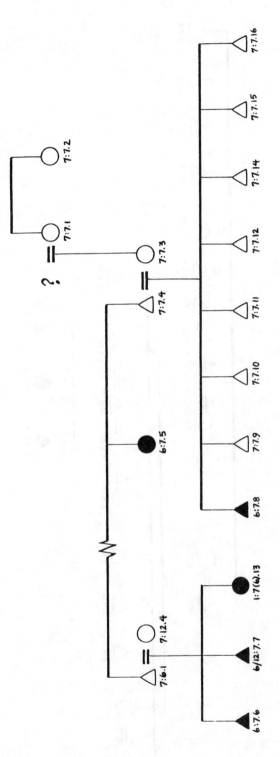

8. HOUSE OF HUNTERS

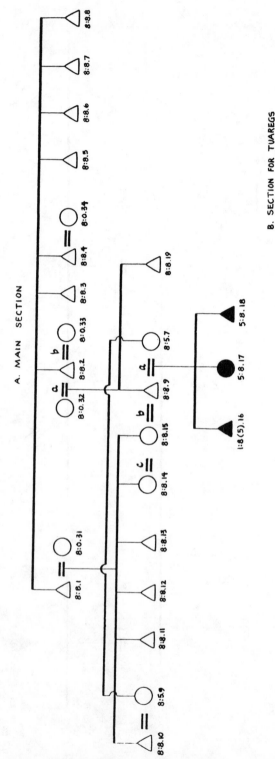

A. MAIN SECTION

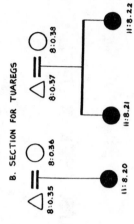

B. SECTION FOR TUAREGS

9. HOUSE OF THE CHIEF OF THE PAGANS

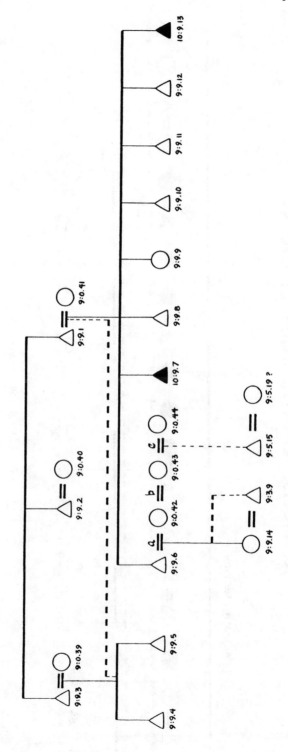

10. HOUSE OF THE CHIEF OF GWARI

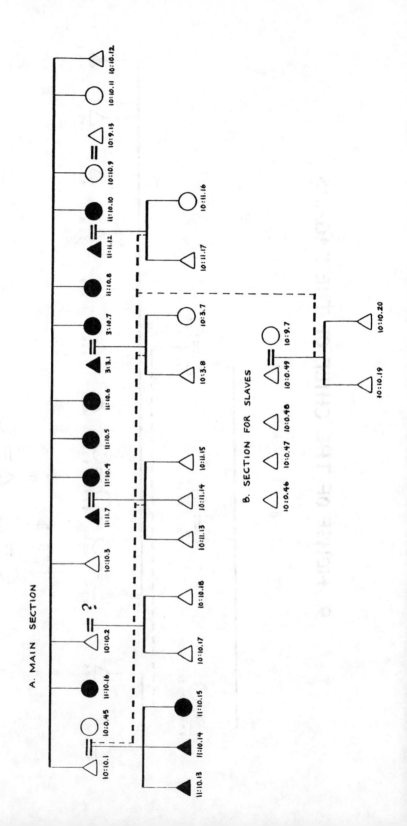

A. MAIN SECTION

B. SECTION FOR SLAVES

II. HOUSE OF THE NORTH AFRICANS

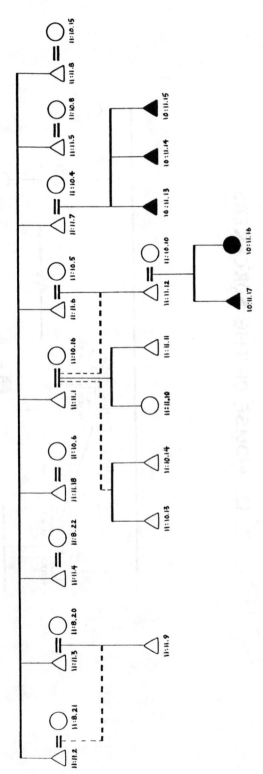

12. HOUSE OF THE SORCERERS

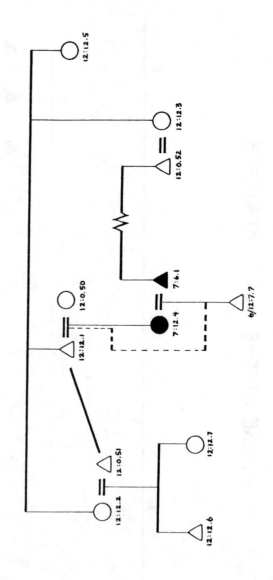

Appendix **B** • *Houses of Jangare*

(2) Numerical List†

1:0.1	Mabuga	1:2.15	Dam Maza
1:0.2	Azurfa	1:5.5	Bakar Doguwa
1:0.3	Ci Goro	1:5.8	Bilkisu
1:0.4	Mai Fitila	1:6.15	'Yar Mairo
1:0.5	Sambawa	1:7(6).13	Ciwo Babu Magani
1:0.6	Bagobiri	1:8(5).16	Wanzami
1:0.7	Afiruwa		
1:0.8	Makera	2:0.9	Magajiyar Jangare
1:1.1	Taiki	2:0.10	Safiya
1:1.2	Sarkin Aljan Sulemanu*	2:0.11	Nana'aishe
1:1.13	Sarkim Makafi Isa	2:0.12	Badakuwa
1:1.14	Yakubu	2:1.3	Kunnau
1:1.15	Malam Ma'azu	2:1.4	Kauran Zugu
1:1.16	Dogari Isa, Sarkin	2:1.5	Yariman Ruwa
	Dogari	2:1.6	Sarkin Rafi
1:1.17	Dogari Mai Jan Kaya	2:1.7	Barade
1:1.18	Sammai	2:1.8	Masakin Zugu
1:1.19	Ta Zuga	2:1.9	Hasan
1:2.6	Ba Gudu Babba	2:1.10	Husseini
1:2.7	Ba Guda Karami	2:1.11	Kurma
1:2.8	Mai Daro	2:1.12	Gambo
1:2.9	Mayanin Gobir	2:2.2	Sarkin Aljan Biddarene*
1:2.10	Mai Garin Daura	2:2.3	Mai Dirmi
1:2.11	Dan Galadima	2:2.4	Baba Rakau
1:2.12	Dan Daudu	2:2.5	Baratse
1:2.13	Mai Gizo (Owner of a Spider)		
1:2.14	Korau	3:0.13	Kuri

*House head.
†A key to the numerical code appears on p. 166.

3:0.13	Alhanza		6:0.25	Sarka, Mai Rikicin
3:0.15	Ɗahe			Gangan
3:3.1	Malam Alhaji*		6:0.26	Jigawan Nama
3:3.2	Alfa Maciɗo		6:0.27	Jam Marke
3:3.3	Malam Balarabe		6:0.28	Bahargowa
3:3.4	Malam Ibrahim		6:0.29	Bambama
3:3.5	Malam Gayya		6:0.30	Zabiya, Maryamu
3:3.6	Malam Habubakar		6:5.2	Sarkin Aljan Zurkalene*
3:3.10	Wawan Yaro		6:5.3	Ja'e
3:3.11	Ɗam Bajari		6:5.6	Hawa'u
3:10.7	Arziki, Bagwariya		6:5.10	Labuda
			6:6.2	Jaƙiri
4:0.16	Almajira		6:6.3	Burungu
4:0.17	Ra		6:6.5	Maimuna
4:0.18	Rakana		6:6.6	Amina
4:2.1	Yahanasu Musaka		6:6.10	Daggu, Sarkim Fawa
4:4.1	Ƙuge		6:6.11	Zainaba, 'Yar Mahauta
4:4.2	Kuturu*		6:6.12	Karɓo
4:4.3	Danko*		6:6.13	Abamu
4:4.4	Damatsiri		6:6.14	Sarkim Makaɗa*
4:4.5	Sarukutuf		6:6.16	Gyangyaɗi
4:4.6	Kububuwa		6:6.17	Dariya
4:6.7	Kwakiya		6:6.18	Ɗan Zabiya
4:6.8	Baƙo Mashi		6:6.19	Ɗan Yarima Na Roƙo
4:6.9	Masharuwa		6:7.5	Kasa
			6:7.6	Kure
5:0.19	Yagwargwal		6/12:7.7	Manzo Maye
5:0.20	Yatakko		6:7.8	Zaki
5:0.21	Yafendo			
5:0.22	Yakumbo		7:6.1	Duna
5:5.1	Sarkim Filani*		7:7.1	Doruna
5:5.4	Ɓaidu		7:7.2	Bazabarmiya
5:5.11	Dosa		7:7.3	Harakwai
5:5.12	Sambo		7:7.4	Sarkin Aljan Shekaratafe,
5:5.13	Ɗam Ba'aboriya			Sarkim Fagan*
5:5.14	Rusku		7:7.9	Babakere
5:5.16	Na Matuwa		7:7.10	Dumurmutse
5:5.17	Muhubbare		7:7.11	Danno
5:5.18	Ciriɗo		7:7.12	Ɗan Ruwa
5:5.20	Falaka		7:7.14	Kwaɗo
5:5.21	Buba		7:7.15	Kunkuru
5:6.4	Hajjo		7:7.16	Celo-celo
5:8.17	Tsatsuba		7:12.4	Ladi Mayya, Zakoma
5:8.18	Kura			
			8:0.31	Tsohuwa Mai Kinibibi
6:0.23	Yadukko		8:0.32	Rangwangwan
6:0.24	Tarnaƙi, Hana Tafiya		8:0.33	Samama

---

*House head.

8:0.34	Kanwa
8:0.35	Ba'auzini
8:0.36	Ramata
8:0.37	Haro, Audu Mai Aiki Da Gora
8:0.38	Dabino
8:5.7	Barhaza
8:5.9	Adamare
8:8.1	Dan Tsoho
8:8.2	Baleri
8:8.3	Duna Rage Iri
8:8.4	Ragiji
8:8.5	Tunku
8:8.6	Gudali
8:8.7	Tsoho Samareci
8:8.8	Wada
8:8.9	Mai Dawa, Mai Baka*
8:8.10	Salihu
8:8.11	Gurgu
8:8.12	Bako
8:8.13	Adan
8:8.14	Awwali
8:8.15	Iyani
8:8.19	Dakari
9:0.39	Motsa Giya
9:0.40	Yero
9:0.41	Uwar Gona
9:0.42	Ci Wake
9:0.43	Kiroro
9:0.44	Taroro
9:3.9	Nakada
9:5.15	Mai Gizo (Owner of Matted Hair)
9:5.19	Zainaba
9:9.1	Magero
9:9.2	Nomau
9:9.3	Sammako
9:9.4	Arne Mai Kanga
9:9.5	Arne Mai Kudundiri
9:9.6	Sarkin Arna*
9:9.8	Sunkwiyo
9:9.9	'Yam Mace
9:9.10	Itace
9:9.11	Mai Suru
9:9.12	Arne Karya Duwatsu (1)
9:9.14	Ta Duri

10:0.45	Ci Rama
10:0.46	Lakataru, Wawan Sarki
10:0.47	Na Dillima, Arne Da Kuge
10:0.48	Daudu, Kilishi
10:0.49	Hazo Jita Rana, Mai Lema
10:3.7	'Yar Yakuwa
10:3.8	Dam Madudduru
10:9.7	Rano
10:9.13	Dan Kurgunguma
10:10.1	Sarkin Gwari*
10:10.2	Lamarudu
10:10.3	Zanzar
10:10.9	Bakar Tukunya
10:10.11	Shegiyar Kafa
10:10.12	Fir'auna
10:10.17	Duna Duba Rana
10:10.18	Kafiri Mai Kaho
10:10.19	Ma'azu
10:10.20	Mammadu
10:11.13	Guntun Gatari
10:11.14	Dodo Da Gashi
10:11.15	Dan Kwalkwali
10:11.16	Adirsuna
10:11.17	Gaduma
11:8.20	Halima
11:8.21	Mai Rukuma
11:8.22	Dagge
11:10.4	Yawo
11:10.5	Kala'ana
11:10.6	Karmana
11:10.8	'Yar Guguwa
11:10.10	Bazar-bazar, 'Yar Mai Ganye
11:10.13	Bawarje
11:10.14	Maci Kare
11:10.15	Galla
11:10.16	Tamba
11:11.1	Barkono, Bature*
11:11.2	Kafaran
11:11.3	Kwatangiri, Dam Mama
11:11.4	Mai Yaki
11:11.5	Gwauro Mai Kwalabe
11:11.6	Karuna
11:11.7	Di'o, Babban Bature
11:11.8	Umaru Sanda Ba Buga
11:11.9	Dan Auta

*House head.

11:11.10   Baɓɓaku
11:11.11   Mami
11:11.12   Sarkim Bicci
11:11.18   Arne Karya Duwatsu (II)

12:0.50   Lashe-lashe
12:0.51   Koƙi

12:0.52   Kwaɗayi
12:12.1   Batoyi*
12:12.2   Kwalan Ta Koƙi
12:12.3   Kafeda Mai
12:12.5   Tari Mai Tad Da Hanƙarniya
12:12.6   Ɗam Manzo
12:12.7   Ƙulita

---

*House head.

Appendix *B* • *Houses of Jangare*

(3) Alphabetical List†

A

Abamu 6:6.13
Adamare 8:5.9
Adan 8:8.13
Adirsuna 10:11.16
Afiruwa 1:0.7
Alfa Maciɗo 3:3.2
Alhanza 3:0.14
Almajira 4:0.16
Amina 6:6.6
Arne Da Ƙuge (*see* Na Dillima, Arne Da Ƙuge)
Arne Karya Duwatsu (I) 9:9.12
Arne Karya Duwatsu (II) 11:11.18
Arne Mai Kanga 9:9.4
Arne Mai Kuɗundiri 9:9.5
Arziki, Bagwariya 3:10.7
Audu (*see* Haro, Audu Mai Aiki Da Gora)
Awwali 8:8.14
Azurfa 1:0.2

B

Ba'auzini 8:0.35
Babakere 7:7.9
Baba Rakau 2:2.4
Baɓɓaku 11:11.10

Badakuwa 2:0.12
Bagobiri 1:0.6
Ba Gudu Babba 1:2.6
Ba Gudu Ƙarami 1:2.7
Bagwariya (*see* Arziki, Bagwariya)
Bahargowa 6:0.28
Baƙar Doguwa 1:5.5
Baƙar Tukunya 10:10.9
Baƙo 8:8.12
Baƙo Mashi 4:6.8
Bambama 6:0.29
Barade 2:1.7
Baratse 2:2.5
Barhaza 8:5.7
Barkono, Bature*11:11.1
Batoyi* 12:12.1
Bature (*see* Barkono, Bature)
Bawarje 11:10.13
Bazarbarmiya 7:7.2
Bazar-bazar, 'Yar Mai Ganye 11:10.10
Bilƙisu 1:5.8
Buba 5:5.21
Burungu 6:6.3

Ɓ

Ɓaidu 5:5.4
Ɓaleri 8:8.2

---

*House head.
†A key to the numerical code appears on p. 166.

---

*House head.

Korau 1:2.14
Kububuwa 4:4.6
Kunkuru 7:7.15
Kunnau 2:1.3
Kura 5:8.18
Kure 6:7.6
Kuri 3:0.13
Kurma 2:1.11
Kuturu* 4:4.2
Kwadayi 12:0.52
Kwado 7:7.14
Kwakiya 4:6.7
Kwatangiri, Dam Mama 11:11.3

K

Karuna 11:11.6
Kauran Zugu 2:1.4
Kiroro 9:0.43
Koki 12:0.51
Kuge 4:4.1
Kulita 12:12.7
Kwalan Ta Koki 12:12.2

L

Labuda 6:5.10
Ladi Mayya, Zakoma 7:12.4
Lakataru, Wawan Sarki 10:0.46
Lamarudu 10:10.2
Lashe-lashe 12:0.50

M

Ma'azu 10:10.19
Mabuga 1:0.1
Maci Kare 11:10.4
Magajiyar Jangare 2:0.9
Magero 9:9.1
Mai Baka (*see* Mai Dawa, Mai Baka)
Mai Daro 1:2.8
Mai Dawa, Mai Baka* 8:8.9
Mai Dirmi 12:2.3
Mai Fitila 1:0.4
Mai Garin Daura 1:1.10
Mai Gizo (Owner of a Spider) 1:2.13
Mai Gizo (Owner of Matted Hair) 9:5.15
Maimuna 6:6.5
Mai Rukuma 11:8.21

Mai Suru 9:9.11
Mai Yaki 11:11.4
Makera 1:0.8
Malam Alhaji* 3:3.1
Malam Balarabe 3:3.3
Malam Gayya 3:3.5
Malam Habubakar 3:3.6
Malam Ibrahim 3:3.4
Malam Ma'azu 1:1.15
Mami 11:11.11
Mammadu 10:10.20
Manzo Maye 6/12:7.7
Maryamu (*see* Zabiya, Maryamu)
Masakin Zugu 2:1.8
Masharuwa 4:6.9
Mayanin Gobir 1:2.9
Motsa Giya 9:0.39
Muhubbare 5:5.17

N

Na Dillima, Arne Da Kuge 10:0.47
Nakada 9:3.9
Na Matuwa 5:5.16
Nana'aishe 2:0.11
Nomau 9:9.2

R

Ra 4:0.17
Ragiji 8:8.4
Rakana 4:0.18
Ramata 8:0.36
Rangwangwan 8:0.32
Rano 10:9.7
Rusku 5:5.14

S

Safiya 2:0.10
Salihu 8:8.10
Samama 8:0.33
Sambawa 1:0.5
Sambo 5:5.12
Sammai 1:1.18
Sammako 9:9.3
Sarka, Mai Rikicin Gangan 6:0.25
Sarkim Bicci 11:11.12

*House head.

*House head.

Appendix C • Musical Transcriptions

Example 1
Song 1. For Sarkin Aljan Sulemanu

Example 1 - *Concluded*

Example 2
Song 2. For Sarkin Aljan Sulemanu

Example 3
Song 1. For Inna

Example 3 - *Concluded*

Example 4
Song 2. For Inna

Example 5
Song 3. For Inna

Example 5 - *Concluded*

Example 6
Song 1. For Dan Galadima, Part I

Example 6 - *Concluded*

Example 7
Song 1. For Dan Galadima, Part II

Example 7 - *Continued*

Example 7 - *Concluded*

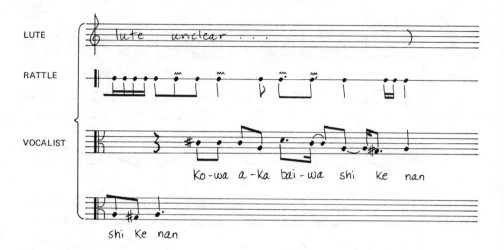

Example 8
Trance Inducing Music For Dan Galadima

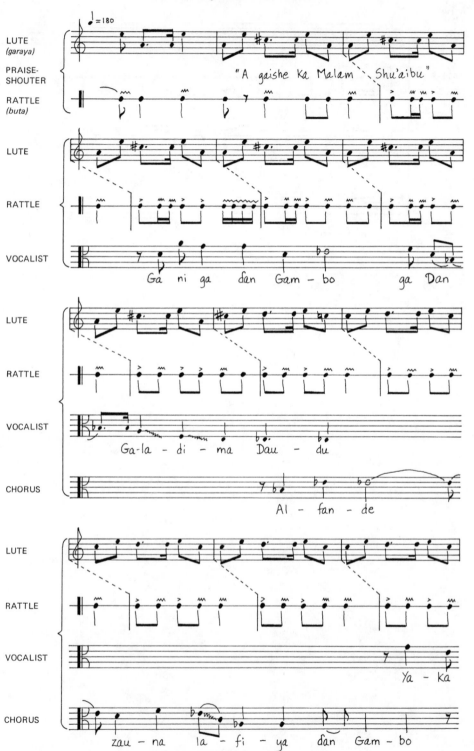

Example 8 - *Concluded*

Example 9
Song For Wanzami

Example 9 - *Concluded*

Example 10
Song For Magajiyar Jangare (Trance-Inducing)

Example 10 - *Continued*

Example 10 - *Concluded*

Example 11
Song For Sarkin Rafi

Example 11 - *Continued*

Example 11 - *Continued*

Example 11 - *Concluded*

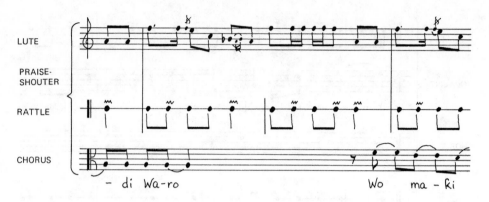

Example 12
Song For Barade, Sarkin Yaki

Example 12 - *Concluded*

Example 13
Song For Malam Alhaji

Example 13 - *Continued*

Example 13 - *Concluded*

Example 14
Song For Bagwariya

Example 14 - *Concluded*

Example 15
Song 1. For Kuturu

Example 15 - *Concluded*

Example 16
Song 2. For Kuturu

Example 16 - *Concluded*

LUTE

PRAISE-
SHOUTER

RATTLE

[beginning of song for Danko ···]

fagen gujiya, ba gurin tsira "

Example 17
Song For Danko

Example 17 - *Continued*

Example 17 - *Concluded*

Example 18
Song For Sarkim Filani

Example 18 - *Continued*

Example 18 - *Concluded*

Example 19
Song For Kure

Example 19 - *Continued*

Example 19 - *Continued*

Example 19 - *Continued*

Example 19 - *Concluded*

Example 20
Song 1. For Sarkim Makada
(The Beginning of a Possession-Trance Event)

Example 20 - *Continued*

Example 20 - *Concluded*

Example 21
Song For Mai Dawa

Example 21 - *Continued*

Example 21 - *Concluded*

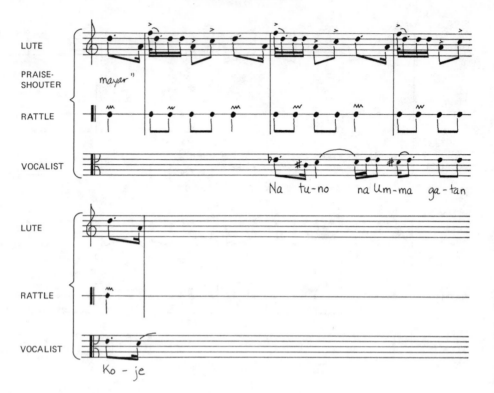

Example 22
Song For Barhaza

Example 22 - *Continued*

Example 22 - *Concluded*

Example 23
Song For Nakada

Example 23 - *Continued*

LUTE

RATTLE

VOCALIST
Ma-hau-Ka-ci Ka-ram may-

LUTE

RATTLE

VOCALIST
-yu dam Ma - lam   dam

LUTE

RATTLE

VOCALIST
Ma-lam Ka ki ha-lim Ma-lam, ga ra-qo da wu-tsi-yar Ka-re dam

LUTE

RATTLE

VOCALIST
Ma-lam, Kai wu-ta ma-tar-Ka ha-ya-Ki ar-ne mai gwan-gwan, a-na tu-wo

Example 23 - *Concluded*

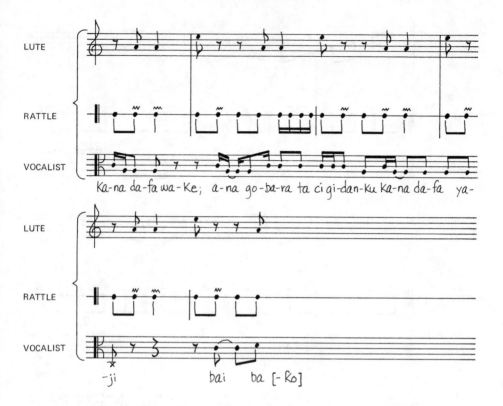

Example 24
Song 1. For Mai Gizo

Example 24 - *Continued*

Example 24 - *Concluded*

Example 25
Song 2. For Mai Gizo (Trance-Inducing)

Example 26
Song For Sarkin Gwari

Sar-kin Gwa-ri mai fa-rar ma-ka ; ya - ya

Example 26 - *Continued*

LUTE

RATTLE

VOCALIST

Kai   Ka har-bu mu-ji-ya?

Har-bi a tsu-li Kum-bu-ri a Ka

Sar-Kin

Example 26 - *Concluded*

Gwa-ri mai fa-rar ma-ka

Example 27
Song For Umaru Sanda Ba Buga

Example 27 - *Concluded*

*Appendix **D** • Photographs*

1

While a possession-trance event goes on around him a cult-adept is possessed capriciously by Maci Kare (Eater of Dogs), a pagan spirit. Frothing at the mouth is a common sign of dissociation.

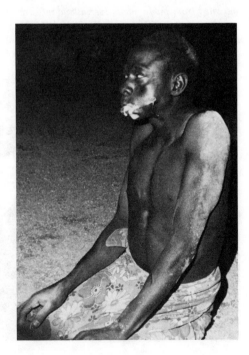

2

The cult-adept's mouth is foaming and his eyes are rolled back up into his head, indicating the presence of a spirit. This medium has entered possession-trance using sensory deprivation, a limitation of bodily activity, and under-breathing.

3

An example of simultaneous induction. Three mediums are falling into trance together, to the accompaniment of garaya *(plucked lute) and* buta *(gourd-rattle) music for a neutral spirit.*

The mare is covered so that the divine horseman may settle himself on her neck concealed from public view. Her attendants are speaking with the spirit, encouraging it to ride peacefully. The cloth may also aid in inducing trance through under-breathing.

4

5

*A medium entering trance using
increased bodily activity (energetic
dancing) and over-breathing.*

*This medium's possession-trance begins
with a cataleptic seizure as* goge *(bowed
lute) and* kwarya *(large hemispherical
gourd) music invokes a spirit on his neck.
The possession-trance cult is Hausa but
in Maiduguri Kanuri women
(background) are drawn in as witnesses.*

6

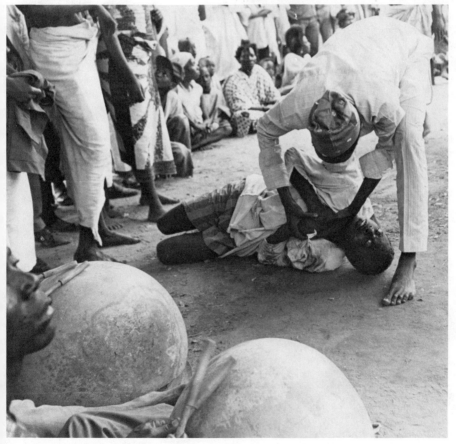

7

Sarkin Rafi *(Chief of Well-Watered Land) prepares to smash a pumpkin at the cult's harvest ritual in Kano. The pieces of the pumpkin are transformed into medicinal ingredients by his actions.*

8

Part of the initiation site in Ningi. On the left is a large baobob tree, which is the resting place for Bakar Doguwa *(the Black Tall-Woman) and the site of* Malam Alhaji's *(Malam, the Pilgrim) Quranic school for spirits. The water pot near the compound fence marks the place where neophytes are taken for daily medicinal washings. The hut on the right contains initiation materials but is also the initiation master's sleeping quarters.*

A new initiate is taught some refinements of the dances and gestures of a spirit who will be with her forever. Mai Baka *(the Bowman) is the spirit, and his possession of this mare is recognized (but not condemned) as weak during this first event after the woman's cure/ initiation.*

9

10

An attendant assists a young cult-adept ridden by Dan Galadima (the Prince). The Prince dances on a new, elaborate grass mat while Barade (a Warrior) sits waiting in the background (left).

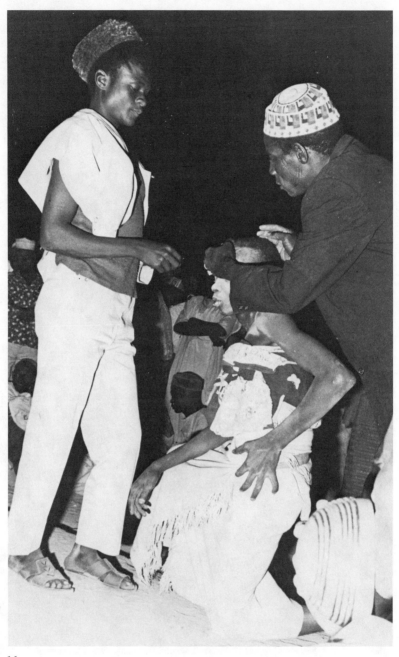

11

The man on the left indicates his support for Sarkin Rafi *(Chief of Well-Watered Land) by placing coins on the latter's forehead. A praise-singer (right) removes the coins, which are placed in a special shoe container in front of the musicians.*

12

A man places a coin on Sarkin Rafi's *(Chief of Well-Watered Land) forehead as two women wait to make similar gifts. Coins are moistened slightly to make them stick. The event is a Friday afternoon performance for wedding-gift distribution, during which guests and hosts compete for recognition of their generosity.*

13

A Kanuri woman places a row of coins on the goge-*playing ensemble leader's forehead. Strictly speaking, it would be improper for her to indicate such support for cult-adepts since she is not Hausa, but she may give gifts to musicians without prejudice.*

14

Dan Galadima *(the Prince) (standing)* greets Sarkin Rafi *(Chief of Well-Watered Land). A spirit is greeted by pressing one's right hand on his horse's back.*

15

Sarkin Rafi (*Chief of Well-Watered
Land*) *greets a man who later gives
him gifts of money as a sign of
support. The bareheaded lute player is
in the foreground.*

16

*A woman supporter greets the Chief of
Well-Watered Land, asking his help
in the solution of a personal problem.*

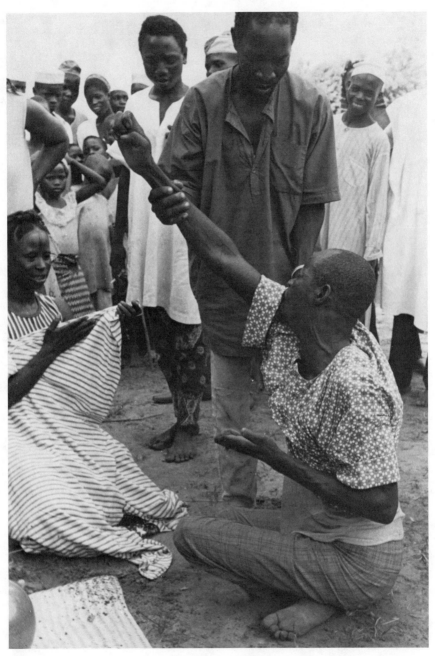

17

Kuturu *(the Leper)* takes possession of
his medium as his attendant tries to
remove his shirt and prepare his
costume. Sarkim Makada *(Chief of
Drummers)* looks on *(left)*.

18

*After demonstrating the possession of
one spirit, this medium returned to
himself and was then possessed by
another spirit. The cloth used to cover
him during the induction of his
possession-trance has just been
removed, revealing a cult-adept being
ridden by an as-yet-unidentified spirit.*

19

Nakada (*Causer of Downfall*), the rebel son of Malam Alhaji (Malam, *the Pilgrim*), prepares to dance. The cloth used to cover his medium as he entered possession-trance is draped over the shoulders of his attendant. Nakada's clothing includes a fishnet shirt, monkey skins, and a long stick which he uses as a phallus.

20

Kuturu (*the Leper*) *sits in a characteristic pose. Over his arm is draped his palm-
nut kernel string, which he uses as a weapon. His alms gourd lies
on the ground at his feet.*

21

Aided by two ritual attendants, a man possessed by Kuturu *(the Leper) administers to a woman who has just suffered a relapse of the illness (spontaneous strangulation) that led to her initiation into the* bori *cult.*

22

Lined up at the race-course in a rehearsal for an arts festival, these cult-adepts display the appropriate clothing for certain female Fulani spirits, Barhaza, Adamare, et al. A man dressed in Barade's (a Warrior) clothing stands behind them.

Mai Gizo (*Owner of Matted Hair*) *is a pagan spirit who is both fearsome and dangerous to bystanders. He shows his power by swinging the metal hatchets he carries down over his back, blade out.*

23

24

Shu'aibi Mai Gayara of Kano at work. His son, a gourd-rattle player, sits to his right and at this performance is the principal member of the ensemble's chorus. The man to his left is the group's vocalist.

A sarewa *(end-blown flute)* and kwarya *(large hemispherical gourd)* ensemble in *Nasaru near Ningi. The vocalist to the left in the picture has temporarily put down his snack tray to assume his role as a member of the ensemble. Similarly, one of the gourd players is a vendor of cigarettes, hard candy, and APC (aspirin).*

25

References

Abraham, R.C. 1962. *Dictionary of the Hausa Language,* 2d ed. London: University of London Press.

Ames, David W. 1973. "A Sociocultural View of Hausa Musical Activity," in d'Azevedo, Warren (ed.), *The Traditional Artist in African Societies.* Bloomington: Indiana University Press, pp. 128–61.

——, and Anthony V. King. 1971. *Glossary of Hausa Music in Its Social Contexts.* Evanston, Ill.: Northwestern University Press.

Bargery, G.P. 1934. *A Hausa-English Dictionary and English-Hausa Vocabulary.* London: Oxford University Press.

Barkow, Jerome H. 1974. "Evaluation of Character and Social Control among the Hausa," *Ethos* 2(1):1–14.

Beattie, John, and John Middleton (eds.). 1969. *Spirit Mediumship and Society in Africa.* New York: Africana Publishing.

Besmer, Fremont E. 1972. *Hausa Court Music in Kano, Nigeria.* Ann Arbor, Mich. University Microfilms.

1973a "Avoidance and Joking Relationships between Hausa Supernatural Spirits," *Studies in Nigerian Culture* (Occasional Papers of the Centre for Nigerian Cultural Studies, Ahmadu Bello University) 1(1):26–52.

1973b "Praise-Epithets for Some Important *Bori* Spirits in Kano," *Harsunan Nijeriya (Languages of Nigeria)* 3:15-38.

1974 *Kídàn Dárán Sállà: Music for the Muslim Festivals of Id al-Fitr and Id al-Kabir in Kano, Nigeria.* Bloomington, Indiana: African Studies Program Monographs.

1975 "Bòorii: Structure and Process in Performance," *Folia Orientalia* 16:101-30.

in press a "Initiation into the *Bori* Cult: A Case Study in Ningi Town," *Africa* 47(1977):1-13.

in press b "Music of the Hausa *Bori* Cult of Spirit-Possession," Centre for Nigerian Cultural Studies Recording No. 2. Lagos: Decca.

Bourguignon, Erika (ed.). 1973. *Religion, Altered States of Consciousness, and Social Change.* Columbus: Ohio State University Press.

Crapanzano, Vincent. 1973. *The Hamadsha: A Study in Moroccan Ethnopsychiatry.* Berkeley: University of California Press.

Douglas, Mary. 1966. "Secular Defilement," in Douglas, Mary, *Purity and Danger: An Analysis of Concepts of Pollution and Taboo.* New York: Praeger, pp. 29–40.

Farmer, Henry G. 1939. "Early References to Music in the Western Sudan," *Journal of the Royal Asiatic Society* 1939:569–80.

Firth, Raymond. 1973. *Symbols: Public and Private.* Ithaca, N.Y.: Cornell University Press.

Geertz, Clifford. 1966. "Religion as a Cultural System," in Banton, Michael (ed.), *Anthropological Approaches to the Study of Religion.* London: Tavistock, pp. 1–46.

 1970 "Ethos, World-View and the Analysis of Sacred Symbols" (1957), in Hammel, Eugene A., and William S. Simmons (eds.), *Man Makes Sense: A Reader in Modern Cultural Anthropology.* Boston: Little, Brown, pp. 324–38.

Gidley, C.G.B. 1967. " 'Yankamanci—The Craft of the Hausa Comedians," *African Language Studies* 8:52–81.

Goodman, Felicitas D. 1972. *Speaking in Tongues.* Chicago: University of Chicago Press. 175 pp.

——, 1974. Jeannette H. Henney, and Esther Pressel. *Trance, Healing, and Hallucination: Three Field Studies in Religious Experience.* New York: John Wiley & Sons.

Greenberg, Joseph H. 1941. "Some Aspects of Negro-Mohammedan Culture-Contact Among the Hausa," *American Anthropologist* 43:51–61.

 1946 *The Influence of Islam on a Sudanese Religion.* New York: J.J. Augustin.

 1947 "Islam and Clan Organization among the Hausa," *Southwestern Journal of Anthropology* 3:193–211.

Hause, Helen E. 1948. "Terms for Musical Instruments in Sudanic Languages: A Lexiographical Inquiry," supp. no. 7 to the *Journal of the American Oriental Society* 68(1):1–71.

King, Anthony V. 1966. "A Bòoríi Liturgy from Katsina; Introduction and *Kíráaríi* Texts," *African Language Studies* 7:105–25.

 1967 "A Boorii Liturgy from Katsina," *African Language Studies VII Supplement.*

Krusius, P. 1915. "Die Maguzawa," *Archiv für Anthropologie* n.F. 14:288–315.

Lee, Richard B. 1968. "The Sociology of !Kung Bushman Trance Performances," in Prince, Raymond (ed.), *Trance and Possession States.* Montreal: R.M. Bucke Memorial Society, pp. 35–54.

Lévi-Strauss, Claude. 1962. *The Savage Mind (La Pensée Sauvage).* London: Weidenfeld & Nicolson.

Lewis, I.M. 1966. "Spirit Possession and Deprivation Cults," *Man* 1:307–29.

 1969 "Spirit Possession in Northern Somaliland," in Beattie, John, and John Middleton (eds.), *Spirit Mediumship and Society in Africa.* New York: Africana Publishing, pp. 188–219.

 1970 "A Structural Approach to Witchcraft and Spirit-Possession," in Douglas, Mary (ed.), *Witchcraft Confessions and Accusations.* London: Tavistock, pp. 293-309.

 1971a *Ecstatic Religion: An Anthropological Study of Spirit Possession and Shamanism.* Harmondworth, Middlesex, England: Penguin.

 1971b "Spirit-Possession in Northeast Africa," in Hasan, Y.F. (ed.), *Sudan in Africa: Studies Presented to the First International Conference Sponsored by the Sudan Research Unit, 7–12 February 1968.* Khartoum: Khartoum University Press, pp. 212–27.

Ludwig, Arnold M. 1968. "Altered States of Consciousness," in Prince, Raymond (ed.), *Trance and Possession States*. Montreal: R.M. Bucke Memorial Society, pp. 69–95.

Marks, Morton. 1974. "Reliving the Call: Sound and Meaning in Gospel Music (Ritual Form in Language)," unpublished MS.

Mauss, Marcel. 1967. *The Gift: Forms and Functions of Exchange in Archaic Societies*, trans. Ian Cunnison, orig. ed. 1925. New York: W.W. Norton.

Merriam, Alan P. 1964. *The Anthropology of Music*. Evanston, Ill.: Northwestern University Press.

Monfouga-Nicolas, Jacqueline. 1972. *Ambivalence et culte de possession: Contribution à l'étude du Bori hausa*. Paris: Editions anthropos.

Murdock, George P. 1959. *Africa: Its Peoples and Their Culture History*. New York: McGraw-Hill.

Needham, Rodney. 1972. "Percussion and Transition" (1967), in Lessa, William A., and Evon Z. Vogt (eds.), *Reader in Comparative Religion: An Anthropological Approach*, 3d ed. New York: Harper & Row, pp. 391–98.

Nicolas, Jacqueline. 1967. *"Les juments des dieux": rites de possession et condition féminine en pays hausa. Études nigériennes*, no. 21. Niger: IFAN-CNRS.

Palmer, H.R. 1914. "Bori among the Hausas," *Man* 14(52):113-17.

    1928 *Sudanese Memoirs: Being Mainly Translations of a Number of Arabic Manuscripts Relating to the Central and Western Sudan*, reprint ed. 1967, vol. 3. London: Frank Cass.

Patton, Adell. 1975. "The Ningi Chiefdom and the African Frontier: Mountaineers and Resistance to the Sokoto Caliphate, ca. 1800–1908," Ph.D. diss., University of Wisconsin.

Prince, Raymond (ed.). 1968. *Trance and Possession States: Proceedings of the Second Annual Conference of the R.M. Bucke Memorial Society, 4–6 March, 1966*. Montreal: R.M. Bucke Memorial Society.

Reuke, Ludger. 1969. *Die Maguzawa in Nordnigeria*. Freiburger Studien zu Politik und Gesellschaft überseeischer Länder Band 4. Bertelsmann Universitätsverlag Schriftenreihe des Arnold-Bergstraesser-Instituts für Kulturwissenschaftliche Forschung.

Rosman, Abraham, and Paula Rubel. 1971. *Feasting with Mine Enemy: Rank and Exchange among Northwest Coast Societies*. New York: Columbia University Press.

Smith, Michael G. 1959. "The Hausa System of Social Status," *Africa* 29:239–52.

Stenning, Derrick J. 1959. *Savannah Nomads: A Study of the Wodaabe Fulani of Western Bornu Province, Northern Region, Nigeria*. London: Oxford University Press.

Tremearne, A.J.N. 1914. *The Ban of the Bori: Demons and Demon Dancing in West and North Africa*. London: Heath, Cranton, & Ouseley.

    1915 "Bori Beliefs and Ceremonies," *Journal of the Royal Anthropological Institute* 45:23–70.

Turner, Victor W. 1967. *The Forest of Symbols: Aspects of Ndembu Ritual*. Ithaca, N.Y. Cornell University Press.

    1968 *The Drums of Affliction: A Study of Religious Processes among the Ndembu of Zambia*. Oxford: Clarendon Press and the International African Institute.

    1969 *The Ritual Process: Structure and Anti-Structure*. London: Routledge & Kegan Paul.

Van Gennep, Arnold. 1960. *The Rites of Passage,* trans. Monika B. Vizedom and Gabrielle L. Caffee, orig. ed. 1909. Chicago, Ill.: University of Chicago Press.

Vilée, James W., and Peter Badejo. 1973. "A Preliminary Study of *'Yan Lela Masu Kidan Buta,*" *Studies in Nigerian Culture* (Occasional Papers of the Centre for Nigerian Cultural Studies, Ahmadu Bello University) 1(1): 52–109.

Wilson, Peter J. 1967. "Status Ambiguity and Spirit Possession," *Man* 2:366–78.

Yusuf, Ahmed Beitallah. 1974. "A Reconsideration of Urban Conceptions: Hausa Urbanization and the Hausa Rural-Urban Continuum," *Urban Anthropology* 3:200–21.

Index